LEAVING DEEP WATER

LEAVING

DEEP

WATER

The Lives of
Asian American Women
at the Crossroads of
Two Cultures

CLAIRE S. CHOW

A DUTTON BOOK

DUTTON
Published by the Penguin Group
Penguin Putnam Inc., 375 Hudson Street,
New York, New York 10014, U.S.A.
Penguin Books Ltd, 27 Wrights Lane,
London W8 5TZ, England
Penguin Books Australia Ltd, Ringwood,
Victoria, Australia
Penguin Books Canada Ltd, 10 Alcorn Avenue,
Toronto, Ontario, Canada M4V 3B2
Penguin Books (N.Z.) Ltd, 182–190 Wairau Road,
Auckland 10, New Zealand

Penguin Books Ltd, Registered Offices:
Harmondsworth, Middlesex, England

First published by Dutton, an imprint of Dutton NAL,
a member of Penguin Putnam Inc.

First Printing, March, 1998
10 9 8 7 6 5 4 3 2 1

REGISTERED TRADEMARK—MARCA REGISTRADA

LIBRARY OF CONGRESS CATALOGING-IN-PUBLICATION DATA:

Chow, Claire S.
    Leaving deep water : the lives of Asian American women at the
crossroads of two cultures / Claire S. Chow.
        p. cm.
    ISBN 0-525-94075-8 (alk. paper)
    1. Asian American women—Interviews. 2. Asian American women—
Social conditions. I. Title.
E184.06C49 1998
305.48'895073—dc21   97-40718
                                                             CIP

Printed in the United States of America
Set in Meridien
Designed by Stanley S. Drate/Folio Graphics Co., Inc.

This book is printed on acid-free paper. ☺

To my mother, Diana
My husband, Jim
and my children, Rebecca and Julian

ACKNOWLEDGMENTS

Richard Simon, editor of the *Family Therapy Networker,* who gave me the push necessary to bring to life the article "Too Great a Price," from which this book originated.

Barbara Lowenstein and Madeleine Morel, agents extraordinaires, who recognized even more than I what I was capable of producing.

Deborah Brody, senior editor at Dutton, who could not have been more supportive or encouraging as I wrote this book.

Judy and Steve, Tae and Greg, Jennifer and Marshall, Cathy and Noel: friends in every sense of the word, who followed the evolution of this project with interest and useful feedback.

Susan Stockdale, my good friend and cheerleader.

Jin Ah Renee Kim, who keeps me smiling.

Jane Chu Thompson, whose felt connection to my story helped me to understand what this project really means.

Linda Kuwatani and Ram Gokul, good friends and good colleagues.

Jim Beattie, my at-home editor and the love of my life, who believes in my work and who believes in me.

Rebecca and Julian, who have graciously accepted the fact that Mom has been spending a lot of time on that "Asian woman's stuff."

Diana Chow, who gave me her story for this book and who always gives me her love.

Barbara Chow, who lived through much of this with me, who provided invaluable assistance when I was researching my project in Washington, D.C., and to whom I owe a debt of more than sisterly gratitude. Steve Ray, who supports Barbara and who supports me.

All the Asian American women I interviewed for this book, including those whose stories I was unable to include: This book would not have been possible without you. I offer my heartfelt thanks.

CONTENTS

PREFACE

Several years ago, I sat for my written exam for licensure as a marriage and family counselor. Looking around the room of a hundred or more would-be therapists, it suddenly hit me: I was the only Asian in the entire room. What surprised me was not so much that this was true, but that I hadn't noticed it before. The experience brought to mind a trip to China I had taken more than a decade ago, during which I watched my blond-haired Caucasian husband try to deal with the discomfort of being the instantaneous center of attention every time we so much as set foot outside the hotel.

Our first night in Beijing, my grandfather arranged for us to be driven by private car from our hotel to his apartment (at that time, there were approximately two hundred cars in the capital city, and he had access to three of them). We were shocked and saddened by the standard of living endured by my relatives (unpainted walls, bare bulbs hanging from the ceiling, dining rooms doubling as bedrooms), but the warmth of arms outstretched to greet us—more then thirty aunts, uncles, and cousins—still burns brightly in my memory. The next day, Auntie Mao Y Mei's husband, a gregarious and kindly man, arranged for us to see my grandmother's lovingly tended grave. Leaving Beijing, our tour took us to Hangchow, and to the famous bridge linking northern and southern China that my grandfather had built. The bus actu-

ally detoured from its prescribed route so that we could see the
landmark built by my grandfather, a man our bus driver described as a "national treasure."

I had grown up virtually without relatives, and in my intense
desire to assimilate, that was quite all right with me. I did not
particularly care to spend time with Chinese people, and certainly not with relatives who were living reminders of the embarrassing stigma of my ethnicity. But all those feelings dissolved
when I walked into that apartment in Beijing. I realized at that
moment that extended family is not just a collection of acciden-
tal alliances, but a living body, a place to be welcomed for being
simply who I am: the daughter of my mother, granddaughter of
my grandfather, niece of my aunts and uncles. We had never
seen each other before and, in some cases, would never meet
again, but in that moment, we shared a sense of connection and
loyalty that was unlike anything I have ever experienced. It was
the first time in my life I had ever felt valued *because* my last
name was Chow, not in spite of it.

That trip to Beijing was an important step in my journey to
integrate ethnicity and identity. I am still traveling that path.
Writing this book has brought a tremendous gain in self-concept,
in understanding who I am as both an Asian and an American
woman.

What, then, does it mean to be Asian American? To me, it
means living in a place where I don't look much like anyone else
but in most respects act like them, knowing all the time that
halfway across the globe is a densely populated region full of
people who look just like me but don't particularly act like me.
It means forever holding the contradiction of belonging and not
belonging, of feeling "at home" and wondering where home is.
It means living with other people's ideas about me, ideas that
often do not coincide with the person I really am. It means
doubting my self-concept. It means working to overcome stereotypes. It means sometimes playing stereotypes to my advantage.
It means occasionally still wishing I was white. It means occasionally still feeling the sting of shame about my ethnicity trick-
ling out from its hidden places. It means wishing, just this once,

that someone could step into my shoes and see what life is like from my perspective.

What else does it mean to be Asian American? Wishing I spoke the original language. Wanting my children to feel good about their heritage and hoping they pass on at least a whisper of their cultural legacy to their own children. Feeling proud of Asian Americans, Chinese particularly, who achieve great things in this country. Not knowing what to do with my feelings of defensiveness when China or someone Chinese is criticized, even if I believe they have acted wrongly. Recognizing a hunger for more knowledge about the land my parents were born in. Finding comfort in the sound of spoken Mandarin, the act of eating Chinese food with chopsticks. Feeling embarrassed when someone asks me a question about Chinese or Asian culture that I can't answer. Wishing I knew the answers. Feeling more than a little embarrassed about the fact that I try to distance myself from recent immigrants who don't speak English, who wear those mismatched and garish clothes. Feeling a certain level of comfort with other Asian American women that I don't find elsewhere in my life.

And this is also what it means to be Asian American: Contending with mixed messages—echoes of the lessons my mother taught me contrasted to the values I am exposed to in my everyday life, in my work as a therapist. Aware, at critical junctures in my life, that I could take two very different approaches to a given dilemma; for example, I could "follow my bliss" and go "bum around Europe" after college (as my mother explains the choice my husband made) or I could go straight to graduate school and start working on the Ph.D. I knew from the age of six I would one day attain. Remembering a time when I was fourteen or fifteen, fiddling at the piano with the melody from Simon and Garfunkel's "Scarborough Fair" and being told by my father to "stop playing that *obscene* music." Trying to convince him that, even though this was not classical, it had roots in an Old English ballad, wondering exactly how this piece qualified as obscene. Aware that it is up to me to define my life and my identity because, in the end, *I* am the one who must live with the consequences of all those contradictions.

When I first started working on this project, I did not have nearly as clear a sense of what I thought about myself as Asian American. This was not a subject I discussed with others (too embarrassing, perhaps, and no real forum in which to do so). I only knew my experience in its visceral reality: a combination of memories, sensations, overwhelming feelings. So this is what I took into my writing, along with certain preconceptions about what I would encounter in my interviews with other Asian American women. That is, I imagined that many people would feel the same way I did, that their experiences would be similar to mine. After all, my sister Barbara and I growing up had so much in common: a fervent desire to be white and a unilateral rejection of our ancestral heritage. But as I started to share my story with others, I was surprised to learn that my feelings and those of my sister were the exception rather than the rule. Or as Barbara put it, "You mean you're telling me we're freaks?"

Well, maybe not freaks, but clearly not the norm. I interviewed over 120 women of varying ages, geographical residence, occupations, and generational status, and I found very few who could really relate to the part of my story about the *shame* I felt being Chinese. Certainly there were women who tried to emulate white standards of beauty (as I did), who preferred their parents not speak that guttural and foreign-sounding language in the presence of friends, who wondered aloud what life might have been like if they had been born to parents with northern European origins. But embarrassment, shame, and self-hatred: These were not descriptors generally used to name a woman's experience.

At the outset, I think I was hoping to find at least a few people "like me." And early on, I happened to connect with a Chinese American woman who wrote me a letter from her heart, saying that I had told her story (in an article I wrote preceding the book), given voice to her unarticulated concerns. She related an incident buried in the memory files of junior high, where an art teacher asked the class to draw a self-portrait. Jane worked hard at her drawing (she is a talented artist), checking the mirror for accuracy. Only when she finished did she step back to realize that her self-portrait depicted a girl with completely Anglo facial features. Hearing this story and sharing other similar feelings brought me a profound sense of relief.

But the kind of connection I shared with Jane was to reoccur only rarely in my interviews with other Asian American women. I still remember my amazement the first time I talked with someone who told me that she grew up without ever having felt different due to the fact of being Japanese American. Even though, intellectually, I understood that Hawaii's racial and sociopolitical situation was unique, something inside me screamed, "But she must by lying! How can anyone in this country grow up not wanting to be white?" Over time, the internal voice of disbelief was crushed under the sheer weight of evidence to the contrary. And actually, I am glad. As much as I appreciate the affirmation of being heard by a person who has tasted my experience, I would just as soon others not go through it. I especially hope that my daughter and my son are spared this particular anguish.

Another expectation I had in the beginning was that I would find many other women who could speak to the topic of racism and discrimination. I believe that I have been the victim of both racism (which I define as a set of attitudes and beliefs devaluing human beings because of their racial origins) and discrimination (which I define as those actions that flow from racist beliefs). In many cases, the acts of discrimination have been subtle, and the racist beliefs about me have been submerged under the veneer of polite social intercourse. But the proof of their imprint is the fact that I spent so much of my life wanting to be someone other than who I am, wanting to be white. I don't believe that young children question their inherent worth unless they get that message from others. I might very well not be writing this book today if I didn't also still carry echoes of "Ching, chong, Chinaman," the ghosts of tears that stung but never fell.

In my interviews, I found women who know that racism and discrimination against Asian Americans exists, because they have lived with it. Clearly, the legacy of the internment continues to shape the lives both of internees and their sons and daughters. And recent statistics indicate that hate crimes against Asian Americans are actually on the rise. But many women who spoke to me either downplayed the effects of racism or denied its existence in their lives altogether. At first, I experienced the same sense of skepticism I spoke of earlier. Over time, however, it became clear that even if I believe racism and discrimination persist on both a person-to-person and institutional level, many Asian American women have not felt its effects.

Why? My unsubstantiated opinion is that women do not glimpse the specter of racism in their lives for several reasons. First is that most immigrants are simply too busy making a life for themselves in this country and/or trying to heal from the trauma of war or political unrest. Furthermore, intra- and intergroup racism is a fact of life in their abandoned homelands. As my mother explains, foreigners in China would receive much worse treatment than do foreigners here. Second is the "model minority" myth. The Asian American women I spoke to were not all professional, certainly not all wealthy, but by and large they could be considered successful. I did not interview (for example) Vietnamese gang members, men and women toiling in sweatshops, or others who fall between the cracks. If you can buy yourself a piece of the American dream, it's easy to believe that racism does not stand in your way. Compounding the myth is the lack of good historical information about the experiences of our grandparents and great-grandparents in this country. Exclusion laws, antimiscegenation laws: These are not generally included in the history books.

A third reason may have something to do with innate cultural characteristics that prompt Asian Americans, women especially, not to challenge authority or question the "way things are." My mother's advice to me in writing this book was to "try not to offend white people." A certain streak of fatalism, of stoic and passive acceptance of one's destiny, is inherent in the original culture. Another reason may be that many Asian American women grew up with access to an Asian community: relatives, family friends, business acquaintances. Such a connection eases the sense of isolation and provides positive role models. Perhaps my early experiences with racism in the neighborhood and on the playgrounds was especially wrenching because I had only white folks to emulate; there was nowhere else to turn.

Finally, I believe that many of us have achieved the somewhat dubious distinction of "invisibility." More than one woman told me that her friends "don't think of her as Asian." She may not be white, but she is also *not* "not-white." She is not seen as a person of color and therefore does not identify with that characterization. This position allows her to "pass" in certain segments of mainstream America and fortifies her image of herself as "one of us" rather than "one of them." For some, this may represent the highest achievement: full assimilation. But for myself, I am no longer willing to pay the price of success with the currency of ethnic self-denial.

Talking to all these women has changed me, continues to change me. My story is included in this book because the process of writing has forced me to look at my ethnicity and my identity at a very deep level. But I am aware that my experience is unique to me, so that even with the preconceptions I carried into this project, I have tried hard to let each woman speak for herself. Thus, my intention has always been to present a variety of voices and stories that, collectively, give an impression of what it is like to be an Asian American woman. I was not searching for unanimity or statistical accuracy. I believe that the truth lies in stories that are told from the heart and from the gut. I hope that they will make you laugh and cry and pause to reflect, as they did me. If you are an Asian American woman, I hope that some part of the truth of your experience will be reflected here. If you are not, I hope that some part of the truth of human experience will find a place of resonance within your heart.

1 GROWING UP ASIAN, GROWING UP AMERICAN

In my favorite picture of myself as a baby, my mother is holding her three-month-old daughter almost as high as the shimmering star on top of the Christmas tree. My face is transformed by awe and wonder, my mother's smile illuminating her whole body. I treasure this record of my first Christmas, as I do many other snapshots in the photo album of my memory. Grainy and faded home movies of Brownies marching in the Memorial Day parade. Kittens unwittingly pressed into service as overdressed babies in prams. School plays and Easter egg hunts and snowmen being manufactured, factory style, on the front lawn. An overdocumented childhood that still exists, in neat rows of labeled boxes, in the family room of my mother's house.

When we go to visit my mother's house, I sometimes take these pictures out and my children ask to see them. They giggle over the lithe and naked bodies of two-year-olds in the backyard wading pool and ask why they can't also have three chameleons, two guinea pigs, and a rabbit. But even as I share the stories that these picture evoke, I am increasingly aware of the pictures that are *not* here.

I know, for example, that it is useless to look through the boxes for a photograph of my family celebrating Chinese New Year's, perhaps with delicate and tasty moon cakes sitting on porcelain plates. Or expect to find myself proudly writing my

Chinese name in large and wavering brushstrokes. Even one of the very few traditional rituals that my parents did honor, on the occasion of my first birthday, is only a story, related in passing when my own daughter turned one. I have no photo of myself sitting in front of a tray full of different objects, each chosen to represent a vocation or direction in life. I was told that I reached without hesitation for the deed to the house! As a child, I would have been embarrassed by such a picture, but now I regret there is no tangible record of that ceremony. A picture to slip between those of myself wearing a hat and trying to blow out the candles on the cake with pink icing. A picture to indicate that I come from a culture with centuries of rituals. A link to my heritage that could make me feel proud.

My parents never pushed us to maintain our Chinese culture. I was bilingual until the age of three, and then when I went to nursery school and switched exclusively to the use of English, nothing was done to stop me. Pictures by Picasso and Klee were hung on our walls, and when my sister announced one day at dinner that she wanted hamburgers, preferably cheeseburgers, none of this "gross napa cabbage stuff," my mother started adding ground beef and Velveeta cheese to her shopping list.

All this served to fortify the illusion I was creating for myself: that I was not "really Chinese." If only I could do something about these eyes and this hair, I could turn into the white person I longed to be.

But this is not what childhood looked like for everyone. Some women grew up with a clear sense of their heritage: its social customs, celebrations, language, values, and beliefs. They went to Chinese or Japanese language school and recall with fondness a grandparent who lived with them and kept alive the mother tongue. They received the red money envelopes or watched the pounding of the mochi, and remember playing with friends or relatives who also had black hair, who also had high cheekbones.

And yet, while I am aware of wishing I had been exposed to more of my Chinese culture as a child, I also realize that this opportunity created, for many women who experienced it, a source of conflict. A common theme is the sense of having been raised in two different worlds, perhaps associating with white classmates and friends during the day, but returning to an Asian household each afternoon. Unfortunately, it is difficult for one child to hold this delicate balance of old and new. Too often, she finds that her attempt to explore the American part of her identity is greeted with anger from her parents. Only later in life, if the parents themselves have become acculturated, can the conflict be resolved. But the sad thing is, sometimes, that never happens.

Diana is a psychologist who has tried to come to terms with the traditional influences that formed her life. Conflict between the old ways and the new ways came most sharply into focus in an incident involving her daughter and her mother.

"My parents were both raised in China in very traditional families and were taught Confucian values of filial piety, obedience, keeping opinions and feelings to oneself. They passed them on to us and yet, at the same time, pushed the family to acculturate, to follow the American way of life. When we were young, we lived in an apartment and I still remember my mother telling me about looking out the window one day and noticing that the neighbors hung a line full of clothes out to dry. She assumed that this was how things should be done and so thereafter would even wash clean clothes in order to have enough laundry to hang on the line. My mother also heard that children were supposed to bring an apple to the teacher. So my oldest sister was given a red shiny apple to bring in on her first day of school. She wanted to obey her mother, yet she felt awkward about presenting the gift. Every day she'd go through that conflict, feel the pressure, and by the end of the year had to throw away a rotten apple left in her desk all that time.

"We didn't celebrate many traditional holidays and when we resisted being taught the language, my parents gave up. And yet it's clear that we were raised with many of the traditional expectations. Studying, getting A's, was all-important; socializing or making friends was at the bottom of the list. In school I was the only Asian, so I tried hard to blend in. I'd pick friends who were supportive of me, not necessarily the best students. That would sooner or later provoke a comment about my sister's choice of friends, who were 'all on the honor roll.'

"Studying hard was considered the best route to success. Originally, my grandfather believed that you had to have a Ph.D. or M.D. to count. Sadly enough, one of my uncles who only got his M.A. felt that he could never please his father and committed suicide. But after living in the U.S. for a while, Grandfather changed his tune—since Westerners seemed to value money so much, he decided that success could be measured in terms of dollars. Recently, my husband and I decided to build our own house. My husband said to me, 'Oh, your parents are really going to love our new place, they'll be impressed.' My response: 'I thought *I* was the Chinese one here.' I don't know how to break the news to my older sister, whose own house isn't as nice. I know it will be hurtful to her.

"Which relates to another dynamic in my family. My parents would often rank us. You're number one in croquet, you're number one in bridge, or whatever. I'm sure the houses we live in now are also ranked. Intrafamily ratings were not directly applied to academic success, but my parents had another way of letting us know where we stood. 'Did you know that Mrs. Shen's son just got into Harvard Medical School? And his brother has a Fulbright scholarship. Such nice boys, those Shens.' My sister and I were very competitive, and it was hard on me because I was older but not quite as good a student. Three out of five of us were valedictorian. I'm not one of them. I'm sure that's one reason I stayed away from the sciences and went into psychology. One way to avoid the comparisons was not to play the same game.

"We were never allowed to 'talk back' to our parents. When those silver half-dollars first came into fashion, my parents started looking for and keeping them. They were worth a lot more than their face value. One day at school, my sister learned that it was a bad idea to hoard these coins, they needed to be in circulation. She came home that afternoon and tried to explain this concept to my parents, who reacted in the extreme to what they considered impudence on the part of their child. How *dare* she try to tell them what to do. They actually told her, 'Go ahead then. Report us to the government and have us shot.' My sister cried all day, and I still have vivid memories of this incident. And when my younger sister started dating a man who was half Puerto Rican, they went nuts. My mother tried to get me to convince her to give him up. When they visited her once and found my sister's boyfriend in the house, they just sat on the sofa through the whole evening, arms crossed in front of their chests. And then threatened to cut her off if she married him.

"This threat of abandonment, this demand for obedience at all costs, was recently tested with respect to my daughter. Our nanny quit suddenly and I was in a real bind, needed child care right away. I had real doubts about whether I should ask my mother for help, and the sad fact is that I should have taken these doubts seriously. Instead, I paid dearly for my decision. One day, my mother was emptying out the dishwasher when my daughter walked into the room. 'No, Grandma, my mom always puts the cups on this lower shelf so I can reach them by myself.' My mother was outraged at this. 'How can you talk to your grandmother like this? You think I'm your *servant*, you can order me around?' My mother was crying and screaming, and my daughter had no idea how to react. But by the time silence reigned, it was clear that an impasse had been created that will never be bridged. The incident won't be mentioned again—that's what our family does with painful events—but I know my mother will never feel the same about her granddaughter. Something has been irrevocably lost and I'm feeling sad and angry at the same time.

"We never talked about difficult subjects. Sex is certainly close to the top of the list. I remember when I got my period, my mother told me how to take care of myself, but she said it in a way that I felt embarrassed that this was happening to me. I tried to hide it. When my sister told me she understood why I was so grumpy at certain times of the month, I was mortified. I knew nothing about sex, except the bare minimum of facts. I used to play with some family friends who happened to be boys. We would always go up to my room to play board games. One day, my mother told me not to take them there anymore, I was too old. I had no idea what she was talking about except that possibly they'd see my box of sanitary napkins on the shelf. As a therapist, for a long time I had difficulty bringing up with my clients the subject of sex. Now I can handle that topic OK during sessions, but I'm still reluctant to talk to my daughter. I tell my husband, 'OK, maybe next year I'll get into that subject.' Maybe next year she'll learn about the birds and bees."

Here is what it's like for a mother and a daughter, loving each other, but looking at the world through different lenses. Holly is a talented and successful young writer learning to negotiate the ways of the dominant culture; Susan is in some ways more comfortable with the world as her parents presented it to her. Holly speaks first.

"In fifth grade, in Manhattan, Kansas, of all places, I got linked up with the only other Asian in class. He was South Vietnamese, I was Japanese American, but what the hell! My teacher, an ignoramus, figured we could work together, encourage each other and thus excel. I'm sure he took one look at us and thought, "Aha! Must be twins separated at birth." But aside from this incident, I didn't notice a lot of overt discrimination as a child.

"What I did notice, however, was the tension between who I really am as a person and who my parents raised me to be. Between what the Japanese American community expected of me and what I wanted to make of my life, I was raised not to value myself—or my sex—very highly. Always to put others first. To be dutiful. And never to question authority; anyone who knows more or even appears to know more merits my deference. I've always felt that the Japanese American men I was supposed to acquiesce to were not as sharp as I, that I could take on many of them with half my brain tied behind my back.

"My mother has pushed me very hard and is genuinely pleased by my success. But I think part of that stems from the fact that she never had a chance to reach her potential. She says she is very happy with the way her life has turned out, but for myself, I know I would be feeling unfulfilled. And in a way, I believe that my parents reinforce my subversive behavior as I act out what they feel but cannot express. However, if you asked them, I'm sure they would deny this.

"By the time I was fifteen, I knew I was going to have to leave school and strike out on my own. I wrote my first novel, about a gay white man, before I was nineteen and I believed all along that I was absolutely doing the right thing. Kind of like the bumblebee who was never told that it is aerodynamically impossible for her to fly. But now, I look back on that period of my life with something like a twinge of regret. Recently, I talked to my parents about precisely this issue and voiced my concern about the repercussions of my choices on their lives. I told them I knew they had been ostracized by their friends for being 'bad parents.' I mean, how in the world are you supposed to explain that your only daughter is a high school dropout? My father corroborated my sense of things; my mother only said, 'Well, things were so bad at home that I didn't really care what was going on outside.'

"I have a curious relationship with my identity as Japanese American. Away from the community, I have a great deal of pride in my heritage. But when my work or my life brings me back in contact, I feel my alliance slipping. So much racism, sexism, classism. Hey, these guys just escaped the ghetto themselves, but that doesn't prevent them from using the soapbox to project their view about who belongs, who doesn't. All the things I am, or have done, are not socially sanctioned: being a writer, being independent, leaving school, flapping my yap in public.

"Raised the way I was, it has been hard for me to get where I wanted to be. I never really liked the traditional Japanese values, but I bought them hook, line, and sinker. I have had to work hard at overcoming the constraints, but I know that the internal self-censoring mechanism still operates. So, at nineteen, thrust into the cruel world of book promotion, I stumbled along. One thing that helped was the development of a mentor relationship with a publicist who works in L.A. She'd watch clips of my interviews and tell me, 'Let's hear a little more enthusiasm! A little more pride in your work!' She has also helped me overcome that self-effacing persona we are supposed to project. At this point, I'm perfectly at ease hearing myself described in glowing terms. I know that, after the age of twenty-five, 'promising young author' can quickly become 'should have/could have.' Youth is wasted on the young, but not on me.

"My family is proud of me. They love the fact that I'm a successful writer, although I doubt that many of my relatives really appreciate what is between the covers of that solid object they call a book. It would have been so much easier if I had chosen a career that was more, well, respectable. Comprehensible, explicable. Something with a road map to point the direction you should take. And it would be nice if it also required a college degree, better yet a master's. When Maria Shriver came to my parents' house to do an interview, she asked my mom what I liked to do besides write. 'Cooking,' said my mother, 'sewing.'

"The contrast between my extended family's style and my own was highlighted at a recent gathering. One of my uncles, who is passive in the extreme, and I were having dinner at a restaurant. And receiving lousy service. My uncle paid the bill, went ahead of me to get the car. He also left a generous tip. What, tip this jerk? I asked to speak to the manager, explained how disappointed I was, and said I would not be coming back. His obsequiousness did nothing to change my views, nor did it deter me from picking up the tip and returning it to my uncle as soon as we drove away. My uncle was mortified, and still speaks about this incident.

"I know that my parents would like me to get married. Hopefully to someone respectable. They want grandchildren, and they know I will be alone after they are gone. I myself am not opposed to marriage, but if I was, my mother would tear her hair out! She'd probably snatch me bald-headed, too.''

Susan (Holly's mother) tells her story.

"I think of myself as very Japanese. I'm a Nissei on my father's side, my mother was raised in Japan. It would have been very difficult for me to grow up any other way than this: as the daughter of very 'old country' parents who raised me to honor the traditional values. I have an auntie in Japan who used to tell me, 'You're more Japanese than the people your age who live here!'

"In my family, the males were catered to. I was never directly told that, as a girl, I was not worth as much as my brothers, but that's the inference I made. I simply knew that less was expected of me. For example, I should go to college, but mainly because it would be easier for me to marry well. Once I got married—to a nice Japanese man—it would be my role to defer to him. And when my mother was stricken with lung cancer, it was my responsibility to take care of her.

"Then we had Holly. She has always had an inner drive, a desire to be her own person. I wish I knew then what I know now about parenting. About helping children succeed in this culture. When she was fifteen, Holly quit school to become a novelist. That was a very traumatic time for all of us. But what could we do?

"Having Holly 'out there' has opened my eyes. Trying to make it in the literary world, she told me that she was not equipped to fight and claw her way to the top. To step on others in order to ascend. Japanese, after all, would say, 'Please, step on *me*!' My own instinct is not to make waves, not to draw attention to myself. I taught this to my daughter. If she wanted to try something unconventional, I would say, 'But what will people think?' But because of Holly's experience, I have changed how I see my own life, my values, my culture. I realize that as nice as some Japanese values may be—for example, the emphasis on kindness, politeness—they won't help you in the business world. If you don't help yourself, no one else will.

"I am very proud of my daughter. Proud of her for taking risks and not being the nail that just lines up with the rest of them. My mother was a pioneer, making her way here from the old country; Holly is a pioneer in the new land."

Carol is a schoolteacher who grew up in an environment she calls "schizophrenic," because it was a blend of traditional Chinese beliefs and inventive adaptations of the new culture. Like others in her position, she has had to create her own reality, her own way of looking at the world. Without role models to follow, you invent your life as you go along, choosing which traditions to hold on to, which to reject.

"When you stand at the threshold, you have to leave the old country behind—the people, the traditions, the way of life—and move into the new country. Our parents made that decision for us. And now we have to move on.

"My father started out in San Francisco's Chinatown, but he didn't like it there. So he picked up and headed for the Central Valley. The story is that he arrived with twenty-five cents in his pocket, his last quarter, and was afraid to spend it. His first job was peddling vegetables on the street, then he bought a truck and eventually a store. There weren't many Chinese in our small town, but there was a community extending across several towns that kept traditions alive. When Dad first arrived, he was denied a haircut because he was Chinese, and later the real-estate agent had to check if it was OK with the neighbors before my parents bought their first house. Still, Dad persisted, made friends with whites in the community, ultimately became well respected. I see it like this: My father was in a place where he did not fit in, but he *made* himself fit. I'm not sure I would have stuck it out the way he did.

"In a way, our childhood was kind of schizophrenic. On the one hand, we were told to go out there, to blend in, but at the same time we always knew we were Chinese. For example, we worked at the store—Dad wouldn't have considered hiring any help. We always knew our parents had made great sacrifices for us and there was no question that we would succeed. They would say, 'You're a Chinese kid, you *have* to be good.' The obligation to stand tall was clear to each one of us. And the fact is, although neither parent went far with their own education, all seven of their children got a degree and are respectable people now.

"Another thing is that doing well is not just an individual achievement, it's a matter of family pride. We were too poor to eat out very often, but every time one of us accomplished something, winning an essay contest, getting elected class president, etc., all would share in the glory by going to a restaurant.

"At the same time, my father knew that we had to be able to make it in the white community. They spoke English at home. In fact, my mother realized just how bad her Chinese was when she went to China to visit the small village she had lived in fifty years earlier. Nothing had changed. A man walked up to her and knew her name. She even found some chalk drawings she recognized on the wall of a house they had lived in. But she did get a letter from the village later alluding to those 'girls who couldn't speak Chinese.' My parents did celebrate holidays such as Chinese New Year's, but instead of being just a family event, Dad would invite customers, all kinds of people to let them share in our tradition. I think this explains why I never felt there was anything wrong with being Chinese.

"This is my opinion about traditions. They teach you a lot about the culture, but they also keep you boxed in, don't necessarily let you be who you really are. Culture is like a magnet that draws you, but not always where you want to go. My father wanted us to be successful in the white world, but he couldn't let go of traditional ways of thinking when it came to the marriage choices of his children. I met and became engaged to a white man, and for a long time my parents simply gave me the silent treatment. I was very hurt. It's hard to be cut off from the adoration of your parents, but I'm also bullheaded, and I was going to marry who I wanted to marry. The feeling of obedience in Chinese families is ingrained in you. But there comes a time when you have to make your own decision or you'll just be chasing a dream. In my case, I dated a Chinese man for quite a while, and he wanted to get married. My parents loved him, it would have been so easy, but I knew it wasn't right for me. I couldn't have been the best person I could be with him. So I broke it off.

"As it turned out, my parents didn't have a chance to stretch our their dismay about my white fiancé for too long. They were so tightly bound by tradition that even if they didn't approve of my choice, they still had to give the wedding banquet or it would have *looked* bad. So I said, OK, but we can't afford it, you'll have to pay. They did. And recently my oldest uncle commented that our family is now like chop suey—a little bit of this, a little bit of that. And it's OK.

"Dan and I have been married now for twenty-five years, and have a seventeen-year-old daughter. I don't think we've had a lot of conflicts due to cultural differences, but if you think you can go into an interracial marriage with no rocks to climb over, you are crazy. Even though I'm married to a white man, teaching in a white community, some traditions linger. When Mom calls to say she needs me, I drop whatever I'm doing. My husband has to understand things like that. It's part of who I am, I can't just erase it. If someone tries to wrest you away from those roots, they are trying to take you away from who you are. So Dan goes to all these Chinese banquets with me and sometimes he's the only white guy there. He's a good sport.

"Now comes the question of raising my own child. From my mother's point of view, kids are born bad, you have to train them to be good. I see it this way: My daughter's seventeen, I'm fifty. I have to make the decisions. Schoolwork is a must. Most things are black and white, very little gray.

"When my daughter asks what box to check, I say, check the one that says 'Chinese.' You are Chinese even though your father is white. It's like this. In our house, we have forks in the drawer. But the chopsticks are right next to them. We use both."

Marcia's childhood also reflected the split in values.

"I grew up in two different worlds—the Caucasian world of my friends and the traditional Chinese world of my mainland immigrant parents at home. In a way, I never felt entirely comfortable in either place, aware that while I was considered part of the group at school, I never saw myself as "dateable," and equally aware that I was not entirely at home in the Chinese circle of friends my parents surrounded themselves with. I never had much chance to socialize with kids from school because there were always so many obligations on weekends—Chinese school, Chinese church, family friends expecting us for dinner. And beyond the external social environment, I also knew that I had been raised with traditional Asian values of duty, respect for parents, and the fear of behaving in a way that would bring shame to the family.

"At times, I would observe my white friends' lives and find myself attracted to what looked like a lot of freedom. But at the same time, it disturbed me how they'd talk about their parents or how they'd make these plans without any concern for their parents' opinions. And to this day, I can still hear my poor mother pleading with me, 'You can't compare me with your friends' parents!' As to living the American way, the idea of necking in the backseat with a boyfriend sounded interesting, but from my Asian upbringing, I knew I wouldn't be comfortable in that situation. Let alone be able to find a guy to test out this concept.

"I can't say I ever felt embarrassed about being Chinese. I guess my parents' strategy of continually reminding us that we are '100 percent Chinese' worked. To this day, they still have a very strong connection to the Asian community. We ate only Chinese food at home. My mother did know how to make spaghetti and something we called 'Gravy Train,' a dish with beef and gravy over mashed potatoes. But we spoke only Chinese at home until second grade, when my teacher explained to them that I might be hampered in associating with classmates because I didn't understand the slang.

"By senior year, I started a small rebellion against my parents' expectations. They got me a car, and I decided to do some things with friends instead of spending every weekend with them. Of course, my mom would lay a guilt trip on me. 'Oh, everyone will miss you *so* much if you don't come!' So the next week, I'd stay at home, but by the following week, when I couldn't stand it any longer, I'd be off again. And so on.

"For college, I wanted a school where I could be with other Asian Americans. I went to Stanford and even lived in an Asian dorm. Still, I had both a white clique of friends and an Asian clique, and I couldn't quite figure out where I belonged. I dated a few Asian guys, but they were never that interesting to me. They didn't quite fit my image of what a man should be, and I could never get over the incestuous feel to our relationship—in a way, these men seemed somehow like brothers. How can you get romantically involved with your brother?

"One thread that kept me connected to my parents was their continued academic expectations of me. My dad was a doctor, and expected his children to follow suit. All my siblings did. I was premed at first, but later majored in biology and took a lot of hard sciences, but I felt even that wasn't good enough for him. I felt I had failed by not pursuing medicine.

"I also provoked my parents to the point of threatening to cut off my tuition when I announced that I wanted to live in a vegetarian co-op interested in recycling. And that I would be sharing a room with four guys, a room I had deliberately selected because I knew the guys planned to sleep on the roof and I'd have the space to myself. Ironically enough, while my parents saw me as getting into some kind of radical behavior, my friends were seeing me as a traditionalist. They nicknamed me 'Dodo' after the extinct bird. I was one of a kind—a college student who didn't drink, use drugs, or mess around. Naive or not, I wore that like a badge of honor and still answer to that nickname.

"The conflict between my two worlds appeared again in my choice of a husband. When I married my first husband, a Caucausian man, my parents were very upset and told me they wouldn't come to the wedding. Then, when I told them I was planning to divorce, they were unhappy again. I couldn't win. Even though they didn't like him, they still felt I should give it a better chance, save face. I shouldn't stigmatize my family like that. After the divorce, my mother kept on beating up on me verbally until one day, we talked and I said to her, 'I know I screwed up. I know I made a mistake and I'm never going to be able to make amends.' I think she figured out that it wasn't going to do any good to keep harping on me, so she dropped the subject and never returned to it. Happy ending: I have since remarried and my parents truly like my husband. Even if he is Caucasian."

For Eleanor, the Chinese traditions that defined her family are also associated with an accumulation of unhappy memories. Her work as an adult has been to try to recreate herself on her own terms.

"A few years ago, I helped my parents move out of their condo and into a retirement facility. My father had Alzheimer's, which was bad enough, but my mother had to make sure that she was sicker yet, that she simply couldn't cope. She has never learned to do the things that would give her some independence: write a check or speak the language adequately. And so she alternates between self-aggrandizement ('Look what a great job I've done raising you kids') and self-hatred for all the things she never accomplished. As I was emptying out cupboards with sixteen years of accumulation, I kept finding empty yogurt containers. Carefully washed and each with its own lid. It hit me again how much emphasis my parents placed on never wasting a *thing*. Not a plastic bag. Not a rubber band, for God's sake. The thought comes back to me, 'Is this Chinese? Or is this just my family? And all the loneliness and lack of acknowledgment I felt as a child, is this the culture or is this just us?'

"I don't know much about my family's history, just some stories that are more like folktales. It's not that important to me. I do know that both of my parents came from wealth, from generations of 'haves,' and that their marriage was arranged. That my mother was sent here by her future in-laws when the Japanese invaded China and, on the boat over, had to sneak down to the lower berth to get rice because she was from a Buddhist family and could not eat meat.

"When I was six or seven, I came home from school one day to find my mother lying on the bed with an empty bottle of pills. She claims she did not take an overdose. But she was very depressed, having just received the news from China that all of her family had perished, all the wealth was gone. This, along with the knowledge that my older dyslexic brother was a perennial source of disappointment to them, left me one clear path: Be good. Don't screw up, be the perfect child so my parents could show me off to their friends. Be responsible for their happiness.

"Everything for Chinese children has an expectation attached. We are expected to get A's; the veiled threat is always there that we won't be loved if we don't. My brother is fifty years old. He's a fine person but he never did that well in school and consequently labeled himself as the black sheep, hated himself as much as my parents hated him for his shortcomings. Just recently, he has started to see himself as something other than a failure. He is part of a church group that accepts him for who he is. It's an incredible blessing.

"When I was at thirteen, we moved from Long Island, where life was actually quite good for a few years, to Los Angeles, where things were brutal. For one thing, my mother could not adjust to the new environment and absolutely flipped out. My father relocated us specifically to Brentwood because it had the best schools. It also happened to be extremely white and life was based on the current TV shows. God forbid you do anything that was not 'in.' I felt like a misfit, but not so much because I was Chinese, more because I couldn't dance, didn't know the lyrics to the top-ten songs. Eventually, I found a set of very nice girlfriends who were all good students, but not the pimply nerds. By eleventh grade, however, they started to date boys from this matched set of guys at school. I was left by the wayside. I knew I was not being asked out because I was Chinese, but this didn't particularly bother me. Surfer girls were in, and I wasn't a surfer. In fact, being Chinese was a good rationalization for my status.

"From high school, I went to UC Berkeley. I didn't really meet other Asians there. In fact, I was kind of scared off by the Chinese Students Association, afraid I wouldn't fit in. They all seemed to come from extended families, to know about their culture. Whereas for me, my parents seemed more like a generation set adrift from China. Their approach to life was 'acultural.' Freshman year I lived in the dorm. But sophomore year was a dilemma. What to do? One, another year in the dorm (too dorky); two, get an apartment (too much work); or three, rush a sorority. I decided to become Miss Perfect and take option three. I still remember so clearly the events of Rush Week and my acceptance into the waspiest, richest, blondest sorority on campus. After I was accepted, I felt I had really conquered something, but once I was living there I felt like a misfit again. I was very involved in house activities, but I never found anyone to be really close to.

"After college, I spent some time in Hawaii. That was strange. All my life, I had wanted to blend in and couldn't, and finally I'm in a place where I don't stand out. But I find that now I'm invisible, not memorable, and I don't like that either. I'm just 'one of the girls.' Literally. And once, when I was introduced to a professor while in a group with other Asians, I had the experience of being completely ignored the next day. When I tried to get his attention, he apologized. 'Oh, you look just like all my other students.' Now, in my work as an architect, I do some traveling in Asia. Recently, when I was in Singapore, I realized that I looked like I might fit in, but I really didn't. The only place I have any sense of being at home is in my own house. And there, the feeling is tenuous at best.

"My first husband, Frank, was a good man from a good family. He was also Jewish, and we used to go to Seders with his family. This brought up for me very painful memories of Christmas and other holidays in my childhood. The other kids at school would all be so excited about their two weeks' vacation. But for me, I knew it would just be going to my dark, sad house, waiting until trees were half price and then finding maybe one present on Christmas morning. A very chintzy, compromised attempt at any celebration. This fanatic control over every penny spent became a big issue in my marriage and, I believe, contributed significantly to its demise. Frank was an architect, very skilled at his profession, and wanted his own practice. He was able to launch his own business, but could never break even. I lost respect for him and eventually we divorced.

"What is this thing about Chinese and money? For a long time, I thought it was just my family, but now I know it's the culture. It's not just being cheap, it's *Chinese*! It was such a relief for me to figure this out and I am now working on trying to overcome this trait. To be able to spend a dollar without feeling guilty. The scene from *Joy Luck Club* about the daughter who keeps track of every penny she or her husband spends, keeps lists and accounts—all that cracks me up. I had just assumed things happened like this only in my family, but now I know better.

"My parents are both in a retirement facility with Dad in a special Alzheimer's unit. I feel absolutely OK about where they are, although the thought did cross my mind that my mother might want to come live with me. But we both know she'd never be happy here, vacillating between feeling used because she had to water my plants or lonely because I'm not around much. I don't feel at all guilty. And I think back to what my parents provided for me. Recently, a friend's daughter graduated from Wellesley. There was such an outpouring of love for that young woman that I found myself feeling tremendously sad remembering my own graduation. My parents did not even show up.

"When I visit my parents now, it's a pretty futile effort. My mother just tells the same story over and over. So I've made an arrangement that is working out great for both of us: I've hired a very good friend to check on her and do the things she needs done. Liz actually gets along with my mother better than I do; there isn't all the baggage. We don't have to go through the 'I get mad, she gets hurt and paranoid' routine.

"My therapist once told me, 'It's never too late to have a first childhood.' Celebrate your own accomplishments! Although I realize my parents did the best they could with me, it wasn't enough. I'm trying to make up the deficits on my own."

2 COMING OF AGE

When I was fifteen years old, my friend Carol talked me into going to a dance at our high school. Of course, we had promised each other we would stick together through the evening, and, of course, she wound up leaving me high and dry. I called my mother in tears and asked her to pick me up early, a very uncool thing to do, which only increased my discomfort and pain. On the ride home, I sat silent and sniffling, while my mother tried to reassure me. She told me that we (meaning Asians) mature later and besides, in the larger scheme of things, a high school dance on a Friday night wasn't very important. She reminded me that I was a talented and hardworking student and that I had a bright future to look forward to. Boys and dating were less important and would happen in their own good time.

I didn't respond, but believed in my heart that nothing could be further from the truth. At that moment, I would gladly have traded all my good grades for one soulful look from a blond- or brown-haired boy who knew how to signal his desirability by the way he leaned against a wall. I hated being passed over for dates or clubs or teams. I hated having to console myself with the thought that the guys who ignored me could end up high school dropouts. I shuddered at the possibility of having to settle for some terminally uncool Chinese boy bound for Cal Tech. But because my mother was offering advice from her heart, because she was my mother, and because I was now stuck in the car with her, I hoped against hope that she was right.

Adolescence is a rough time for almost everyone. For me, there were particular issues that made this period of my life if not harder, then at least more complicated. Adolescents yearn to be just like everyone else, but everyone else around me was white, not Chinese. Adolescents are expected to start pulling away from the family. However painful this may be to parents, it is seen as a necessary task. But in Chinese culture, there is far less emphasis on transforming the parent-child relationship. It is OK to remain "dependent" on one another for a lifetime. Adolescents are attuned to the most minute details of physical appearance, each blemish a new agony. I lived with acne on a face that, even without pimples, was still repugnant to me because of its Asian features. Adolescents are notoriously embarrassed by their parents. Mine were not only uncool in the generic sense, they also kept gross-looking food in the refrigerator and spoke with something of an accent. Adolescence is also the time of struggling with identity. I realize now that I could not have begun this process, because there was so much of my *self* that I rejected, cut off.

And then there is that awkward, passionate, groping attempt to experience oneself as a sexual being. I spent my first night away from the college dorm with my boyfriend James, a senior at Cal Tech. I was a freshman, still very sheltered and very much in what I considered to be love with a tall, dark-haired man of Scottish descent who was studying at a very prestigious university. We had dinner at his cafeteria—tough steak and desiccated potatoes, which I didn't taste anyhow—and decided not to drive the twenty-five miles back to my school. Admittedly, sharing a single bed with a six-foot-tall man required some physical agility, but mostly what I remember about that night was the warmth and tenderness. I don't think we got much sleep, but I do remember waking up in his arms.

The next day was a different story. We drove back to Scripps. I drifted through the remainder of the afternoon on a cloud, until later that day when I was notified of a phone call. It was my mother, calling to let me know that she had heard about my night away. A Chinese student at my boyfriend's dorm apparently saw us, put two and two together, and called his mother to tell her what he had witnessed. His mother immediately informed mine, and the rest, as they say, is history.

The ironic part of this whole story is that James and I, while sharing an intimate night together, had not actually made love. Yes, part of me did want the same freedom that I saw my white friends experimenting with (and recounted to me in explicit detail), but something held me back. Fear, standards of morality, questions of honor, concerns I couldn't articulate at the time. James knew this and managed to honor my wishes for the duration of our relationship.

Later in that year, I would confide to a good friend who was a junior that I was very embarrassed about other people imagining me some kind of inhibited virgin, but I could not bring myself to engage in the activity that would alter my status. You could have heard my sigh of relief when Jeannie confided to me that she didn't mind the *impression* she created when she allowed her debonair French boyfriend, Pierre, to spend the night in her room.

I cannot say how much of my reluctance to explore the full measure of my sexuality has roots in my experience as Asian and American. However, I now see it as a part of the picture. I remember my mother telling me that "nothing is more wonderful (maybe she said romantic) than two virgins on their wedding night." I knew she believed that sex should be reserved for marriage. But that was not the real impediment. What kept me locked in passionate but chaste embrace in single beds with men I was attracted to was the fact that I had disliked the way I looked for so long that it was almost impossible for me to feel safe and comfortable in my own body. Also, I think a part of me believed that my best, my truest self was not grounded in a physical reality. All those years of feeling like the uninvited guest, the little girl with her nose pressed to the window of other people's parties, the white child imprisoned in a Chinese body, led me to this invention: that my value lay in my intelligence, not my physical self.

And so, for me, those years were marked by a curious mixture of desire and detachment. The desire to do what anyone else was doing, the desire to project a certain image of sophistication, tempered by the inability to truly come to terms with my self and my own body.

I think most Asian American adolescents experience the same highs and lows, the same angst that is prevalent in the culture at large. But their experience, like mine, is often colored by the fact of ethnicity and minority in ways that are not always obvious. For example, to the obvious fact of adolescent rebellion must be added the concept of culture clash. To the process of identity consolidation must be added the complication of ethnic self-image. And for some, adolescence simply begins later in life—perhaps not until you go off to college and are exposed to different viewpoints.

Margaret is a Sansei and a schoolteacher. She remembers her adolescence as a time of learning more about her ethnicity, both in positive and in negative ways. For Margaret, as for many other Asian American women, the conflict between home values and school, or dominant-culture, values, did not manifest itself until this point in her life, when peer influences gained the upper hand.

"I've visited Japan a few times, and each time I tried to arrange a trip to our family's small village near Hiroshima. The family cemetery is still there, some of our land, even a Samurai sword. But I haven't made it yet and now I understand the family home is falling into disrepair. That makes me sad. I grew up in Salinas (rural central California) in a very westernized environment. Both of my parents came from large families, so we did see the cousins a lot, especially on holidays. For New Year's, we'd spend the whole week cooking all the traditional foods, but that was the only really Japanese thing we did. My older sisters learned some Japanese, but my parents stopped teaching their children the language after the war, after their internment in camp. And even though my grandparents were originally Buddhist, they became disillusioned with the religion and converted to Christianity. We went to an all-white Methodist church.

"I never really thought that much about being Japanese until I was in eighth grade and did a project about the camps. My parents didn't ordinarily say anything about camp, it was too painful. But they would answer my questions if I asked. It wasn't until my father was dying, however, that we found out some of the hardest truths of his experience there. Dad used to leave my mother—who had two small children—every morning and go wandering around the camp's perimeter. Mom always felt abandoned, very bitter. Finally, we learned that he had been subjected to abuse by Japanese who faced deportation because they, unlike him, had refused to sign the loyalty oath. He left my mom and her babies in order to protect them from also being harassed. But he could never talk about it, and so my mom never knew.

"After that, my next real encounter with my ethnicity came in high school. I was very shy, not popular, didn't like the way I looked, had no boyfriends. I came home very depressed one day and I remember my mom saying to me, 'You know, maybe boys don't ask you out because you are Japanese. This town we live in has a history of being anti-Japanese.' This was a real eye opener to me and it didn't make me feel better, although I'm sure that was my mother's intention. My reaction was—Great! Here you're telling me something I can't do anything about. This is only going to make it harder for me.

"My sophomore year, I got into this thing about people changing their eyes (to look less Asian). I'd read stories in the papers, in magazines. It wasn't that I really wanted the surgery for myself, but I was always drawn to those Maybelline commercials and how the women looked in them. After a while, this preoccupation gradually faded and I went on to something else. I wished I had a better figure—or even a figure at all. This didn't really have to do with being Japanese or not, and when I started to look around, I realized that I wasn't the only one who was still wearing a training bra. I became more accepting of who I was. Still, I sometimes wondered if I wasn't dating because of my race or because I didn't own enough Capezios. There was no real way of finding out and nothing could be done anyhow.

"My best friend at the time was Jani, this popular blond girl who also had lots of money. Enough to buy Capezios in all the hues of the rainbow. My mother tried to discourage my friendship with her, feeling I would be influenced badly, but I held my ground. I wasn't consciously trying to act white by hanging around with her, but maybe that's what I wanted.

"Until this point, I had always been the good child—obedient, good grades, no one ever had to call home about my behavior. Fay, my older sister, already had the role as the difficult child, would mortify my parents by falling asleep in church. And then, Jani and I discovered the Beatles. I became a Beatlemaniac, it was my *whole* life. This drove my parents crazy. They loved classical music and they had never dealt with a child that liked rock and roll. My junior summer, we found out that the Beatles were going to be in concert in San Francisco. Jani and I just *had* to go. I got a job working in the strawberry fields so I could earn enough money for tickets, a hotel room, and transportation. I even made reservations, knowing full well I could not tell my mother the truth of my plans. Well, she did find out and almost prevented us from going, until Jani's parents intervened and said they were planning to drive us. I really didn't feel guilty about defying my mother, but to this day, she is still upset with me about this incident. I know she will carry that with her to her grave.

"I also wanted to wear makeup, in an abortive effort to make myself prettier. One day, I came to the dinner table all made up and my dad says, 'Go wash that off. You look like a raccoon.' So I did run some water over my face and came back to dinner, but I didn't touch my food, just sat there sniffling. That did not prevent me from wanting to experiment with cosmetics, even if it made me look like a 'hakajun' (white person). In retrospect, I see this and my obsession with the Beatles as a way to escape all the high school stuff that was so painful for me.

"Going off to college gave me a very different perspective, especially regarding my ethnic background. I had a chance to experience the opposite swing of the pendulum. I first went to UC Davis and was very lonely there, called my mother every weekend. But then I transferred to Berkeley just at the point where being Asian was a big deal—the whole ethnic studies thing just taking off.

"I happened to hook up with a cousin who took me under his wing, made a 'project' out of me. He tried to convince me that there was something wrong with me because I didn't want to hang around with and date Asians exclusively. 'What's the matter—you ashamed of us or something?' He took me on the Asian circuit—all the parties, etc. After a while, I found out that he had been using me as a kind of cover—there was this woman he was interested in and he would ask if I minded getting my own ride home. He stopped taking me places but by then I was already connected to the community. In a way, it was nice. I started to get in touch with what it meant to be Japanese and to make some Asian friends.

"But in the end, I gave it all up because I found myself under this increasing pressure to decide—are you one of *us* or are you one of *them*? There was a certain plaza at Berkeley frequented by Asian students. If I walked through with a white friend, my Asian friends would all pretend they didn't even know who I was. The all-or-nothing attitude was too much for me.

"Now I'm married to a Japanese man. His family, unlike mine, is very Japanese and he even thought at one time about living permanently in Japan. But in terms of looking for the traditional submissive female, I think I've actually gotten more of that from Caucasian men. This one white boyfriend I had used to tell me that I was 'too nice,' but when I did become more assertive, he didn't exactly like that either, and so we broke up. With Ken, if I really want to get to him, to drive him nuts when he's being impossible, all I have to do is act superagreeable. 'Oh, of *course*, sweetheart. Whatever you want is just fine with me!' "

When trauma is added to the experience of coming of age, it becomes even more difficult to sort out issues of identity. In addition to the problems usually encountered by adolescents, Jeannie also had to contend with her family's move to Singapore and the devastating consequences of being sexually abused.

"I have moved a lot of times in my life. The other day, I figured that we must have moved eighteen times before I was in
sixth grade. My dad was a pastor, and so we were always going
from this apartment to that house. When I was twelve, we made
a major move. My father got a job as a missionary in Singapore.
At that time, I had no idea where Singapore even was, and I
imagined we'd be living in a grass hut or something. Seven years
later, I moved back to the U.S. on my own. Each of these changes
was a difficult transition for me, and with each one, I had to
spend a lot of time trying to figure out who I was. I've been back
here for three years now and I'm still trying to work out my
identity.

I remember before we left for Singapore, I was at the age
where I really wanted to fit in with everyone else. At my school,
there were the white girls and also the African American group,
but very few other Asians to hang around with. I tried very hard
to be accepted by the popular girls and felt that, because I was
Chinese, it would take more on my part. For example, I knew
you had to earn the right to be their friends by owning the right
things. So I'd sit with them at lunch and try to impress them,
saying, 'Oh yes, my mom just bought me that kind of jeans or
tennis shoes or whatever' even if she really hadn't. Actually, I
mostly wore hand-me-downs, but I worked on saying things
that would get them to say 'WOW!' Part of me felt uncomfortable, but the need to fit in was greater. In some ways, I guess
I'm still that way.

"Just when things were finally going OK at school, we moved
to Singapore. The first thing I saw when we got off the plane
was a McDonald's, so I breathed a sigh of relief. But once we
started school, I had to again go through the whole process of
trying to be accepted, even though everyone around me this time
was Chinese. I still felt different because I knew I was American.
I was conscious of being 'too white,' of standing out. I was louder
than they were, my language had too much American slang, and
girls would say things to me like, 'Don't think you're so great
just because you're from America.' Believe me, I wasn't putting
on any airs. It's just the way they perceived me. My clothes were

no longer fashionable, but this time I really didn't care. I started to develop my own style and very slowly I made friends, got accepted. I was proud of the ways that I was different from them, the ways I was American.

"Academically, however, it was a different story. When we left the U.S., I was studying fractions. By the time we got to Singapore, they were already on pre-algebra. I'm no good at math and science anyhow, even if that's what they expect of Asians. I had a very hard time with my studies and never got good grades. My parents got me these tutors, but even that didn't help. They used to threaten me that I'd never have a good future, never be able to make money. To this day, I'm haunted by the fear of turning into some kind of bag lady and having my parents proved right. What really sucked was that my younger sister had no trouble adjusting to the new school. She also liked to show me up.

"At some point, my parents talked about sending me to school in the Philippines because they thought I'd do better there. The Philippines at that time was a dangerous place, and I remember being furious that they would even consider sending me away just because my grades were bad. Part of me was angry at myself, but part of me was also angry at them for pushing me so hard.

"By the time I was sixteen, they gave up on me. I was the black sheep of the family, and they didn't want to be disappointed in me anymore. I was also turning into a rebel, sneaking out at night to go with friends to a dance club and so on. We didn't do anything bad, but they would have killed me if they knew.

"There are only three good universities in Singapore and I didn't get into any of them. So I really had no future there, and my parents agreed I could return to the States and try to make a life for myself here. At first I lived with godparents, but they have an 11:00 curfew, which I considered unreasonable. Also, they were very religious, which I no longer am. So I moved out on my own. I'm now working at a restaurant and going to school. I'll probably major in liberal or fine arts, which wouldn't be my parents' first choice, but at this point, they're happy I'm in school at all. They say, 'Just go study what you need to.' But they add, 'Don't bring shame to the family.'

"Coming back to the U.S., I had to figure out who I was again. I no longer had the feeling of pride at being different that worked for me in Singapore. And I recently experienced my first real taste of prejudice to my face. It was a rude awakening.

"One thing I do know is that I'm attracted to white men. My first date was with a Cantonese boy, but since then I haven't gone out with any other Asians. I once went out with this guy who was half black, but I never told my parents. When I was eighteen, I got this letter from my parents saying it was OK for me to date now. I'm like, if only they knew! But it still felt good to get their blessing.

"I'm still seeking my parents' approval. I'd like them to be proud of me even though I know I've disappointed them. But there's a lot I can't even tell them. The worst, the most hurtful thing is that I was sexually abused by my brother. At the time, I just thought, 'This can't be wrong because he's my brother and he loves me.' I haven't been to therapy or anything, but I am healing now. One of the best things I do for myself is to be alone and write music. I don't share this with anyone, but I can say what is there in my heart through my songs. Some day I'd like to release an album, but I know that's not practical. When I got my electric guitar for Christmas, my parents told me 'not to play any rock and roll music, just Christian songs.' But in my own room, I play whatever I like, I play what I really feel, and now I am moving toward feeling better and better about myself."

When an adolescent has to come face-to-face with racism and its myriad challenges to self-esteem, her response can take many forms. Some girls retreat, others internalize their experiences, and still others fight back in whatever way they can. Sarah found within herself a spirit of resolve and determination inherited from her parents.

"My mother is Spanish and my father is Filipino. Both suffered from discrimination on the job and elsewhere in their lives. I still remember Dad coming home one day and saying that he had scored the highest grade *ever* on the test to become a mail carrier. But it was clear to him that they didn't believe a Filipino man could do that on his own. So he asked them, 'Do you want me to take the test again?' Mom never used to talk much about her experiences. She managed to climb the corporate ladder, but now I know that she had to prove herself every step of the way. I think that's where I get my determination.

"When I was around ten years old, my parents decided to move us out of the city of San Francisco and into the suburbs. I will never forget the day we went to the sales office of the new subdivision we were interested in. We walked in. Not a word. They treated us as if we didn't even exist. Finally, my dad told us to leave. On the ride home, my mother started to cry. We asked why. Dad responded, 'They don't like the color of our skin.' I didn't understand what he meant, so I pressed him. 'We're not *white*' is what he said. Until that moment, I had always been aware of feeling different, of feeling that I didn't fit in, but never quite knowing why. Now I had a reason.

"When we finally did manage to find a house to consider buying, the real-estate agent took us over to see it. The owner of the house was white, and when we showed up at her door, she took one look at us and commented to the agent, 'I'm not sure how the neighbors are going to feel about this.' My dad's response: 'Why? Isn't our money as good as anyone else's?' I remember being scared to death to go to school. The kids would just look at us and then start whispering to themselves. I'll never forget folk-dancing class. No one would ever ask me, so I always ended up with the fattest boy in the class, William Hughes. After a while, it was like, 'Well, shall we dance?' 'Might as well.' Then there was the time we were doing some kind of performance. Mrs. Paine stood up onstage in front of the microphone trying to pair people up. Someone asked her something and so she answered, 'We do have this one little dark-complected girl here.' Meaning me.

"When I was in sixth grade, there was this popular girl named Andrea. She always wore party dresses to school. One day we had to give an oral report to the class. She gave hers, and they all hung on to her every word. My turn next. I got up to speak and this boy Gary says, 'Oh, we don't have to listen to her.' Then he started his 'Ching, chong, Chinaman' routine. I ran out of the room in tears. The only thing the teacher said was, 'Well, kids are like that.' The next day, Gary told me I was a big crybaby.

"But something inside me just couldn't accept all this without a fight. For example, I wanted to play tetherball, but the kids would never ask me to join. So I got my dad to buy me a set to put in the backyard. I still remember him pouring the concrete and all. I got really good. Finally, I was good enough to beat some of those other kids, and when they saw that, they let me play with them. And one day this kid named David started in on me. He told me my mother was a black Aunt Jemima and my father was a Fu Manchu. I got so mad, I just beat the holy crap out of him.

"At this point in my life, I was a real tomboy. My parents were in despair. But I think part of the reason might have been that this helped me be strong in standing up for myself and also gave me a way not to have to compete with girls in matters of clothes, looks, etc. In eighth grade, I finally went to a dance. But all I did was hide out in the bathroom, where I told fat Alice, 'I don't want to be here.' She said, 'I know, I don't want to be here either. My parents made me come.'

"Things got somewhat better in high school. I did get asked out on dates, but I won't forget Ralph and the freshman dance. My dad drove me to his house. His father opened the door and did this obvious double take, looking at my father out of the corner of his eye. When we got to school, his friends started to kid him about bringing me, a 'ching chong.' So I just told him we didn't have to dance, I'd call home for someone to pick me up.

"I also got this thing in my head that I was going to be a cheerleader. I practiced and practiced until I could do all the routines in my sleep. I made the squad. The teacher never liked me, never once addressed me by name. "You over there—move to your left." But when I wore that uniform, I felt *good*, I didn't care what anyone thought.

"Those years are over, thankfully. I went to my thirty-first high school reunion a few years ago, and my husband commented, 'Hey, everyone here knows you!' 'Of course they do,' I said, 'I was a cheerleader and a minority.' But what I learned at that event helped put things in perspective. Several people confided that they had wanted to approach me back then, but just didn't know how to bridge the racial differences. In a way, it felt good to hear that.''

Adolescence can also be a time for working through attitudes and issues about ethnic identity in positive as well as negative ways. Tracy's experience is typical: She went through a period when it was embarrassing to bring friends home, but then she moved past that point to find pride in her culture.

"Until I got to college, my friends and acquaintances were primarily Asian American. I never consciously sought this out, it just happened, in part because many of the people I knew were children of my parents' friends. But I also think I felt comfortable in this circle of friends because certain things were understood without having to be explained, i.e., how your parents acted.

"With white friends, things were different. I remember in junior high school being embarrassed that my parents would speak what we called 'Chenglish' [a mix of Chinese and English]. I would be like 'Mom, speak *English* around my friends.' Sometimes, if white friends came over, we'd just kind of stay upstairs, out of her way. And as my mother became more devout in her Buddhist practice, I'd avoid the family room altogether because that was where she'd keep a shrine and some incense. If I was having a sleepover, we'd tiptoe past my mother practicing her early-morning meditation, and I'd just be hoping my friends wouldn't ask me to explain what she was doing.

"But by the time I got to high school, I didn't care about this anymore, it no longer bothered me. I guess you could say I matured. I went to a private school where they stressed multiculturalism. A white friend of mine even decided to become a Buddhist, and so my mom was able to give him a lot of valuable information. That was kind of cool.

"Preparing for college, I expected that I'd develop a new circle of Asian friends, that I would just naturally gravitate to them. That's not what happened. I'm still in touch with some of my Asian friends from high school, but now my best friends are black. I went to a few meetings of the Asian student organization, but I still haven't made any close Asian friends. Some of the girls I've met seem very focused on image—clothes and appearance. That's not me. And others are very serious. I couldn't, like, party with them and not feel restrained.

"One thing I *don't* like, however, is when black or white guys tell me, 'I'm really into Asian girls.' Usually they say this when they are drunk. I'm like, 'Why?' I know they have this stereotype of Asians as exotic, mysterious. They like long black hair, think it's trendy. To me, that attitude is annoying.

"I have dated both black and white guys, but not seriously. With Asian guys, I sometimes feel I can't be who I really am. If I want to drink, for example, they'll be offended. Still, all things being equal, I'd prefer to marry an Asian American man. For the same reasons that I had mainly Asian friends as a child. There is a common ground there, an understanding. I think it will be easier on the kids not to be racially mixed, not to have to try to decide what they are. My godfather is in an interracial marriage and I see the effects on the kids. At first they just assume the identity of the dominant culture. It's easier. But as they get older, they want to know more about the other side, and that's hard for them. If, for example, they go to Taiwan and don't speak the language, people there will look down on them. "Oh, you're *half* Chinese? And you don't speak any Taiwanese?" Whereas I can go there and feel pretty comfortable.

"I think my parents were pretty good about how they raised us. I appreciate that. They pushed me, they were stricter than the parents of my white friends, but not as strict as some of my Chinese friends' parents. They didn't like make me practice piano five hours a day. I know those kids did it just because they felt compelled to, would feel guilty if they did not. Still, if I get a C on a paper, I wait until I get an A in the class before I call home. But the bottom line is that *I'm* the one who is most disappointed with a mediocre grade."

Sometimes, it is necessary to leave home to find out who you are. Debbie was born and raised in the heart of San Francisco's Chinatown but always felt herself drawn to living in a totally different environment. Her experience of coming of age by necessity involved embarking on a voyage of self-discovery. Only with the security of knowing who she was could she return to the Bay Area.

"About eight years ago, I headed off to the wilds of New York City. Of course, my parents hated this idea. 'You're going to end up on the streets! . . . Since this is your idea, don't expect us to help you! . . . Why don't you go to law school instead? . . . What are we going to tell your friends? They'll think we've been so horrible to you that you *had* to leave!' Even my bank teller asked how I could think of doing such a thing. But overriding all these concerns and the guilt they produced was my fear that, at age thirty, I would hate myself for not ever having taken the chance.

"I was born in San Francisco's Chinese Hospital and went to grade school at St. Mary's in Chinatown. The other kids in my classes were Chinese, but I felt different anyhow. I knew from an early age that I wanted to leave the area. It was too much like a small town, where everyone had already pegged you and fixed your identity by first or second grade. And my identity was that of the little girl who always had her nose in a book, who was never any good at sports. From St. Mary's, I went to Saint Rose High School, where I was suddenly thrust into the role of a minority both from an ethnic and religious standpoint.

"I still remember my first day. I was very excited about the new school, but on the way to lunch, I overheard a girl talking to her friends, who were also white. Standing not more than five feet away from her, the conversation was very clear. 'I *hate* Chinks,' she said in a matter-of-fact tone of voice. Contrasted to the high I had been on earlier in the day, this provoked in me the worst possible feeling. It changed how I felt about myself, because until then, I had never considered being Chinese a particular burden. From this experience, I went into a period of trying to de-emphasize the Asian part of myself. I didn't tell my parents when the parent-teacher conferences took place because I didn't want to have them, with their less-than-perfect English, show up at my school. I also distanced myself from my friend Rhoda, who was very into being Chinese and had this embarrassing habit of practicing her Chinese characters on the chalkboard between classes. There were all these feelings that I never shared with anyone. My own personal agony. And again, I felt the urgent need to leave San Francisco, to go somewhere else where I could reinvent myself.

"I have this 'inferiority-superiority' thing. As a result of my high school experience, I felt bad, ashamed of being Chinese. But I also harbored the secret fantasy, 'Someday I'll come back and show you!' I think my mother's style of parenting, which is very Chinese, contributed. She'd pull me up and push me down at the same time. Sometimes in the same breath. 'These grades aren't too good. But you don't *look* stupid!' And when I was in the process of applying to college, we'd go through this thing where she'd run down to the mailbox every day before I could get there and then announce, 'Well, no letter from Berkeley! You didn't get in. You probably won't even get into City College.' And this was months before they were actually sending out acceptance letters. Looking back, I think she was just externalizing her own anxiety about my future and possibly trying to protect me from disappointment. At the time, however, my only thought was, 'Mom, I wish you'd just shut up.'

"Actually, I did get into Berkeley. When I got there, I realized that my social life had been stunted. I wanted to live in a co-ed dorm, but my mother intercepted the application for housing and checked the box marked 'single sex.' So I ended up in the only all-girl's house on campus. There happened to be a number of other Asian Americans there, and we all ended up on the same wing. Part of me hoped to be accepted by them, but part of me was still in the mode of rejecting the Chinese in me. Others noticed this dichotomy, these two opposite poles battling for my identity. 'In some ways, you are *so* Chinese. Always going around boiling your water before you use it. And you look like us.' But at the same time, I was also very Western in my thinking. I was into New Wave, punk music. None of my friends from the dorm wanted to go to these concerts with me.

"I felt I had to move away. I knew I would make mistakes, but I wanted them to be *my* mistakes, not just reactions to the actions of my parents. For example, this three-and-a-half-year relationship I was in with a Caucasian guy who really wasn't right for me. My parents didn't like him because he was white, but also because he was too much of a dreamer. My mother kept dropping dire hints: 'Interracial marriages never work out! If you spend too much time with a white man, you'll become damaged goods and no longer of any value to a worthy Chinese man!' Against even my better judgment, I persisted in the relationship, as much to assert myself to my parents as to be with him. It became increasingly obvious that I needed to leave San Francisco and my family in order to figure out who I really was.

"Eventually, I was able to realize my dream. I landed in New York without a job, but managed to work my way into a position as a publicist with a major publisher. I felt comfortable with my colleagues, I made good friends. And slowly, I learned to be comfortable with myself as Chinese and American. In all, I stayed seven years. However, I almost went back a few times before I was really ready to return. At one point, my parents were having real problems with my younger brother, who was probably going through the same kind of crisis I had experienced. My mother wanted me home to run interference. 'How can you justify being three thousand miles away at a time like this? Don't you care about your family?' I felt guilty, but I managed to resist the temptation to take the next flight out of La Guardia.

"In time, I did get burned out on the book business. I was ready to go home. Ready to do something else. And I knew I was returning not because my parents were pressing me, but because I wanted to. For myself. I returned to San Francisco, and to my delight and amazement, found that my parents had mellowed, had opened their minds, even accepted my boyfriend (who is now my fiancé), a white man. I find I no longer have to regress

to childhood whenever I am in their presence. And that in itself
is remarkable enough!

To conclude, a story from a woman whose life history is certainly out of the ordinary. Nona was raised in Chinatown by
white Christian missionaries. And yet, many of the dilemmas
and feelings that she experienced as an adolescent are similar to
those of Asian American women from more "typical" families.

"I have very few memories of my early days in San Francisco's Chinatown, just a vague picture of my mother—of walking
down a narrow dark hallway those times when she would occasionally drop me off with a neighbor. However, I vividly remember the day she left me at the Ming Quong orphanage in Los
Gatos, California. I was three years old and terrified. I wasn't
able to see her backing out the door, but I *knew* my mother was
leaving without me. To this day, I still don't know why.

"The white missionary women who looked after the thirty-
five girls at Ming Quong were basically kind people who cared
about us. We also had each other, so even if children at school
made fun of us because we were Chinese (not very often) or
because we were poor (more apparent in this rich community),
we could always find comfort and support among ourselves.
Much later in life, when I would watch mothers and children
coming into my store together, I felt a sense of longing for a
mother's love, had an idea of how different my life might have
been. But at the time, I accepted things as they were. When we
were given the opportunity to be adopted at age sixteen, most of
us chose instead to go to work as domestics for a rich white
family. Who needs parents? we asked. Who needs to go through
all that?

"Although we were well provided for, the missionary women
did not show us any affection. They also did not push us to go to
college, with the exception of a few really brainy girls (whom we
labeled the bookworms). Our attitude became, 'Why work so
hard at studying? Why not just try to make money instead?' We

got courses in typing, office skills. The missionary women were realistic about our job opportunities. One thing they didn't know much about, however, was how to handle us when we became teenagers. They never discussed sex or men or relationships. Somehow we learned what was right and what was wrong. We all paid very close attention when a certain pretty girl with a headful of wavy hair was sent *back* to live with the younger girls. You got the message.

"Of course, I wanted to be white. This became more of an issue when I became a teenager. I remember trying on dresses one time and one of the white teachers told me, 'Oh, Nona, you can't wear *that* one. You're not "big" enough on top.' I was mortified. I dated a few Chinese boys, those who had been interviewed and found acceptable. But I yearned for someone white. After all, they were the Superior Race. To my mind, they were better looking and had more advantages. The Chinese guys I knew were passive, not outgoing. Older girls at Ming Quong had been instructed to marry a 'nice Christian Chinese man.' But when it came to me (I was the youngest child there), somehow they forgot or chose not to give me this advice.

"I did marry a white man whom I met at a party. His first concern was how my parents would react if he asked me out. Once I explained my situation, things were fine. Our marriage has worked out all right. Let's put it this way. I adjust to things pretty well.

"Today I own a store that sells Oriental gifts and clothes. I call it Ming Quong, or the Radiant Light. I love my customers! I take the time to learn from them. I find Caucasians to be more open and broadminded. One day, this woman was explaining to me how things like bowls had a 'vibration.' Put this in the palm of your hand and you can feel it. At one time, I would have thought, 'How weird!' But now I'm more accepting. I compare myself to others in my Chinese women's club. They tend to be staid, old-fashioned. They would find my customers strange. A white girlfriend just told me, 'Nona, you amaze me!' Now *that*, I like!"

3 ONE OF THOSE 4.0, PIANO-PLAYING ASIANS

From a very early age, I had a clear picture of what my parents expected of me. My sister and I were told that a good education is not just something parents give to their child, it is the only acceptable avenue for a son or daughter to repay their parents and bring honor to the family. I once asked my mother if, like my white friends, I could get paid for good grades. The look on her face spoke volumes. I might as well have asked if I could get an allowance for sleeping at night, or eating dinner, or breathing air. Years later, I made the grave mistake of commenting that if my six-month-old daughter, Rebecca, would be happy flipping hamburgers at McDonald's, it would be OK with me. My mother was appalled.

My mother also made it clear that she had a right, even a duty, to help me live out her vision for my life. She wanted me to be a writer. Her dream was that one day she would see my name at the end of a poem or short story in *The New Yorker*. Even when I was a little girl, my mother would look at me and be reminded of her beloved sister, Mao Y Mei, a gentle woman, poet, and lover of the English language who could have had an even more illustrious career had she not been caught in the maelstrom of the Cultural Revolution. My mother herself had literary opportunities, which the politics of the times had not allowed her to pursue. To this day, she treasures letters from an

English teacher who believed that she should have gone to London to study Shakespeare. By embarking on a career studying literature, I could live out the dreams of a previous generation.

Accepting a parent's authority without question was another strong family legacy. When my uncle discovered that one of his daughters had become involved with a foreign scholar studying in China, he instructed her to end the relationship and marry someone more appropriate. Against the wishes of her heart, she complied. For my part, I knew what would make my mother happy, so I accepted an offer from the University of Chicago's well-regarded master's program in English literature instead of embarking on the career in mental health that I envisioned for myself. I wrote home about the splendors of the Regenstein Library and what a privilege it was to study with the great James Joyce scholar Richard Ellman, but I also stayed up late at night talking with dorm buddies who were studying in the School of Social Work.

It was not until thirteen years later, when I was finally sure enough of myself to risk my mother's disappointment, that I enrolled in a training program for marriage and family counselors. Although I was married and had just had my second child, it was with great trepidation that I called to tell her about my decision. I could picture her sitting there in the kitchen at the ancient Formica table trying to balance encouraging words with a deep sense of disappointment and failure. I was not going to inherit my aunt's academic and artistic legacy; and I was not going to live out my mother's dreams. As much as I wanted to follow the direction of my own heart, I did not want to break hers.

The great weight of parental expectations is perhaps one of the most common themes in the lives of Asian American women. From a young age, we are aware of our parents' vision for our lives. We knew what we should study, how we should act, whom we should eventually marry. If we find ourselves drawn to other pursuits, other partners, most of us will make our own choices. But not in the spirit of rebellion. Even if we fail to do what was expected of us, we are always aware of the tension between parental approval and personal choice.

What makes life especially tricky for Asian American women is that the range of expectations is often very limited. Only A's will do. No dating in high school. No need for extracurricular activities. No serious romances that could get in the way of academic success. Only certain colleges, certain majors, and certain career choices are acceptable. Hard sciences are good, medicine in particular. If you can ask the question, "How do you think you are going to make a living doing that?" don't even consider it a choice. And then, degree in hand, marry a professional and well-educated Asian man. Have kids (preferably at least one son). Along the way, practice the piano diligently, show off for company, but don't think about music in terms of a career.

What further complicates the picture is that parental expectations really have more to do with the parent than with the child. Mothers and fathers do not generally advise their daughter to become a doctor because they believe she has a natural inclination for this work. They push her because medicine is a respectable, prestigious career that generates a good income. As soon as the daughter is able to add "M.D." to her name, parents can feel good about the job they did in raising her. Not inconsequentially, they also secure some pretty solid bragging rights. In traditional Asian culture, this makes sense. Children are to make choices that bring honor to the family, not that fulfill individual dreams. The culture is family-centered, not child-centered.

Cindy, a senior at Berkeley, reflects on the path that her parents' expectations have set before her. At small junctures, she has made deviations that allow her a taste of personal freedom, but on the whole, the destination they have in mind is the one she is trying to reach.

"I know that, in the end, I'm going to do what my parents expect of me. Basically, I always have. But looking ahead to my senior year at Cal, I'm starting to feel that it's time to move on, to be more of an adult. I lived in a dorm my first two years of college, but for the past year, I've been at home. I like it that way. The laundry gets done, the food is better, and I get a needed break from campus. Even when I lived in the dorm, I went home on weekends. My friends were like, Why? But I found that the party scene wasn't all that great and at least at home, someone is around to take care of you if you get sick.

"I used to be very, very shy, never spoke up at all. In junior high, however, I realized that if I wanted to go to Cal (and I wasn't about to be the first of my generation not to get in), I'd have to be more than one of those 4.0, piano-playing Asians. So I got involved with sports, student council, and eventually speech. I blossomed, found new friends, opened up. My parents, however, didn't exactly see things that way. 'So-and-so got into Berkeley and he didn't do half the extra stuff you're doing.' Later, I'd come back at them with 'I'm a business major' or 'I'm going to Cal because you want me to. You couldn't make me into a doctor, so you had to settle for this.' 'No, no,' they would protest. 'You think we're asking you to do all this for our sake. No, we're just looking out for your best interests.' I've had a hard time with that one, but now I can see their point of view. My parents were immigrants from Canton, and they worked very hard—still do—at the restaurant they own so that we could have a better life. They feel satisfied with their efforts as long as they know the sacrifice was worthwhile. Sometimes I look at other kids my age, and it bothers me to see how incredibly much they take for granted.

"One thing I know my parents expect of me is to marry a Chinese man. I had this friendship with a Japanese guy who is a few years older than I, but I told him it could not turn into a romance because I wasn't ready to cope with my parents' disapproval. My mother has informed me point-blank that even after she dies, she's still going to want me to marry Chinese. And not just any Chinese will do. My brother dated this woman for a while, but my parents didn't like her, Chinese or not. She demanded too much of his time, they complained. If she really cared about him, she'd encourage him to study harder.

"I have my own reasons for preferring an Asian, but not necessarily a Chinese man. One, shared personal experience. Two, someone who understands my culture and shares my anger about racism. Three, someone who can understand why a lot of what I do is for my parents. Four, someone who has been through the same childhood. Being asked questions like, 'Do you celebrate Christmas? Why do you always take your shoes off when you go into your home?'

"One thing we never discussed in my family was sex. This is a very awkward topic of conversation and one even my girlfriends and I skirt around the edges. I know, however, that if I was to get pregnant, my parents would totally kill me. If my older brother didn't get to me first. When I first went to college, I was shocked to find out that some of my friends had already had sex. I was very uptight and those first few frat parties—where everyone gets so drunk—were hard for me to take. As time went on, I got to see that these girls weren't bad people, and I stopped judging them. But for myself, I'd still prefer to wait.

"In some ways, I see myself as very much of an adult. I'm driven to be successful in my profession. I am committed to improving the status of my fellow Asian Americans. In part, my commitment comes from a relationship with two mentors I found in high school, teachers who encouraged me to set my goals high. But I'm probably also reacting to my place in the family where, as the youngest sister of a very smart older brother, I was always just 'little Cindy.' Even when he took two full years off from college, doing nothing but working out at the gym, he was still able to maintain his royal status. For me, I've had to prove myself and I still feel the need to sell myself to prospective employers, realizing that my height and the fact that I look so young work against me.

"But in other ways, I realize I still have some growing up to do. I'm older and more experienced than when I was a protected and sheltered high school student surrounded by others in my honors classes. It was a nice protective shell, but I have yet to break out of it completely."

Sometimes, our parents' expectations and our own expectations are inseparable. How can I know if I am doing this for myself or for them? Perhaps what they want for me is so deeply embedded that it has, in a sense, *become* me. This kind of struggle, even this question itself, would rarely be asked by a young woman living in traditional Asian society. But here, we seek answers to these dilemmas.

Paula has achieved what many Asian parents dream of for their children. She is a successful doctor in a private practice. She believes she is doing what she wants to do. But the questions linger. . . .

"My sister is only two and a half years older than I but we're very different. She has always been rebellious, even as a little child. After she got her degree in pharmacy, which she pursued because it was the only field of study that my parents would financially support, she married a Caucasian man who did not have an advanced degree. In fact, he didn't even finish college. Then she had two daughters, and feels no particular pressure to heed my mother's advice to 'keep trying for a boy.' Watching her screw up like this, disappoint my parents to this extent, it was clear what my role should be: I would do what they expected of me. I would restore honor to the family where she had shattered it.

"My parents are both from a small village in Guangzhou. Their marriage was arranged, and it has never been fully satisfactory for either of them. As a child, they seemed to me distant from each other. Now that we are out of the house, they tend to fight a lot. My father is old school, gets his way. They both preferred to have a son, although they would not come right out and say this. In junior high, it sometimes bothered me to see the preferential treatment given to my younger brother. I'd say, 'You like him better because he's a boy,' and they wouldn't answer me.

"Sometimes I wonder if I am allowing my parents' expectations of me to take precedence over what I want, but it's really hard to know for sure. Even if my parents were no longer alive, would I live my life differently? Or are these values so thoroughly ingrained in me that they have become an inseparable part of who I am? For example, I am a doctor in a group practice. My parents were overjoyed when I graduated from medical school. But did I do it for them, or did I do it for me? After college, I had considered med school or law school. My parents would have been happy with either choice.

"I remember playing the piano as a child. We all took lessons, and whenever we'd go to a relative's house, we'd have to perform for them in order to determine who was better. No one made any real comments while we were there, but once we got home, my mother would say something like, 'Your cousin Irene is so good at piano,' implying that we were not up to par. Ironically, I had enough talent that my teacher encouraged me to consider a career as a concert pianist. She suggested I enter this concerto competition and tried to entice me by saying that, if I won, I'd get to play with an orchestra in front of a lot of people. But for me, the early memories of those forced recitals was enough to take away all the appeal of her suggestion. And so I quit piano altogether. Plus, my parents had always encouraged us to play piano, but never seriously, never to think of it in terms of a career.

"In high school, I got straight A's. I also became interested in the debate team, and slowly worked my way into competition. My parents felt it was a distraction to my studies. Getting an award was OK, but on the whole they would have preferred that I simply didn't do it at all. When it came time to look at colleges, I got the full brunt of their feelings. 'Well,' they said, 'you could have been accepted by X, Y, or Z college if you hadn't spent all that time off making speeches.' I'm like, 'But I got a 4.0! You can't do better than that.'

"My parents' expectations have also affected my social life. I haven't dated a lot of men and, at the age of thirty-two, am still single. They ask me every opportunity they get, 'When are you getting married?' But what they don't realize is that I feel so much pressure to marry the right man, to marry the man I think they will like, that it greatly complicates my search. Every time I meet someone new, I think to myself, 'What if my parents don't approve?' And there are many men I encounter that I probably don't even give a second thought to because I know in advance what my parents' opinion would be. I'm also aware that it's not enough for me to marry Chinese. He needs to have an M.D. or a Ph.D. He needs that title of 'Dr.' in his name. My mother told me quite directly that if I don't marry a Dr. So-and-So, then I will lose my title as well, because we'd be referred to as Mr. and Mrs. —— instead of Dr. —— and Dr. ——.

"Sometimes this makes me angry. Sometimes I think, 'Just because you're unhappy with my sister, why do I have to right the wrongs?' But at the same time, I don't really see myself living any other way. Even when I left home to go to college, I pretty much continued to do things in the way that they would want me to.

"Was becoming a doctor enough to satisfy my parents? Unfortunately, I think the answer is that I will never reach the point where I feel I have fully met their expectations. There is always another corner to turn. Now I'm a doctor, but I'm not married yet. And then there would be the matter of having a son. I do not feel imprisoned by my parents' standards, but there are moments when the weight of their expectations falls very heavily on my shoulders. But not heavily enough for me to take the path my sister has chosen."

Debby, too, followed the direction prescribed by her parents, but as a young adult, she made a conscious effort to find out who she was outside of her parents' views. For many other women like her, this need for personal exploration is both a source of conflict and an opportunity for growth.

"My personal and lifelong battle has been to get my parents to see my point of view, to acknowledge what is true about my life. I have Korean American friends in their thirties whose parents still think they are virgins. That's what they want to believe. But finally, at the age of thirty-two myself, I have resolved my conflicts to the point where my parents and I can be friends. I can understand that they brought over the values they had when they left Korea. I see that in a sense, they were frozen in that period of time.

"Until recently, I felt confined by their expectations and restrictions. I led a very regimented existence. For example, there was to be no dating until marriageable age, around nineteen or twenty, and then the push was on. You were not supposed to date anyone who wasn't serious marriage material. You shouldn't be 'soiling' yourself. There was no point in dating as a means of self-discovery. Koreans were the number one choice, followed by Americans. There was no number three. I did date Korean men. But now my parents are no longer pushing me as hard after having lived through some memorable and traumatic relationships with me. They realize that simply being Korean doesn't automatically qualify a man as a good spouse.

"When I went to college, I continued to live at home. My parents could not see any reason for me to stay in a dorm. The curfews were horrible. Even as a sophomore in college, I still had to be in around midnight. My siblings and I did not have any secrets from my parents, and there was never any real sense of privacy at home. But there was a great and pervading sense of fear. If I was let out into the world, I'd surely go wrong, get pregnant, find someone in a black leather jacket. Who obviously rides a motorcycle. I obeyed my parents because the anger I'd face if I broke a rule wasn't worth the hour or so later return. I would be grilled about my activities to the point that it was better to get in on time. Plus, I was financially under their control.

"In college, I experienced the premed pressure. My parents really wanted me to be a doctor. I bought the whole line about medicine, but I hated dissection and I knew I would have to prove to them I couldn't hack it before they would release me. So I continued in the major, knowing it would screw up my GPA. Not exactly the Western way to do things, but I didn't see any other choice. 'Doing my own thing' was not an option.

"I finally managed to break away, but not until I had finished graduate school. I was still at home through grad school, but afterward, I was determined to become financially independent and move out. I told my parents my plans and my dad tried hard to make me feel scared and guilty. He even threatened to disown me, but I refused to take on the guilt.

"Today, we get along. Through it all, I retained the Asian value of the importance of family. But I also think my parents now see who I really am, and that makes all the difference."

Expectations can be, and often are, exacerbated by guilt. When Mom and Dad struggled and sacrificed to give you the opportunity to get straight A's, it's pretty clear what your report card better look like. Terry tells her story.

"In Korea, where I was born, I was apparently some kind of 'wonder kid.' My parents made up a false birthdate for me so they could get me into school sooner, but I could not take the pressure. By the age of five, I was in second grade, but I was wretched. At one point, I cried so continuously that I got a hernia.

"Then, my father got a student visa to come to the U.S. My parents saw how happy I was and decided to stay here permanently. But the move was not without its price. We left a very nice life behind: servants, a house with a fountain. My father used to get calls, at least once a year, from Seoul, begging him to return because his expertise as an urban planner was in great demand. That is just one of the reasons for which I feel guilt. For all I know, if we had stayed in Korea my father could have become president of the country. But they sacrificed all that for the sake of their children.

"To make ends meet, my parents bought a combination Chinese/American take-out place, and my mother had to go to work. She had a hard time adjusting. Some days she'd come home smelling of grease and say to me, 'You know, I'm just a hamburger lady.' I got the message unequivocally that the only way to repay her for her years of sacrifice was to get straight A's and then go to an 'Ivy' (Ivy League college). Otherwise, all that aggravation and hot cooking oil would have been for naught. When my brother went to the University of Virginia, notwithstanding the fact that it was rated one of the top public schools in the country, my parents were mortified. My other brother and I, being absolutely brainwashed, were equally mortified.

"I went through my little rebellion and refused to apply to Harvard or Yale, but I did go to Dartmouth. That, however, did not merit a college decal on the back window of the Volvo. In fact, the decal did not get affixed for me until I went to Yale for graduate school, at which point, my mother could say, 'Yes, my daughter did go to Dartmouth. Which is a good school, even if you don't know it, and at least Ivy League—but now look where she is!'

"I could write a book about responsibility and guilt. After all, I'm Korean, and I was also raised Catholic! The story, still circulating in family legends, is that I'm responsible for my younger brother's fall, where he hit the corner of a table and almost lost an eye. If I had been better about practicing the piano, my mother wouldn't have had to be sitting on the bench next to me and instead she could have been supervising the baby, and obviously this never would have happened.

"One summer vacation during college, I was standing at the kitchen counter cutting up a watermelon. Out of the clear blue, my mother asked me if I was still a virgin. That was a shock, but since I didn't ever lie to her, I said, 'No.' So we talked about birth control. Actually, as a Catholic girl, I had more problems with this than she probably did. At that point in my life, I was sure I'd burn in hell if I didn't marry the guy. Luckily, I didn't; he was a very controlling man who had already picked out names for the children we were going to have. I also gave up my Catholicism.

"I married a Caucasian man even though my grandmother came from Korea for a visit when I was twelve and made me promise to marry someone Korean, after bribing me with this outrageously expensive TV. My mother also tried to tell me horror stories about how all these interracial marriages never worked, always ended in divorce because the kimchee stank too much or the husband couldn't get along with his mother-in-law. But she has come to accept and love Gregor very much. And I always keep my kimchee in the refrigerator.

"In college, my mother took me on a trip to Korea. We stayed with her very wealthy sister, whom she loves but also does not particularly like. My aunt would sigh and say how sad it was that my mother had to suffer so much, and her daughter only went to Dartmouth. On the plane ride home, my mother told me, 'All things considered, I'd do it again. The money we left behind is not important. I'm proud of how you turned out. I may be just a hamburger lady, but my kids went to Yale, Harvard, and MIT.' That statement of hers helped to erase a lot of the guilt I felt. Not all of it, but it helps."

Western philosophy emphasizes individual choice and personal responsibility over loyalty to family. The idea is to "follow your bliss," to take the initiative in clearing a path of your own making. Sacrificing personal dreams and ambitions in order to satisfy parental expectations is not considered a noble, or even healthy, choice. Continuing to seek parental approval into one's mature years—as I find myself doing—is viewed as a sign of immaturity rather than a piece of the process of fulfilling obligations. For an Asian American woman to choose a life very different from that envisioned by her parents, it is sometimes necessary to draw the line firmly and have the tenacity not to deviate. Ginger tells her story.

"My parents immigrated from Toishan and never learned English very well. So, at a young age, I translated for them, which forced me to become assertive. My mother had health problems. By the time I was twelve, I was accompanying her to doctors' appointments and learning early on to become an aggressive medical consumer. The fact was, her life depended on the quality of the questions I asked. It also helped that I was the youngest child with three older brothers. They blazed a trail for me, they were my mentors. I didn't experience a lot of prejudice at school. It was just, 'Oh, here comes another Lew kid.' Any racism I did encounter, I simply ignored.

"When I decided I wanted to go to law school, my parents were surprised. This was a new concept to them, and law as a profession is not well respected in the Chinese community. But I'm pretty headstrong, so I went and paid for my entire education by myself. After that, I got some of the 'marriage and kids' pressure from my family, but not quite to the same extent as my brothers. I married a Caucasian man. My parents weren't exactly thrilled about the marriage, but I gave them no choice. Then, when we decided to divorce, they tried to talk me out of that. I refused to discuss it with them, I drew very firm boundaries. The way I see it is this: I'm fulfilling my idea of what a good daughter is. If you don't like it, that's not my problem. I believe that if you take on the guilt thing, you are giving your parents tremendous power, and I don't choose to do that. And I don't see this as an Asian thing. It's a human choice—whether to say yes or no to your family.

"And yet, when my mother was declining, I was her primary caregiver. I was living in D.C., but flying back to California every three weeks to be with her. I think we both felt that I had fulfilled my obligation to her.

"Being bicultural has also helped me in my present position as general counsel for the Commerce Department. I can adapt to situations with greater flexibility than I might otherwise. Every meeting in D.C. constitutes a different culture, and I'm able to come into a new situation and get the lay of the land through my intuitive assessments of people.

"Coming to D.C. from California, I have felt more keenly the stereotypes of Asian women. There is still a lot of the 'old boys' network here, and Asian American women worry about whether people see them as too assertive. In response, I have chosen to be aggressive and it has served me well. I don't have time to worry about what others think. If they don't like my style, it's their problem.

"I'm now the third-ranking person at Commerce, a position that required Senate confirmation. But I still feel I have a lot to achieve. For one thing, I'd like to see more of us in public service. If we're not part of the political landscape, we're not going to be counted. Where is our voice on affirmative action? Civil rights? Where was our list of nominees when Blackmun retired?"

The ways in which our parents' expectations have shaped our lives is sometimes brought most clearly into focus when we have our own children. We learn, perhaps to our dismay, how much of our parents is embedded in us. How much we are passing on instinctively, without reflection. But at the same time, we are trying to parent our children in ways that fit the current climate better, in response to the child's individual needs, not the parents'. Martha's story.

"I don't think I really understood how traditionally Chinese and conservative my parents were, Dad especially, until I grew up. I know that I still carry a lot of those values, but on the whole I see myself as more American than Asian. I am married to a Caucasian man and we want our children to feel good about being half Chinese, but we aren't passing on all those expectations I grew up with. For example, even though my parents kept asking, I didn't start Matthew with piano lessons until he wanted them himself. And he's crazy about baseball, convinced he can play professional ball some day. So I encourage him, it's fine with me. I want my children to have a good education but I don't see it as the only way to be successful.

"Growing up, I got the clear message that education has to be the number one priority. Number two is the ability to be self-supporting. My parents would say, 'What would happen to you if your husband dies? You are going to need to be able to make it on your own.' I know that my mother came from a very wealthy family and my dad from a very well educated one. Although both of these were valued, I could always sense that my dad's background was considered superior. My parents valued education to the point that they have always been willing to help me out financially with school. The Ph.D. program I started in speech pathology (but didn't finish) was a cause for great rejoicing! They bragged to all their friends about my doctorate before I even finished my first quarter in the program. Education, however, was not valued for its own sake; it had to lead to something productive. My sister is a very talented artist, but my parents always discouraged her interest. 'What are you going to do with that degree?'

"When my sister found out that our parents were paying for my dental school education, her reaction was, 'That's nice they're doing it, but you know you are going to feel eternally obligated.' She was right. Now my parents get all their dental work done free at our office. Expensive stuff that I sometimes have to pay out of pocket. I never say anything. I feel I owe it to them, but there are times I wish they'd at least acknowledge what I'm doing for them.

"Another Chinese thing in our family is my father's lifelong regret about not having a son to carry on the name. This was very clear to my sister and to me from the start. In fact, my husband is so aware of my father's feelings that he even offered to let us name the boys after my dad—to let them use the family's last name instead of his own. I thought that was very kind of him, but frankly, I'm more interested that they carry my husband's name, not my father's. Plus, the fact is that my parents aren't all that close to my kids anyhow. Bill's parents are much more like the kind of grandparents you'd want for your kids. My parents don't know how to talk to their grandchildren. They expect respect because that's how you should treat your elders but they don't really do anything to earn that respect. And while they're perfectly happy to attend Matthew's piano recitals, they have never been to a single one of his baseball games.

"Like many other Chinese parents, mine were very protective. Towards the end of high school, I got very antsy to be out on my own, but as long as I lived at home, I lived within the boundaries they set for me. I knew I wanted to date, but I was too shy, too naive. I had no idea how to approach a boy and no idea what to do on a date if a boy even asked me out. My parents would occasionally try to set me up with the sons of their Chinese friends, and I acquiesced, but was never interested. At the time, I wasn't aware of it, but I must have had some prejudice against Asian males. They were not physically or otherwise attractive to me.

"In college, I got involved in some political activity, even joining the picket lines when a group of minority students decided to protest. But I never had a serious romantic relationship until I was almost twenty-one. And when I found out that my sister was no longer a virgin by her senior year, I was both angry and shocked. Angry that she shared that information with me, but also shocked at her behavior. Most of my friends were white, but these were not the kinds of friendships where we discussed things like sex.

"I met my husband in dental school. Early on, he told me that his father was a bartender. I didn't believe him! I asked him to name the restaurant, and I looked it up in the phone book. Sure enough, it was there! His dad is a very intelligent man and we get along quite well. But I know that my parents, true to Chinese form, have a much easier time with my sister's in-laws, who better met their expectations. This is uncomfortable for me. I don't like the feelings I have when I hear them discuss an upcoming trip to see my sister in Colorado. You can just hear it in their voices, the admiration they have for her husband's family.

"But even as I recognize the ways that my parents' traditional values and expectations have made my life difficult at times, I also realize that a certain amount is ingrained in me. I'm very supportive of my son's interest in baseball, but if his grades started to slip, I'd probably find it necessary to limit that involvement. I do value my education and all the benefits it has given me. Once, I almost married this guy who never even finished college. He used to bring this up as an issue and I would tell him, 'Hey, that's your problem. If you believe in yourself, you don't have to worry what others think.' But, in the end, I have to admit that my parents were right. Paul's lack of a college education would eventually have come between us. And this is clear to me: If my sons ever felt ashamed of or tried to reject the half of them that is Chinese, I would feel offended. I would feel that they were denying a part of *me*."

My question is, How do they do it? How do generations of Asian parents make their expectations so unfailingly clear? Even an ocean crossing does not seem to slow down the process. I ask this question because I don't believe that, even if I wanted to, I would be able to instill in my own children the same sense of expectation that I grew up with. Most Asian American women do not remember their parents particularly harping on themes of education or careers. The expectations become ingrained in us, almost as if they could be encoded onto some type of parental microchip and emplaced at birth. One thing we do remember is the inevitable comparisons. "So-and-so's son is valedictorian. He's going to Harvard. To be a doctor." But this strategy only reinforced a system already well in place. Our parents did not need to add, "And I expect the same of you." That much, at least, was obvious.

4 BETWEEN MOTHERS AND DAUGHTERS:
Love and Guilt

My mother and I have always been very close, but our relationship has not always been easy. For me, there is the constant, subterranean pull to fashion my life into a form that will please her. Sometimes it seems very clear: I have the power to make her happy or unhappy. It would be selfish to make choices that would disappoint her. But at other moments, I am aware only of the little girl inside who wants her mother's approval but fears she will never merit it.

In my own sphere, I am a reasonably competent, mature forty-two-year-old woman with a psychotherapy practice, two school-age children, and a stable marriage. But within the purview of my mother's influence, I still feel more like a child than an adult. I regress, I lack confidence, and I lose faith in my carefully constructed self-concept. I cry more often.

One night, when my daughter was about six months old, my mother rocked her to sleep and then placed her gently in the crib. We lingered outside the door for a few minutes, talking, dreaming our dreams. "When Rebecca gets older," she said, "I'm going to send her to private school." My husband was in the kitchen finishing up the dishes. He happened to overhear this conversation and motioned to me. "What did your mother just say?" he asked. "Please tell her she can't just make that kind of decision on her own."

I did no such thing. Because I am genuinely torn between the desire to please my mother, recognizing that she has my child's best interests at heart, and the desire to be autonomous, to conduct my own life in my own way. What do you do when you are locked on the horns of a dilemma such as this? When there is no acceptable middle ground because someone will be angry or someone's feelings will be hurt no matter which course you take?

In some ways, it would be easier if we lived in China, if the culture as a whole supported this less autonomous, more fused type of mother-daughter relationship. But I am American born and psychologically assimilated. I have lunch with a good friend who tells me she vowed after college never to accept another penny from her mother. She would be financially independent and thus her ties to her mother would be voluntary and consensual, not based on obligation of any kind. That's a nice idea, I think to myself. Maybe I should move in that direction. But then I realize that (a) my mother would be hurt and rejected if I didn't accept her financial generosity and (b) her giving is one of the ways she demonstrates her love for us. I'm aware that there are emotional strings attached, but I cannot reject the gift without also rejecting the giver.

Mother-daughter relationships are emotionally intense and complex in any language. But when the daughter's values and beliefs are influenced by her Western peers and the mother is more firmly grounded in the culture of origin, conflicts are often unavoidable. Western thinking places a premium on independence and self-reliance, while the Asian culture is more concerned with rules about interconnectedness. Within Western families, it is considered desirable for the parent-child relationship to evolve over time, to reach a point where a mother and daughter can relate to each other as two adults. But many Asian American women see no such progression. Once the child, always the child. When my mother visits, she tells me what time she thinks my eleven-year-old should be in bed. Then she turns to me and says, "And you go to bed, too! You look tired. You need to get more sleep." When we leave the house on a chilly day (or even a not particularly chilly day), she grabs a heavier coat for my son and then she chides me for running out of the house with wet hair. "You know better than that," she says. "You want to catch a cold or something?"

The connections of love and guilt that bind mother and daughter together can sometimes have lasting repercussions. This is how Margaret, a forty-year-old Hong Kong–born program administrator, sees her relationship with her mother.

"I have always felt guilty, always felt I could not do enough to please my mother. I married young, in part to get away from home, in part because that was what my friends and I spent all our spare time daydreaming about. A knight in shining armor. I dropped out of college and my mother was very unhappy. 'So embarrassing. It doesn't look good. What am I going to tell people when we go to those banquets?' To add insult to injury, the marriage did not work out and I got a divorce.

"How can I make it up to her? Here I am, twenty years later, successfully remarried with a good job, a master's degree, and a daughter, and I'm still trying to atone for my mistakes. Maybe I could win the lottery. Because that's another thing about Chinese families. Even mothers don't show a lot of outward affection to their children. They let you know how they feel by overbringing stuff, by spending lots of money, and by cooking more food than you can possibly eat. My daughter, at ten, is a very picky eater. Whenever we go to my mother's, I know it's going to be a struggle. Mom will have spent all day in the kitchen, then feel absolutely crushed when my daughter just picks at her food. I have to whisper to her, 'Please eat that. It'll make your grandmother happy.'

"What complicates my relationship with my mother even more is this thing she has about Chinese superstitions. She takes all those beliefs very seriously, and you never know when you risk offending her by some innocent action. It's like walking through a minefield. I once borrowed a clock radio from my mother when mine was broken. Bought a new one, and I wanted to return hers. Unfortunately, I tried to do this on a day that just happened to be my brother's birthday. I still don't understand the whole thing, but there is something about the Chinese character for clock that has to do with death. So you shouldn't be messing with a clock on someone's birthday. When I tried to hand it back to her, she went berserk, refused to accept it. Another time, she was at my house for a visit. I happened to be going out that evening to a formal party and I was putting on a black dress. Such a bad-luck thing to do that my mother literally had to leave the house. The hard part for me is not just that she believes all this stuff, it's that she takes it personally if you forget—or don't know—one of the rules. 'How can you do this to me?' she asks with the kind of look on her face that can only mean one thing.

"Even knowing how this has affected me, I recently caught myself getting down on my daughter. 'You're not trying hard enough! You're not putting in enough effort,' I told her. I felt awful, realizing how much I've picked up from my mother. All that guilt—all those expectations, and here I am, passing them on."

Elaine, a journalist in her mid-thirties, puts it this way.

"Always at the back of my mind is this thought: What will my mother think? I find myself compelled to share most things about my life with her. Increasingly, this includes news or ideas she's not necessarily going to want to hear. So, I'll be having these conversations with her and I can see my husband in the background shaking his head. Giving me the body language. But he has no such compulsion to talk to his mother this way.

"When my first child was born, also the first grandchild, my mother came in, camped out, and just took over. She did everything that needed to be done. When I'm with her, I feel like a child again. I know perfectly well how to cook, but all of a sudden I find myself asking her how long to microwave this. Or what size pot I should use to boil that. I don't get this same feeling when my mother-in-law visits.

"Another issue is the Chinese value of perfection, which is stressed over actual achievement. On my Advanced Placement Exam for English, I scored a 4, which is very respectable. Good enough to get me out of freshman English. But all my mother said to me was 'How come you didn't get a 5?' Every now and then, she tells me 'I'm proud of you!' and I cherish these words, hold on to them tightly because I know it might be a very long time before I hear them again. To this day, I still don't feel I'm that smart. I think this is partly a consequence of the way I was raised. I went to an Ivy League school, my articles are published in national magazines, and I'm working on my first book, but it still doesn't entirely add up. A cousin recently told me about her trip to Thailand to visit her parents. Coming back, as soon as the airplane touched ground in the U.S., she could feel her self-esteem rising again, as if the thermometer of her self-concept had been restored to its natural environment.

"Neither of my parents understand my career as a journalist. They would have liked to be able to tell their friends that I was a doctor, but writer is a choice they cannot fathom and frankly do not make the effort to. Whenever I publish a piece, I always send a copy to them. I'm sure they never read it. My mother-in-law, however, is very interested in my work, buys extra copies of my magazines, passes them around to her friends. That feels good. Now, I suppose if I got something into *Time* magazine, my mother would like that, but otherwise, I feel fundamentally misunderstood.

"At the same time, I'm aware that I will never be able to change my mother. I'm learning just to accept her brand of loving. And there are times in my life when nothing is more important to me. A year ago, my husband and I were going through a rough time. My mom came in, took over, mothered us. Her advice, her matter-of-factness, were just what we needed to make it through."

For Irene, separated from her family by more than an ocean's worth of space, the pull for mother's approval is still a strong influence that captures and threatens to hold hostage both the head and the heart.

"Right now, I'm between a rock and a hard place. I'm finishing my master's degree in clinical psychology and if I don't find a job—or get married—in the next few months, my student visa will expire. I would have to return to Singapore and that would mean returning to a place where I was very depressed, where I knew I was alive only because my heart was beating. Staying in this country would allow me to continue to grow, to expand personally and professionally, to learn more about who I am and what I want in life. It would also mean a better chance to find a man who could be a real partner for me, someone that would value me for who I am. In Singapore, men would most likely see me as threatening: too assertive, too career-oriented, and I would probably end up a spinster. Unfortunately, it's not as simple a choice as it may seem. My mother is expecting me to come home, and the rest of my family sees it as my *responsibility* to do so. I'm viewed as selfish for putting my career before my family, and while I don't agree, I am still torn. These expectations tug at my heartstrings.

"I'm the youngest child in my family, and I think it's been hardest for my mother to let go of me. She only got as far as the sixth grade, and could never understand why I wanted to pursue my education. After high school, I got a teaching credential and found a job teaching PE. As far as my mother is concerned, I had a perfectly good position and only needed to find a husband, have children, and my life would be complete. But I have known for many years that I wanted more. I've always been interested in learning why people do the things they do, what 'makes them tick.' In my family, I feel like a puppet, pulled here by this one, pulled there by that one. My opinions, my desires, were disregarded. Even my choice of friends was continually questioned, and my mother never approved of the people I sought out.

"Living in the United States, studying psychology, and working through my issues in therapy, I feel much more alive than I have in many years. Free to find out who I really am. Free to be my true self. So it is with a great deal of anxiety that I look ahead to my graduation in a few months. My family is expecting to come here for the ceremony and then help me pack and move back. I've been unable to tell them that I am thinking about staying here, that returning to Singapore would be professionally a dead end. I'm afraid my mother would tell me that, in that case, she and my brothers and sister would just forget about coming over. I'm concerned that later on, my sister might even conspire to tell me that Mom was very sick or something and that I needed to return. And that I'd regret that decision for the rest of my life if I chose not to.

"There's also a lot of pressure on me to go back, get married, and raise children in order to make my mother happy, to make her feel that she has done her job well. Regardless of how I feel about the matter. She wonders how I can possibly choose a career over marriage, and my behavior makes my family members accuse me of having 'lost my Chinese roots.' And even if I did get married, if I married a Caucasian, my family would be extremely upset. My children would be considered pariahs. In Singapore, I once dated a man who *was* Chinese but spoke a different dialect than ours. My mother had never even met the man, but she told me to drop him. She tried to convince me that all those kind were wife beaters.

"I did make a brief visit home last September to see how things might work out for me careerwise. There happened at the time to be a regional conference of counselors, and I was very excited to hear that one of the men was presenting on narrative therapy. After his talk, I went up to say how pleased I was to hear him, but he just wrote me off. Didn't pay any attention to me at all. He was very threatened that anyone—especially a woman—would even know about this type of therapy. I realized then that this is the type of treatment I would receive if I tried to work in Singapore.

"I don't want to feel like I am dying inside anymore. I know what my life can be like when it is lived with passion and a sense of freedom. And yet I still want, I still seek my mother's approval. The thought of disappointing her, of not being the person she wants me to be, brings tears to my eyes. I cannot stop them from coming."

Sometimes it is the mother's inability to deal with her own cultural conflicts that is transmitted to the daughter. In a sense, the daughter inherits genetic characteristics along with unresolved emotional trauma. Linda, a Japanese American, grew up as part of the only nonwhite family in town. She remembers being blamed for the mistreatment of POWs, for the war. Children made fun of her for her "monkey hands" and large ears. In appearance, she felt reduced to an animal.

"My childhood was further complicated by the way my mother treated me. She had not realized she was marrying a man with more traditional values than hers, that he would place his original family above his own children or expect her to serve his parents. Both of my parents also had the whole internment experience in their history—all that shame and bitterness buried behind years of silence. So she took it out on me, her oldest daughter. I used to wonder if it was because I looked like my dad and like his mother, the real targets of my mother's aggression. Is that why she used to beat the hell out of me after I had vacuumed the living room just as she asked? Or why she would point to a baboon on TV and say, 'That's what you look like'?

"I also have this memory of my mother sending me to the store to buy some things for her. I was barely tall enough to reach the counter, and I would have to wait for what seemed like hours as they served all the white customers before turning to me. Did she send me in order to avoid having to deal with that painful situation herself?

"My parents wanted me to marry a Japanese man. So I did, it's what I thought I was supposed to do. At that point in my life, my self-esteem was at a very low ebb, I was self-denigrating and pathologizing. I didn't believe a Euro-American man would be attracted to me. I wasn't even sure an Asian man would want me. But the marriage did not work out. And the therapy I sought to help me deal with issues around the divorce only served to increase the strain on my relationship with my mother. My therapist convinced me that my mother had been abusive to me. And that I should put some real distance between us. I tried to comply with her directives. But I found I just could not close things off as the therapist suggested. My mother had no idea what I was trying to do. So I'd have to go into session each week feeling like I'd failed yet again.

"And then, I started learning more about my own culture, about child-rearing practices in Japan. I discovered that many of the things my mother did to me were well within cultural norms. I started to feel differently about her, about myself. Now, after years of working through these issues, I have a better sense of what in me is culture bound. I remember as a child wearing the cloak of deference to authority to such an extreme that if another kid blamed me for something I did not do, I would take the punishment anyhow. So I spent a lot of time sitting outside the classroom.

"Recently, my mother and I had it out. She said some awful things to me, which reminded me of how she had treated me as a child. I told her that it hurt to hear her talk that way, that It made me feel I didn't want to spend time with the family. And in response, I withdrew for a time. But then, as if in a stroke of grace, she told me something I had been yearning to hear all my life: that she and my father would always be there for me. That single statement released a tremendous amount of the pain from my childhood and I let her know how deeply it moved me. How liberated I felt. We ended that remarkable conversation with her asking for my forgiveness. With a sense of elation, I granted it."

Lori, a sophomore in college, who is fourth-generation Japanese on her father's side and second-generation Chinese on her mother's, is intimately acquainted with the painful struggle between the push for autonomy and the pull toward mother. One of the questions that comes up: Is this the culture? Or is this just my family? Gaining a broader cultural perspective on the mother-daughter relationship can be helpful.

"I've read the book and seen the movie several times, but I never before gave much thought to the fact that the characters in *Joy Luck Club* are Chinese. I saw it again last night, and suddenly it was a very different experience for me. For example, in the scene where June's mother is escaping from China and has to leave those two babies behind, it occurred to me that they were doing this in 1949 and that's the year my mother, a baby herself, left China. I realized I was relating to the movie as an Asian American and I really wanted someone else Chinese to talk to about it. I have never felt like that before.

"One scene in particular really struck home. Waverly is on the phone asking her mom if she can cancel their lunch date. Her mom is putting on the major guilt trip. Plus, you can see Waverly's white boyfriend in the background. Well, I'm planning to spend spring break with my boyfriend, and when my mother found out, she had a fit. Not because I was going off with a guy, but because I wasn't coming home to be with *her*.

"I feel so torn. Mom wants to know she's the priority in my life. I know I am her greatest priority. And I do love her, do feel a real family bond. At the same time, I've been raised with very definite American ideas and believe in asserting my individuality, being true to myself. So it's very awkward when she calls. Often she starts crying, telling me how much she misses me and how upset she is that I don't call or write more often. Then, I feel *obliged* to say certain things like 'Well, you know how much I love you,' or 'I miss you so much, too.' It's not that this isn't true, I just don't like feeling I'm being put into a situation where I have to say those things. Once she told me that after Dad retired, they were going to move to 'wherever I was.' I didn't say anything, I had no idea how to react. So, she starts crying again because I didn't say how great that would be. At this point, I don't think I want any children. But if I change my mind, I'm sure some of these same Chinese threads will emerge in my relationship with them. I just don't want to end up crying over the phone like this."

Relationships between Asian American women and their mothers are further complicated by differences in the way the two cultures view the role of the family. Family, and extended family, is extremely important in Asian culture, but from the point of view of what is best for the larger social order, not from a consideration of individual need. A daughter's behavior toward her mother, mother-in-law, grandmother, and older siblings is dictated by precise rules that have been handed down from generation to generation. She is required to honor her parents not because she loves them and knows that they love her, but because it is the *right* thing to do. In fact, even in the absence of affectional bonds, she is still expected to play the role of dutiful daughter.

When Lisa was an infant, her parents left Korea and placed her in the care of her ayah (nanny). This was not an uncommon event in the lives of Asian families trying to emigrate to the United States. Six years later, Lisa's mother sent for her and her brother and sisters. But when they met at this point, they were like strangers, with no experience of intimacy or connection to draw upon. A high school teacher, Lisa wonders if the opportunity for bonding had been irretrievably lost. Today, she feels little emotional attachment to her mother. There is only a painful wall of silence between them, built out of the mother's disappointment in her daughter's failure to act according to her assigned role.

"A friend once asked me when I felt most protected, most cherished in my life. That's an easy question to answer. I was two or three years old, still living in Korea and very close to my ayah, who would occasionally carry me around, piggyback style. One evening we were taking a walk. I was securely attached to her back and wrapped in a cozy blanket. I remember looking up at the stars, aware that it was cold outside and cold on the tip of my nose. But I was held so firmly and held so lovingly that I only felt warm, secure, and happy.

"Unfortunately, I don't have similar memories involving my mother. I can't really say how much of her behavior is due to intrapsychic conflict, how much to the culture, the dynamics of the Korean family in which she herself was raised. All I know is that I've never felt close to her, never had much of a bond, and now we are not even on speaking terms. I feel some sadness. Christmas comes and goes without so much as a card, but I can't really see a way to resolve our differences.

"Things between us were never great, but as adults, at least we were cordial to each other, maintained the proper appearances. Then, a couple of years ago, all hell broke loose. My mother was visiting from Indiana and I had planned a family get-together at my house. I spent several days cooking, trying to prepare an elaborate spread. The dining room table was literally groaning under the weight of all the dishes I had cooked. My middle sister walks in the door of our house, takes one look at the food, and asks, 'Can I get something out of the kitchen for Nick [her son] to eat?' My husband Newman was outraged and told her so. 'Don't you even realize how much work Lisa has put into this meal? There must be *something* here that he can eat.' In response to my husband's comment, my mother became even more outraged. 'How *dare* you let your husband speak to your older sister that way?' she demanded of me. By this point, Newman realized that he had created more of a scene than he had ever intended. So he tried to back off. He apologized to my sister and to my mother. But my mother refused to accept the apology. She stormed out of the house and has refused to communicate with me since.

Conflicts between mothers and daughters are sometimes made more visible when the daughter marries out and a new perspective is introduced into the relationship. A Caucasian husband may have difficulty understanding or accepting the ways in which his mother-in-law demonstrates concern for her daughter, who happens to be his wife. Then, the daughter is placed in the difficult position of trying to negotiate competing expectations. I have known that place. Once, my mother decided that we should cut down an ornamental plum tree because it was blocking off too much natural sunlight. She told me to tell my husband to get out his ax. My husband told me to tell her "No way." I responded by leaving the house and refusing to communicate either party's request to the other. Rene also knows what it is like to be in this position.

"When Tom and I first started thinking about marriage, I had a concern that his parents might have a problem with the fact that I'm Chinese. So I asked him. His answer has become a private joke between us. 'No, they won't care that you're Chinese, but they're not going to like the fact that you're from New Jersey!' As it turns out, I think we share a lot of the same beliefs and values, even accounting for the Midwest–East Coast differences. So that even if he grew up in Nebraska and I grew up in New Jersey as the first generation of Chinese immigrant parents, we can draw on our similarities to make our marriage and family life work.

"One area in which we are not quite in agreement: my mother. Tom says, 'She's living her life through you.' I tell him, 'Well, you can look at it in a negative way, make it sound bad. But the fact is that in Asian families, mothers do get their sense of self from their children's accomplishments. That's the measure of their success.' One thing in my family growing up is that there was never much communication of any kind. You just didn't talk about how you felt. There were no open lines. So I've had to work hard to be more direct, more open about how I feel. But my husband would say that I'm not as honest as I could be, I hold too much in. What I reveal, he says, is only that which can be used to manipulate a situation. I get that from my mother, he says. For example, even if I don't agree with her about something, I'll tell her yes, I'll think about that, etc., etc., instead of just coming out and telling her the truth.

"We used to live in Massachusetts, and my parents would come out to visit one or two weeks at a time. *Inevitably*, by no later than the end of the first week, my mother would say, 'I should bite my tongue, but . . .' That is of course a clear signal that she is not going to hold herself back from telling me exactly what she disapproves of in the way we are living. Everything from the pots are too heavy to cold water in the shower is no good for your joints. My husband and I are both architects. Once my parents came to visit just at the time we were trying to redo our house from the bottom floor up. My daughter was a baby at the time, and there was dust everywhere, the plumbing had not yet been completed. 'I should bite my tongue,' she blurts out, 'but *how* can you possibly live like this?' She also wanted to tell me that the bank of cellular phone towers near the house were not safe. So what should we do? Sell the place? Luckily, she never found out about the asbestos in the roof tiles. After she tells me her concerns, she expects me to do something about it. I feel bad myself because I just mumble some words of acquiescence and don't stand up for myself, say what I really think.

"But I have to say that things are getting better. I don't think my mother takes things so personally anymore. A few years ago, my husband and I were trying to decide whether or not to accept offers from UC Berkeley. My parents were already living in the Bay Area and they would dearly have loved us to move out. But they told us that they understood this was a big decision that we would have to make for ourselves. Earlier, I'm sure my mother wouldn't have hesitated to lay on the guilt. Thickly. I think the thing that has changed is that she now understands there are certain things about my life that she has no real knowledge of, and so she can let them go. Those she *does* know, however, i.e., the proper way to raise kids, she doesn't hesitate to pass on to me.

"Now, the conflict is over my brother. He wants to move to Florida because the San Francisco area is no longer nearly as good for cardiologists as it once was. My mother is crushed that he would even think of leaving. But in this case, I can say things to her about her approach. I can tell her I don't think it's fair to try to keep him from relocating because she would be hurt. Interestingly enough, my brother did all the things my parents wanted him to. I don't really believe he has a sincere interest in medicine, but of course it's a prestigious position with the potential for a very comfortable life. Except that in San Francisco that's not so true anymore. So he just wants to go someplace where he can practice medicine and continue to live the life he has grown accustomed to. Which is the very life she wanted for him in the first place.

"This same thing doesn't happen with my mother-in-law. With her, I have an adult relationship. With my mother, it's parent-child. My mother-in-law knows more about my research and professional interests than my mother does. And with her, I can have conversations about politics, current events, etc. It's just a whole different feeling."

Sometimes, the relationship between mother and daughter influences the whole of the daughter's sense of self. For Betty, who travels around Asia gathering Buddhist temple recipes for a series of cookbooks she is writing, the painful memories of her mother's disapproval form the counterpoint to the texture of her life.

"When I was not more than five or six years old, my mother told me that she was disappointed in me, that I wasn't Chinese because I didn't speak the language. That remark has stayed with me all my life. It has profoundly affected who I am and what I do. Six years ago, I published my first temple cookbook [a cookbook based on recipes used at a Buddhist temple]. I'm now working on others in my series and spend most of my time abroad. A world apart from the small farming town in which I grew up as the youngest of eight children, but an integral part of my journey into confronting the issues that haunt me, into accepting myself for who I am.

"My parents were married through an arrangement made in China. They had two sons, the oldest of whom died, and then my father had an opportunity to come to the United States under a 'paper name.' He became a Jung and, ten years later, sent for my mother. Their oldest son, Bud, was born in China, Jack in Hong Kong, and then five children in five years after they got to Reedley. My mother was tired of having babies and went to her doctor to get some kind of birth control. After five childless years, my father asked what was happening, and when he found out, he was very angry. He told her to 'take that thing out,' and that is how I came into the world.

"Like many other immigrants of their generation, my parents had few options when it came to jobs. They opened a grocery store and we all worked there. I hated it—sorting soda bottles when it was hotter than Hades. And then when I was seven, Dad suffered a severe stroke and became a semi-invalid. Most of my mother's time was spent with him and I was left with the short end of the stick.

"After my dad's stroke, I had to put in even more time at the store. I couldn't join the swim team or the tennis team and I didn't have much time for a social life, which is just as well because I never got asked out anyhow. A consequence, I believed, of not being white, although I did have a Korean American girlfriend who had boyfriends, and she was fat! That I couldn't figure. I had good friends in high school, but I still felt like an outsider.

"College at Berkeley was a whole new experience. So many Asians hanging out together, but I didn't really feel I had a right to join them. The ethnic studies thing affected me. I was going through my identity crisis when I met Dennis, a Korean American man from a good and loving family. I had already tried bringing home a guy who was half Japanese, hoping I'd score a few brownie points for his being part Asian. Unfortunately I didn't know about the animosity between Chinese and Japanese. And I remembered how my parents reacted when my oldest sister married a Caucasian. She got kicked out of the house. But after my marriage to Dennis, it was just, OK, so you married Asian. So where's your house? So where's your son? When are you going to have a son you can send to Berkeley?

"I didn't tell my parents of my divorce until after the fact. My mother wasn't particularly supportive, but she did express the concern that since I was now thirty, I would never find a husband, someone to take care of me in my later years. My sisters' contribution is simply this: They don't say anything about it. Sixteen years later, I'm still single and I can't say I'm not lonely, that I wouldn't like to get married. But I am very happy with my life and finding a man is not my number one priority. Maybe number five. After my divorce, I decided it was my turn to please myself, to figure out what I wanted to make of my life.

"One thing I knew was that I hated my job at the lab. I'd look around at all these women older than I, still working at the same place, and think, 'No way, I can't see myself here for another fifteen or twenty years.' I figured a robot could do my job as well as I could. So I took up scuba diving as a hobby and ended up working for Club Med. What did my family think? Frankly, at that point, I didn't care. By now, they know better than to say things to me. I'm determined to do what I want to do. One thing led to another and eventually to Martin Yan's (*Yan Can Cook!*) cooking school in Foster City. One day, someone at school said to me, 'Betty, if you really love Asian cooking, you should go to Asia.' I said OK! I looked at the newspaper and decided to head for Bali, Singapore, Thailand, where I met a woman who spent three weeks teaching me Thai cooking. Then it was back to the U.S.

"The next year I returned to Asia, did my trek in the Himalayas thing, got sick, and just happened to catch a notice in the local bakery about a Buddhist meditation class offered at a monastery. I thought, 'This is for me!' My experience there was great and I wanted to thank them, so I offered to write a cookbook of their recipes as a fund-raiser. I had to persist, but they finally agreed and that's how the Kopan cookbook was born.

"I'm at a place in my life where I feel proud of being Asian American, but it's still confusing. In Asia, I blend in with others on one level, and yet my mannerisms, my way of thinking, are clearly Western. I'm not Chinese from China, but am I really accepted in the U.S.? And when I visit my parents' small village in Guangzhou, it's the same thing all over again. I arrive at my relatives' with a box of See's candy because I hear it's something they like. They take one look at me and say, 'Oh, you're the one that doesn't speak Chinese.' I think to myself, 'Oh shit. It's coming back to haunt me again.'

"Maybe it's only the small cadre of travelers I've met in Asia and keep in touch with who truly understand what my life and experience are like. The work I do to collect temple recipes is extremely satisfying but extremely exhausting. I'm always having to knock on doors, to beg for things. And whenever I'm back in the U.S. I'm aware of how much I feel like a misfit. I'm never going to have financial security or a steady job and sometimes it scares me.

"My family doesn't have a clue. After I had been working on

my project for six years, my brother-in-law says, 'You mean you go to temples and cook for them? How long have you been doing this?' I can't say this without crying, but I think it's only my nieces and nephews who have any appreciation for my work.

"I wish I could say my time in Asia has helped me to heal all those painful childhood memories. Unfortunately, I realized as my mother was dying that it was still there. Two years ago, I was summoned back from Korea to care for her. The only child who wasn't occupied with a family of her own, it all fell on my shoulders. I had to take her to the doctor, knowing full well that whatever he told me, I would not be able to translate for her. It was agonizing. Finally, before she died, I felt I had to be able to communicate with her. I enlisted a cousin to speak for me, to try to explain why I had forgotten all the Chinese I learned as a very young child. Why my friends had become so important, why I relied on them to provide connections I didn't find at home. She listened to me and acknowledged what I was saying. 'I'm your mother. I know these things.' But she died soon after that, and I believe she had simply lost the will to live.

What we want from our mothers, I think, is something at once simple and timeless, yet difficult to achieve. I am aware of my own longings. I want my mother to be happy with herself, to be able to look back at her life with a sense of satisfaction and achievement. I want her to be happy with me: the person I am, the person I am becoming. I want her to be happy with my children and to approve of the way we are raising them. I want her to join with me in celebrating the triumphs of my life and to support me though the hard times. But not to judge. And not to give me the impression that I have let her down when I make a decision for myself or for my family that does not meet with her approval. And not to view differences of opinion as an expression of contempt for our relationship. What I long for is a pure sense of connection strong and enduring as the arms of the mother holding her child. What I want is simply this: to be the well-loved, well-respected Chinese American daughter of my well-loved, well-respected Chinese American mother.

5 FATHERS AND DAUGHTERS: *Love, Power, and Control*

M y father and I were never close. If I knew that he loved me, it was only because the alternative was too painful to contemplate, or because my mother would tell me so, or because I was instructed to view the material comforts he provided for us as evidence of his caring. I don't remember him taking much interest in my life. I don't remember him showing me any affection. What I do remember is lying on the living room carpet at the age of twelve, feeling alienated and awkward and unhappy with myself, and hearing my father tell me I looked like "a pregnant baby elephant." But even as a child, I think I knew that not all Asian fathers, although it might be in their nature to be undemonstrative, were quite *this* peripheral. And that thought makes me sad to this day.

When Asian American women have complicated relationships with one parent and it is the mother, they usually speak in terms of guilt and manipulation. If the problematic relationship is with the father, the issues are more likely to be about power and control. Marion, a writer, tells her story.

"It's hard for me to say how much of my father's behavior was due to his being Chinese, how much to his innate personality, and how much to the fact that he was a well-respected physician who was also addicted to prescription drugs. From the outside, our family looked fine, affluent. Dad's first car was a Volvo, and then he decided he had to have a Mercedes. He had the material trappings of success, but on the inside of the family, it was a different story: verbal and sometimes physical abuse, threats, chaos, and instability.

"We grew up with the notion of filial piety crammed down our throats. It is probably one of the first concepts we learned. Our number one duty in life was to obey at all times. My father used to get angry about the stupidest things. If the newspaper wasn't where he thought it should be, he'd go around interrogating us to find the culprit. If no one confessed, he'd beat us all. Once, my sister walked through the house wearing wooden clogs when those first became popular. Dad had come home from the hospital on the late shift and was trying to sleep. The sound of her shoes woke him up, so he got out his chain saw and cut them in half. Another time, when my middle sister, the rebel, came home from an all-night date, he took her clothes, threw them in trash bags, and told her he had burned them all. In fact, he hadn't, but he didn't relent until three weeks later.

"Things got really bad in high school. We were arguing about something—I'm not even sure what—when I made the remark, 'Why did you even have kids when you don't want them to be happy?' My father stared at me and then headed up the stairs. He came back with a shotgun. 'Marion,' he said, 'if you don't like your life, I have a solution for you.' He had shown us that gun before, shown us also the bullets, but never had he used it in such a context. When we were growing up, we just thought he was mean. Now I'm aware of other issues—-how badly he was treated at the hospital because other doctors were resentful of those Asians who were willing to work longer and harder, how the pressure, in all likelihood, led to his abuse of prescription drugs.

"I coped by retreating to my room and to my studies. I became studious and antisocial. At school, I got cast as the 'brain' by default, because the few other Asians were all very bright. I never felt as smart as they were. I was more artistic, more verbal, and not as good in math. But the standard operating procedure was to lump us all together whenever there was more than one in a class. I still remember a teacher in seventh grade who had started the year with an open seating arrangement. I was in the back of the class, but I used to daydream about a cute blond guy who sat in the first row. He happened to be sitting next to an Asian I had no interest in. The teacher caught my roving gaze and moved me next to the Asian guy. She smiled at me, a secret acknowledgement of the 'favor' she was doing for me.

"We were all supposed to go to medical school. My oldest sister tried, but was unable to get in, so she did the next best thing, married a medical student. My second sister could not get into medical school in this country, so she is now in the Philippines. I went to college where a third of the undergraduates were premed. I started school with every intention of being a doctor myself, but I lacked guidance and common sense. I didn't know you were supposed to have an academic advisor. So I primarily took the classes I liked most and fell into writing and philosophy courses. I'd look around at all these other Asians, feet firmly planted, heading for a career in medicine. I thought, 'That would simplify life,' but somehow it didn't seem to be working for me. Junior year, I went into a panic, realizing I hadn't taken enough science, so I changed all my classes to premed. That lasted exactly one day. I had no direction, no goal for my life. My real purpose in attending college had been to get away from my parents, but I found myself recreating the chaos I had known for so many years as a child.

"Finally, some of the philosophy I was reading sank in. I remember being very taken with Kierkegaard's idea 'It is not the way that is narrow, it is the narrowness that is the way.' So I decided to pursue a liberal arts major. To placate my parents, I told them at least I could always go to law school. Which I tried to do. I took the LSATs, but very halfheartedly, and came up with probably the lowest score in history. So, no law school, no med school. What could I do with a degree in writing except teach? After graduating, I went to Japan for a year to teach English. Then I heard that people who had done that could get some job in D.C. writing for a Japanese newspaper. And so on. At every step of the way, I had no idea what I would do next.

"I used to blame my mother for what happened in our family, but now I realize she was clueless. She was, in a sense, a child like us. My father treated her like a second-class citizen. He took away her sense of self through his abusive behavior, but then he lost respect for her, because she was just a housewife with no real opinions of her own.

"My father eventually went through detoxification and rehab. The whole family had therapy also. He's now mellow, and he's forgotten the bad stuff. There is a grandchild in the family, and it's wonderful to see my dad play with him, shower affection on him in a way he never could with us. There is a kind of healing that has taken place.

"It's odd how it turned out. My father always had a life plan for us. We would all go to medical school and then we'd come back home to live. He was going to buy a big plot of land and each family would have its own house on the 'compound.' Very feudal. We thought it was a crazy idea at the time, but now it's almost like that has come to pass. Several of us live near our parents. We get together almost every weekend. I think the turbulence of our early years united us, brought us together in a way that might not otherwise have happened. And even if some of the messages were delivered virtually at gunpoint, I'm still grateful for the sense of family, the values I have today. We hated that filial-piety notion as kids, but the indoctrination has kicked in nevertheless. I'm very much aware that, although I can't be a doctor, I'm determined to be as successful in my work as possible so that I can help support my parents financially when they get old. In fact, they probably won't need my money, but that's not the point. It's my obligation, and I intend to fulfill it. Still, it makes me sad sometimes to catch a glimpse of my father at some family dinner staring off into space, as if he's not really part of the family anymore, contending with a private and residual guilt.

"These days, I think to myself, if Dad hadn't been the way he was, I wouldn't be who I am now. And I'm happy with who I am. I'm working on a book and a novel, and I'm living in New York, which was the place I wanted to be. The sound of my father's door scraping against the carpet, which used to alert me to potential trouble, no longer intrudes into my dreams or my waking hours. I believe I can use my experience in creative ways. After all, you could say the envelope of my emotions has been pushed further than the normal range. I'm not one of those successful Asian doctors, but I'm doing something I love."

Considering the historical role fathers play in Asian culture, the conflicts between fathers and daughters seem not only understandable but almost unavoidable. Traditionally, Asian men are at the top of the pecking order. With power comes privilege in many cases, from resources for education all the way to better quality and greater quantities of food. Not only are married men permitted concubines, in some cases they are encouraged to seek them out (a symbol of prestige for a man with a high position). But with power also comes responsibility, and men are expected to provide for the family's material needs, pass on the lineage, care for aging parents, and represent the family in the larger world—in a sense, to secure the family's honor, without which the family has nothing.

In China, Confucius set down the system of kinship relations that has remained in place for centuries, codifying behavior between husband and wife, father and son. In both cases, the father and the son occupy superior roles. Conflicts arise when fathers attempt to transplant this patriarchal system onto the less accepting soil of the United States. In their attempt to hold on to the authority they were once granted as a birthright and to replicate the relationships they grew up with, fathers may view their daughters' notions of freedom and self-determination as very threatening. In the name of filial piety (Confucius's idea that the family is more important than its individual members), fathers try to control their daughters' lives in matters of education, career choice, and marriage. Simply laying out a plan for a daughter's life may be enough, but if that doesn't do the trick, he may threaten, disown, or use physical violence to accomplish his goal. If the daughter envisions a different life for herself, recognizing an inner drive to discover who she really is, she will, at some point, likely find herself in conflict with her father. Often, it is not until she lives away from home that she can begin this journey of self-discovery. And this may be at a rather late date because fathers generally insist that their daughters live at home as long as possible.

The remarkable thing is that some women, like Marion, do not condemn their fathers or harbor much bitterness about their childhood. Marion is not alone among Asian American women who have come to terms with their family history and with themselves by seeking to understand their fathers' behavior rather than simply to place blame. Somehow, they manage to find a point of equilibrium in the tension between making their own path and their recognition of both the abiding importance of family and their father's right to mold its shape. In the end, sometimes these fathers come around: A new grandchild in the family can be a source of redemption and healing for the whole family.

The story of June's relationship with her father contains more than one level of paradox. She understands that her father sacrificed much to give his family—children especially—a better life in the United States. But she is also aware that her definition of success does not coincide with his—that, ironically, the very act of moving his family away from Korea meant that his daughters would be exposed to social messages of nonconformity and independent thinking, ideas that run counter to his notion of how their lives should evolve. The move to the United States also meant that his daughters would grow up in an atmosphere tinged with racism and exclusion. The "better life" he sought would have to be lived, at least in part, in a place where his children simply were not wanted.

"I was born in Seoul and lived there until I was six years old. In Korea, we had a beautiful house with servants. But when I think back to that time, it feels like a dream, perhaps because I don't speak the language anymore. In order to make the move, my parents had to sell everything, even my mother's wedding ring. They struggled in the new country, worked hard to make ends meet. I remember a little purse I had full of Korean coins.

One day it disappeared, and I asked my mother where it went. She wouldn't answer me.

"We first lived in Ohio, and I started school without knowing English. The kids teased us incessantly, but, for a while, it didn't bother me. I couldn't understand a word of what they were saying. By second grade, I did understand, and I cried every day. My mother's English was so limited she was terrified to answer the phone. Once, the principal called her and said she'd have to come take us home. 'Your children are both here gibbering away in Korean, and we have no idea what to do with them.' My sister and I had the feeling that something was wrong with us, and we felt ashamed.

"In fourth grade, we moved to Indianapolis. I remember thinking the kids weren't teasing me as much, but I always felt like the brunt of their jokes. I wanted very much to make friends, and so when a girl offered me this potato chip at lunch, obviously stale and green around the edges, I debated. Should I accept it? She must have been approaching me as a friend. As soon as I reached for it, everyone at the table burst into laughter. The only ones who were willing to befriend me were outcasts themselves, like the black kid who terrified everyone at school, probably in response to the treatment he was subjected to. He used to harass me about whether I knew judo. One day, in a fit of bravado, I said, 'Sure!', kicked back my leg, and accidentally hit him in the jaw, knocking him to the ground. There was a dreadful moment of silence in which I thought, 'I am going to die now.' He picked himself up, slowly turned around to face me, and smiled. As if we were friends.

"By junior high, I understood not only the spoken language but all the subtext, the gestures and the body language. I was playing the violin at the time and threw myself into practicing. I would actually practice more than I would study. I loved playing in the orchestra because I felt at home there—I had a place, I fit in.

"At home, my father was incredibly strict and demanding. He gave us the message that we were not to depend on a man for support, and in fact, all four of his daughters are very accomplished women. That may be part of the reason he went through the heartache of moving from Korea—in order to give us a better chance to succeed. The Korean word for *marriage* can literally be translated as 'losing your daughter.' When a girl marries, her name is crossed off the family records.

"My father's determination to propel us forward also had its downside, which took me years to come to terms with. He had a Plan for our lives. I found out about this when I asked his permission to date in high school. 'No,' he said the first time I asked. A little later, I tried again. His answer was the same. Then he told me what he had in mind. 'You will go to Indiana University. Then you go to medical school. After that, you find a successful man to marry. Asian would be nice but not a requirement. Next comes children.' At the time, I didn't think twice about his statements. It didn't occur to me to object or even to ask if this was what I wanted for myself.

"So I went to the University of Indiana. I had tentatively expressed an interest in the University of Chicago, but Dad told me, 'Well, I've checked around, and it seems all they do there is smoke marijuana.' In college, I realized for the first time that I had grown up never questioning anything, never figuring out what I wanted for myself. Somehow, I landed in what was called the 'artsy-fartsy faggot dorm.' I went wild! Weird hairdos and fads. My parents were mortified; they might have to be seen in public with me. Still, they called every week to ask the standard questions, 'Are you going to church?' 'You'd better not be messing around with boys.'

"I did not do well at premed. In fact, I almost flunked out of school that first semester. I never told my parents this, but I desperately worked with the university to find a way to stay. I knew I *had* to be in college. Until this point, my worst grades ever had been two B's, one for handwriting. I caught hell even for that. Second semester, I decided to change my major to English literature. When my father found out, he disowned me. On the phone, he told me, 'You are no longer my daughter.' I believed him. I really felt I did not have a family anymore. And that is when I began the process of becoming my own person, of fighting back with my father and standing up for myself.

"A few days later, my mother called to say that Dad hadn't meant what he told me. It was always like that—my father never directly apologizing for anything, but I would hear through my mother that he was sorry. Then he did it again, disowning me a second time when I wanted to take some time off from school. I was spiraling downward into an increasingly debilitating depression. I knew that I couldn't just say I wanted to leave school, so I worked out this whole plan of action. I found an internship, deferred my student loan, etc., but this was unacceptable. 'At least finish your undergraduate education,' my father demanded.

"In college, I decided that, since I had been treated as such an anomaly my whole life, I was now going to stand out, but on my own terms. I was going to make a statement. So I started dating this tie-dyed motorcycle-riding hippie named Bruce. And I told my parents exactly what I was doing. Of course they objected, which was partly my intention anyhow. My father's idea of the perfect man for me: 'Three-piece suit, banker, commanding presence.' My mother would add, 'Tall and handsome (but not too).' The man I actually married did not fit the bill. He is an artist, and he is white. After dating for a while, we decided to live together. I told my parents. My sister was aghast. 'You *actually* told them?' 'Yes,' I replied, 'and I think you should explain about you and Greg.' 'No way!' 'But what if they call and he answers?' 'Hey, listen, there are always separate lines, you know!' One day my father called me. He had two questions: One, were we serious? Two, did I have a recent picture of myself I could send him? I answered affirmatively to number one and wondered what in the hell he wanted with my picture. Turns out he had just been to a wedding and ran into Dr. ——, whose son was studying to be a cardiologist. 'Get real, Dad,' I said. 'You think you can make me into some kind of mail-order bride?'

"Announcing my engagement to my parents was very traumatic. Through my sobs, I did manage to let them know that we wanted to take their wishes for the ceremony into consideration and that we were willing to have a church wedding at their church. Nick's grandmother threw an engagement party for us. My parents had a chance to meet his family, and that helped them to begin the process of acceptance. In Korea, you don't just marry the person, you marry the family, and here they could see firsthand that my husband's family was stable, responsible.

"I live in New York now, where I'm aware that not *everyone* is *always* staring at me. My father still thinks I should move back home. He says he could find me a good job. The important thing is that we are friends now. We accept each other. And in the process, I have learned to feel proud of myself and value my own accomplishments."

Margaret is a doctoral student in psychology. She uses her knowledge to give her a better perspective on how things must have been for her father. Through all the hurt, there is at least the promise of healing and reconciliation.

"As a child, I didn't really have a way to understand the things I saw and heard in my family. Because we lived in a white suburb, isolated from other Asians, I tended to believe our problems had to do with being Chinese. Now, as a psychology doctoral candidate, I can see the larger picture. I know that spousal and child abuse cuts across the ethnic and socioeconomic lines. I'm also better able to understand the particular stresses my father endured, but I'm still left with the memory of lying in bed, fully awake, and paralyzed with fear as I listened to my father slapping my mother around. 'Why don't you hit my other ear so I'll go deaf on that side too?' she would scream. Or she'd threaten suicide. And I, the eldest daughter, was overwhelmed with the guilt of not being able to help her.

"My parents both emigrated from Taiwan to seek a better life. They met and married here, but, as is often the case, my mother acculturated more easily. I believe my father dealt with all the losses he had suffered, including a loss of masculinity when his wife went out to work, by asserting physical control over the family, particularly his spouse. He became jealous and possessive, which is a trait of battering men but also is a traditional Chinese thing—you're my property now, you need to leave your family behind and become part of mine. When my mother would get home late because the BART trains were late, he'd be convinced that she was having an affair. I'm aware that this tendency of my father's is one I've inherited and it affects my relationships. I find myself assuming the worst when there is any ambiguity at all in a situation.

"My father never learned to speak English well. He wanted to be part of American society but never felt he really could fit in. That's one reason he became kind of a recluse, choosing to stay at home and work at what became a very successful investment business rather than negotiating closer contact with the dominant culture. Just how insecure he felt about himself became painfully evident to me a few years ago. My parents had finally decided to buy an answering machine, since the five of us had all left home and there wasn't always someone around to take a message. I happened to be at the house one day, and I heard my dad's voice. It sounded like he was talking to someone, but when I went downstairs, I realized he was standing at the answering machine trying to record a greeting. He did it over and over and over. He must have spent nearly an hour trying to get that one line to sound the way he thought it should. Gaining this private glimpse of my father's struggles brought tears to my eyes.

"My mother did the best she could under the circumstances. I used to wish she would divorce my father and have some kind of life of her own, but I understand the Asian thing about divorce. She was always there for us, always trying to protect us, but in a way she was also very intrusive. She put herself in the middle of conflicts, pleading our case to him and then pleading his case to us. 'He's not really a bad man,' she'd say. 'His heart is good.' The inadvertent effect of her taking on the mediation role was to increase the stress on their marriage and slowly to cast my father as a villain, an outsider to the family.

"Another thing about my father is that he had very set expectations for my life. For many years, I just drifted along on the path he envisioned for me, with no sense of self-agency, or else I deviated and kept my choices a secret from him. When I was seventeen, I wanted to be a musician, I even got a contract with a recording studio, but before anything could come of it, my dad got wind of the story, threatened to sue the guy, made a big scene. So I just dropped the idea. I went through college directionless, not even aware that I needed to declare a major until I was in my junior year. I lived at home instead of in a dorm because my father wanted me to. I didn't particularly like it, but neither did I fight it.

"When I look at old photographs or one of the zillion home movies we have, I can see evidence of the fact that my father really loved and cherished me, his firstborn child. I can remember being absolutely stunned, but also so pleased, to receive this big bear hug from him when I graduated. But mostly, the good memories are clouded over by all the bad years. The evidence of closeness is mainly a photographic record. I don't feel the connections in my heart. Lately, I've been trying to make him feel needed by asking my father questions on subjects he knows something about, like stocks, investments, and business. Outside of that, we really don't have a relationship. For too many years, all my siblings and I tried to skirt his wrath by never telling him anything that would displease him. It got to the point where, now, there really isn't much left to say.

"It is still painful for me to think about my father, to remember what happened, and to try to come to terms with the influence he has had on my life. But I'm now in a better place to understand how he came to be the person he was. Understanding does not erase all the sorrow, but it helps."

Lisa, a journalist, looks back with frustration and anger at the central role her father played in the life of her family. But she is also careful to place his behavior within the wider cultural norms for men of his generation. Thus, the traditional and the contemporary are brought into a form of reconciliation through the perceptions of the daughter.

"My mother, whose parents owned a laundry in New Orleans and had a black nanny to look after their children, thought she was getting the best of both worlds when she married my father. He seemed to be very Western, an Eagle Scout even, and a professional man. All this, and Chinese too! In truth, however, she was fooled. My father turned out to be every bit the traditional Asian man, and both he and his family had many expectations of my mother that she found difficult to meet.

"Growing up, we all had to scurry around to make Dad happy. The single biggest incentive to get anything done was the omnipresent threat, 'If you don't do x, y, or z, your father will be mad.' His litany for many years was, 'Three women in this house and still nothing is ever clean!' My father was an engineer and he expected us to be good at math. He tried to help me with my homework, but he only believed in one way to approach a problem. If you didn't understand, he would just yell louder.

"One Thanksgiving, long after I had graduated from college, I called my mother to ask if my boyfriend at the time, Roger (a Caucasian man), could come. She said fine. Next thing I know, I get another call from her. 'Your Dad says . . . blah . . . blah . . . blah,'' which meant that Roger had been disinvited. 'Fine. If he doesn't come, I won't show up either.' Then, my mother put the screws on. 'You mean . . . you're not . . . coming . . . home . . . for . . . Thanksgiving?' So, of course I knew where my obligations lay. It turned out that Dad had invited some people from his clan for dinner, and family—no matter how distant—always takes precedence. After dinner, my sister and I had to take on the role of dutiful daughters. That meant clear the table, get out the dessert, and then meet one of my father's goals for the evening: trotting us out like small trophies to present to his relatives. 'This is my daughter Lisa, who writes for a Major Newspaper. And this is my other daughter, who is getting her Ph.D. from that World Renowned University, Stanford.' We always dreaded this part of the evening, but knew it was inevitable.

"It is difficult for me to communicate with my father because he never tells me anything directly. His way is just to grumble through Mom, and her job is to transmit his complaint to me. Like his desire for me to marry someone Chinese. I did date a Chinese man once, but all he wanted was a green card. Now I am seeing a Latino man. My father and I don't discuss it. I'm at the point where I feel nothing I could do, no one I could choose, would make any difference to him anyhow.

"But while I have these issues with my father, I am also aware of how things must be from his side of the fence. I realize that he is a product of his upbringing and society, both American and Chinese. While his American-born daughters had the luxury of essentially picking and choosing what they would retain of Chinese culture, my father, I think, did not. My sister has often pointed out that he had the worst of both worlds. He was the eldest son, with all the responsibilities and none of the benefits. My grandfather expected all kinds of things of him (getting the family out of China when the Communists came, giving them a place to live because he had a professional, white-collar job, paying for a big-show, big-face eightieth birthday party, paying the real-estate agent's commission on the family house when they backed out of selling it at the last minute, etc. etc.). When they died, they left the lion's share of the estate (such as it was) to two of his sisters. That probably accounts for ninety percent of his terminal curmudgeonliness."

When fathers make absolute choices for their daughters, the daughter may feel that she is being forced to choose between herself and her relationship with her father. But unlike her Western contemporaries, deciding for herself is not so much a question of rebellion, of defining the self in opposition to the parent, but more of a painful necessity if she is to honor her own voice. Cynthia's story.

"In some ways, my father was himself a rebel. He married a Japanese woman for love, against the wishes of his Chinese parents, but before the marriage, he tried to fulfill his role as a dutiful son by joining the army to try to 'forget' the young woman he had met at a dance. It didn't work. He found himself driving from Seattle to the Bay Area to see her.

"I grew up in Los Angeles with access to the Japanese community through my mother and to the noisy, gregarious Chinese community through my father's family. In school, I had a circle of friends who were very much like me, all highly competitive and academically motivated. One friend graduated number one in our class, another number three, and I was number twenty-five, but even as I was keeping stride with my peers, I always had this insatiable curiosity to find out what life was like 'out there.' Plus, I got tired of all the anxiety over grades. So I decided I wanted to go to a college where I could 'learn for the sake of learning,' not just for a GPA.

"I went to UC Santa Cruz, which resulted in the first significant conflict with my father. All along, I had been receiving mixed messages from him. He'd tell me to think for myself, but then he'd be just as likely to turn around and tell me, 'Do as I say!' As far as my choice of colleges was concerned, it was clear that he wanted to do the thinking for me. 'What, a school with no grades? That's not a real school! You need to go to UCLA, major in biology, and then go to med school.' At that moment, I felt absolutely torn: Either I choose my way and lose him, or I choose his way and lose myself. This has been the central struggle of my life, to come to terms with my father's voice within me. Twenty years later, even with much water under the bridge, he *still* wants me to admit I made the wrong decision about schools.

"I sensed that my mother had had some of the same struggles with my father, but my siblings and I were still shocked when, in my junior year of high school, they announced their decision to divorce. As far as I could tell, we were a model family. Now I understand that my mother finally got tired of being last. She never had any say. If, for example, Grandma wanted to come on vacation with us, that's simply how things were. Of course, reasoned my father, you don't tell your own mother that she's not welcome. As the kids got older and my mother started working, she became more assertive. Dad found this very threatening.

"After college, I spent some time with Asian issues and community activism. I also knew I didn't like being on my own, and I fell into a relationship with a man my father couldn't possibly accept, a black man. My father disowned me, virtually refused to communicate with me as long as I remained in the relationship. Part of me was probably trying to define myself by rebelling against his expectations, but it was *never* a conscious thing. It was simply too painful to deliberately provoke this kind of reaction. My father saw my choice of partner as a personal affront, an emotional slap in the face. This much I can say: I never intended to hurt him, it's not what I was about."

Fathers and daughters, love and control. Understanding the context for a father's violent actions may put a name to the behavior, but it does not necessarily assuage the pain. Teh Min, a writer and a teacher of English literature, speaks.

"To me, violence is like a death. A sudden flash: incomprehensible, brutal, unpredictable. I remember a night when I was already asleep. I couldn't have been older than seven or eight. It was past 11:00. My father burst into my room. There was never any question of privacy. He started beating the living daylights out of me, and, of course, I had no right whatsoever to question him, to speak up in my own defense. Only later did I find out that he was unhappy with the quality of my brushwork on that day's lesson. 'How can you do such poor work? How do you expect to get anywhere like this?'

"Now I understand something about my father's life. He was the youngest son, but he never became as successful as his siblings. He fled China because of the political turmoil and always felt ashamed that he did not return. He never once talked about his family. But understanding his life is one thing, reconciling with my father is another. I haven't spoken to him for over twenty years, and I'm not sure I'll ever be able to confront him. When my sister's second child was born, I was with her in Paris and my father called. Somehow, she gave him the impression that I would talk, but I couldn't say a thing. All I could do was cry. That's how it was whenever my sister and I tried to talk about our childhood. All we could do together was cry. What can you say about a man who slept with a cleaver underneath his pillow? Who used to threaten, at least once a year, to hang me because I was such a disobedient child?

"My parents were divorced in the 1940s. This was virtually unheard of in Taiwan at the time. My father got custody of my sister and me because that's how the laws operated. For this, we were stigmatized. It was assumed that 'Because you're from a broken home, you'll never amount to anything.' Most of the time, as we were growing up, my father wasn't even around. We grew up like street urchins, true Dickensian characters, but when he was home, he treated me like the boy he never had and always wished for. He expected me to succeed like a boy and he believed I should be able to take what a boy can take—for example, physical punishment.

"My father had strong hands. I remember them when they came like a rain of blows against the back of my neck. But what is even harder for me to remember is that, when my mother left my father—and I'm glad she did it, she had to leave—she distanced herself from everything that reminded her of him. Including me.

"That's why I think I'm drawn to existential writing. It reflects the reality of my life, but I can't read my own writing, it's too painful. Others read my short stories and grimace. That's how it is. The stark truth is that you make it on your own or you don't make it at all. There's also the Chinese philosophy: This is my destiny, my fate. It can't be changed."

Sometimes, the overtones of the story are less harsh, the pain more muted, but the conflict is still there. Ellen's story unfolds in the present tense.

"I think the hardest and most important lesson I've learned so far is that I have to do things the way I want to, live my own life or I'm not happy. I'm fourth-generation Japanese, my parents came through the camps, but we grew up in a very middle-class neighborhood. I think my parents were influenced by both cultures. For example, Dad thought it was important for his daughters to be independent, to be able to change the tires on the car. At the same time he was very protective. Both of my parents want me to start thinking about getting married. I am thirty years old, with no significant relationship on the horizon. For my mother and father, family is of utmost importance; their whole social life revolves around family. But for me, I don't buy the Asian belief that women get their identity through marriage.

"My parents aren't overt about their expectations. It's subtle and nonverbal, but I know it's there. Outwardly, it's like 'Do whatever you feel you need to.' They are very supportive of me, but I still know what they expect. They don't have to say it. I grew up very quiet, very shy, very 'good.' Always doing the things to please others, never making waves. I still remember my first date at seventeen. Dad told me I had to be home by midnight. So we actually left the movie early to be on time. I was on autopilot, doing what was expected of me. I lived at home while attending college, but I was starting to make plans to live on my own as soon as I graduated and got a job. I'd see a set of dishes or something I thought I'd need and buy them. I was very organized and determined.

"At twenty-three, I got a job and found my own place, moved all on my own. I think I really needed to prove that I could make it by myself without my parents' help. It was very exciting, and I find I love having my own space. I look around and think, 'This is all mine, it's great!' But I'm also aware that my parents were somewhat shocked at how easily I made the transition, perhaps a little hurt. Going to school, being exposed to new friends and different ways of thinking, was the turning point, showing me I needed to find my own way.

"Right now I'm in the middle of a difficult situation, very emotional and hard to resolve. It's related to the conflicts I've spoken about. My dad is a brilliant engineer, and several years ago, he invented this ergonomic work surface, a healthier way to handle paperwork. This project is extremely important to him. All his investors are family, and he has put a lot of his life into it. I have a degree in marketing, and about three years ago, he was having trouble with his consultants, so I offered to come in for one year to help get his enterprise up and running. The difficulties started when I would make suggestions having to do with the business. It boils down to an issue of roles. At home, my father is my father, and I'm not supposed to question his authority, but when I'm at work, I'm used to thinking independently and raising issues that need to be raised. I also know I'm good at what I do, and I cannot do my best work when I have to worry about everything I say. Anyhow, I have ended up staying with his business several years more than I had originally agreed. Now I really want to spend my time developing my own business, but I know that doing so would leave my dad feeling abandoned and me feeling guilty.

"I go to this support group for women, and I recently asked for their advice in handling this situation. They said, 'Are you confident? Are you ready to be on your own?' I answered that I was, and they all told me, 'Then go for it! Do it!' Ironically enough, the name for my business, a marketing and consulting firm, is 'The Whole Picture.' What the women encouraged me to do reflects one part of the picture. The other part of the picture is this. It's an ongoing story, but recently I tried again. I often work on my dad's stuff until ten or eleven at night, but this particular night I finished early and told him I'd like to talk with him. I wanted to discuss when I could announce the launching of my own business. Timing is important in terms of referrals, etc. So Dad says, 'Go ahead and make whatever plans you need to. I'll be all right.' But if I try to get anything else from him, he won't answer. *I* know it upsets him, but I wish we could just discuss it. I also know that, although he won't say so, he probably believes that if you have a choice between work and family, you should always choose family. So I tried to tell him once again how I felt, but he just walked away, saying he wouldn't talk about it anymore. I cannot see the whole picture without also seeing him slowly walk away, his back turned against me."

Then there are the times when things come full circle. The adolescent daughter thrown out of the house by her father is now living with him, driving him to doctors' appointments, and watching, with profound joy and gratitude, as he showers his granddaughter with the affection she never received. How could this come to be? Taeko and her Caucasian husband are both willing to honor the traditional Asian concept of respect, the core of which says that an older person, father especially, is entitled to respect simply by virtue of his age and family role. It is not a question of earning respect. In this culture, one might well take the attitude,

"Just because you're my father and have lived for seventy years, that's no reason that I have to treat you a certain way. If you are inflexible, rigid, refuse to try to see things from my point of view, or to make any attempt at compromise, that's your problem. If you want my respect, you are going to have to earn it."

"The first time my mother ever laid eyes on my father was when she stepped off the boat. Her marriage had been arranged by her parents in Japan, and once she arrived in the U.S. in the early sixties, there was no turning back, even when she discovered that he had a violent temper. Once, she was trying to sew some buttons on my father's shirt. She missed one, and he went to get another. But the lid of the button tin wouldn't budge, so my father simply got out a hatchet and smashed it open. Mom started screaming. She was petrified, but she had no choice. To even contemplate leaving the marriage would have brought great dishonor to her family.

"Growing up, I never had the concept of love. Not until I was a teenager and saw how my Caucasian friends treated each other in their families: hugging, sharing affection. Then, I wanted to tell my mother how much she meant to me. She started crying, didn't know how to react. My father was just Dad. Domineering, stoic. He was like the ice man, and I was scared of him. You just didn't know what was inside—what he was really thinking or feeling. I remember that he used to like to read the paper at the dinner table. One day my mom decided this wasn't setting a good example for the kids, and she asked him to stop doing that. So, instead, he would spend the whole meal picking at one or the other of us. She told him to go back to the newspapers.

"When I was eighteen years old, my friend Jane and I decided to go to the Cherry Blossom Festival. I got back a little later than I was supposed to, and as soon as I stepped in the door, my father started in on me. I told him I was old enough to make this type of decision on my own. He didn't like to hear that, so he slapped me. That's when I said that this was unacceptable to me and I was leaving. 'If you leave,' he yelled back, 'don't expect to come back home.' I didn't. For two years my father refused to have anything to do with me. He told the rest of the family I was not to be seen or spoken to. So I got an apartment, lived on my own. And then I had this asthma attack. My boyfriend at the time panicked and called my mother. She still had some of my medications at home and was just leaving to bring them to me when my dad caught her. 'What are you doing?' he asked. 'Taking Taeko some medicine. She's having an attack.' 'If you go,' my father warned her, 'don't come back.' Mom said, 'OK, but I'm going anyhow.'

"After that, things slowly got put back together. My father had axed me out of his life, but I had never done so to him. I always made sure to send him a Father's Day card, birthday card, etc., even if he never once wrote back. One day, I was at my parents' house doing laundry. I heard my father's car pulling up; he was home from work early. I almost jumped I was so nervous. He saw me and then asked if I was planning to stay for dinner. Mom was in the background letting me know it's OK. So I said yes. I'm part of the family again. My dad acts like nothing ever happened. To this day, I think if you asked him about the time I lived away from home, he's say, 'What time?'

"My father never apologized, but I don't really care. That's all behind me now. I'm just grateful we are all back together, literally, because my husband, our three children, and I now live in my parents' home with them. We've all had to make adjustments, but I am very happy with our life the way it is. We were in a tight spot financially four years ago, and my parents suggested we move back home. It just so happened that my dad's friend was retiring from a landscape maintenance business at the time and suggested my husband buy him out. So there was a job—which has worked out great for us—but we would never have been able to afford a house on our own. At the same time, my parents could use our help with the mortgage and so on. Mutual benefit.

"What really makes this work is that my husband, who isn't even Japanese, understands my culture and knows that he has to respect my father. Even if we're helping out financially, it's still my father's house, and what he says goes. So Chris has learned very well how to bite his tongue. I guess it's because, in some ways, my husband and my father are very much alike.

Chris likes to domineer and have things his own way. But he can see where my father's coming from. He knows my dad worked extremely hard to make it possible for us to enjoy the kind of life we have now, and he is truly appreciative.

"At the same time, Chris also knows that in my culture, when you get married, you are no longer the daughter of the father, you become the wife of the husband. So if my father tries anything with me or with our children, Chris will step in. One day, my dad got so mad about something that he threw his glass on the floor. It shattered into a million pieces and just missed the baby. Chris, who is six three, gets up, looks my father, who is five three, in the eye, and makes it clear that this is not an acceptable way for him to behave.

"The funny thing is, my older sister is married to a Japanese man, but he would never put up with my father the way my husband does. My father knows this. He recognizes that he has a good deal, and so he expects more of my husband than his Japanese son-in-law. Then again he's also much closer to my husband.

"What's hard for me is knowing how my mother feels. I'm sad that her life wasn't happier, that my father doesn't treat her the way she deserves. She doesn't say much, but I know how she feels. The other day I said to Dad that he should go easier on her. All the stress is really bad for her blood pressure. I also warned him that, even though I'll always take care of him, if Mom dies, I won't be catering to him the way she does.

"The other hard thing about our living arrangement is that when Chris and I argue about something, Mom will always be pushing me to go make up with him. If I stop making dinner or something, she'll step in and do it. You don't exactly want your mother to be making meals for your husband when you're angry with him. So I tell her to stay out of it. I can handle him myself.

"You could say my father was very strict with us as kids, but the way I see it now is that I'm very *grateful* to him for making me the person I am. Furthermore, I realize that I was the rebel. I caused my parents the most heartache, so they deserve something back from me. Although my dad never showed me any affection when I was a child, he's so good with his grandchildren that I just have to say I feel blessed."

6   CHOOSING A PARTNER

When my cousin came of marriageable age, her mother gave her this advice: "Finding the right husband is like looking for someone to row the boat with." In other words, a good partner is one who can match your effort stroke for stroke, someone to help you navigate the unpredictable waters. What my aunt failed to mention was precisely those qualities that I, as a young woman, most ardently sought. A man who took my breath away. A white knight who desired me above all others. A man in whose liquid blue eyes I could see reflected the promise of limitless possibility.

Traditional Asian views about choosing a partner are clearly in conflict with contemporary Western ideas. For one thing, fathers did the choosing for their daughters, not daughters for themselves. Parents were believed to be in a better position to assess the important things: whether or not this man came from a good family, could provide well for his wife. Of course, this did not mean their judgments were infallible. My mother tells me the story of her aunt, who was married to a man from a family with very nice furniture. Not only did he turn out to be an unkind man, the furniture was deceptive, indicating a degree of wealth the family did not in fact possess. But fathers had the power nevertheless. They could also consider factors such as the potential husband's ancestral history: Are there skeletons in the closet? Relatives who were mentally retarded or crazy?

For another, love was not the point. A man and a woman in an arranged marriage may, over the years, develop real affection for each other, but "falling in love" was not considered a prerequisite or even an issue in choosing a partner. Additionally, the success of a daughter's marriage is not just a reflection on her as an individual, it speaks to the honor of the family as a whole. So a decision of this magnitude cannot be left in the hands of a mere girl.

Asian American women today are sometimes caught between these two expectations: finding a partner who suits our parents (while parents no longer arrange marriages, they may still state very strong preferences) and finding someone who meets the requirements of the heart. We have a good idea of the kind of man Mom and Dad would like us to bring home. And most of us would just as soon have that parental seal of approval. Yet, overwhelmingly, we reserve the right to make our own choices. Based on love. So even if I marry the handsome Chinese doctor, it is because he is the right man for *me. I* picked him.

In my case, I knew what my parents wanted for me, and although I did not make a dream match in their eyes, at least I was in the ballpark. Jim is not Chinese, but then again, he's not a "minority." He had been married before, but at least he doesn't have children from that marriage. While he does not have a Ph.D., he does have two master's degrees. And he comes from a good, solid family.

Still, I know my mother had her reservations. One of her concerns, not directed at Jim personally but at white men in general, was that white men have the most "desire," followed by white women, Chinese men, and finally by Chinese women. A Chinese woman marrying a white man would be like mixing apples and oranges, or perhaps oil and water.

We will make our own choices about whom to marry. But if we act against the wishes of our parents, the results can sometimes

be enormously painful. Parents of daughters who choose an unsuitable mate may have no hesitation letting her face the full
force of their anger and disappointment. In order to cope, some
women use denial, telling themselves that they have the right to
marry the man or choose the partner they love. Feelings of guilt,
feelings associated with familial ostracism, are cut off. Other
women hold on, quietly but tenaciously, both to their choice and
their hope that parents will eventually come around. Tranh, a
Vietnamese immigrant who came to the U.S. in the seventies,
tells her story.

"In refugee camp, I learned to eat many things I had previously disdained in Vietnam: bananas, tomatoes, green vegetables. Food was scarce, water available only if you were willing to
walk a mile and carry a bucket. For the first time in my life I
knew what it was like to be poor, to live with uncertainty, to
know that my parents had spent their life's fortune paying for
our passage out of Vietnam. A few years earlier, I had helped my
mother in her charity work assisting war refugees. I had seen
hungry children and offered them cookies, but that was only a
glimmer of understanding, not real knowledge.

"Living in camp also taught me how much I had taken for
granted. We came from a wealthy family, I was the youngest of
eight children. I remember crying in the morning because I
didn't want to go to school. But in camp, my view of life changed
completely. I blamed myself for not appreciating the things I had
had. I wasn't so much angry at my situation, but I felt it was
terribly unfair to my mother, who had sacrificed all of her wealth
and all of her possessions to get us out of the country. At times,
waves of guilt and remorse would sweep over me when I thought
about something like a gold bracelet my mother had given to me
in that long-ago childhood. If I hadn't carelessly lost it, that piece
of jewelry could have meant a few more meals for us now.

"We eventually made it to the U.S., with $500 in our pocket.
At first the ten of us lived in a two-bedroom house and we had
to accept welfare in order to survive. This was very shameful, but
we had no choice. I remember being embarrassed about bringing
friends home from school because there was so little furniture.

And our clothes were different; we couldn't afford to buy anything fashionable. We were also very depressed, my mother and I, and at times I felt that it was very hard to think about the future with any optimism at all. I didn't know the language and I wondered if I would ever be able to graduate from high school. Sometimes I thought, 'This is it. This is the end.'

"But I was able to finish school with the help of teachers, all of them Caucasian, who made a special effort to reach out to me. I applied to UCLA because it was the only school close to home. And there I began to be introduced to new ideas, new ways of looking at the world. One course I took was in the Asian American studies department. We had to come up with a skit to present to the class. That's when I started to realize how much my views were changing, specifically my attitude toward Asian men. Before, I had never been interested in any Caucasians. I had always assumed I'd marry someone Chinese. But in this skit, I found myself writing about Asian men as too traditional, too controlling. Men who reminded me of my older brother, the most indulged of the children. Or my father, who communicated with me primarily to criticize something I had done. Yet, I knew I didn't really want to date white men either. Somehow I was in a place that didn't fit into either world. The solution offered in my skit: Don't get married at all!

"I was no good at math, never have been. I tried a few different majors that allowed me to avoid math classes but they were never satisfying. One day, an advisor suggested I consider a master's in social work. My mother asked, 'What's that?' In Vietnam, there is no such concept as mental health. Either you're normal or you're crazy. And if you're crazy, it's probably because of a bad spirit in your body or a mistake in your past life. Maybe you buried your ancestors in the wrong place. A priest could help you, but a social worker?

"I told my mother that social work was like the charity work she had done in Vietnam. That she could accept. At least it made more sense than 'Asian American studies,' which even I found difficult to explain. Her only concern was that social workers don't make much money. I felt guilty about that too. My older siblings had been working long hours to support the family, and I wanted to contribute as well.

"Still, the master's program was wonderful. I loved the classes, and found that I could draw on my own years of trauma to help others in need. I got active in community work, and this is where I met my husband and where the very painful conflict with my parents got its start. Michael was an attorney who took the issue of social responsibility very seriously. He donated many hours of his time to help people who couldn't otherwise afford his services. His heart was in the right place and his work touched me. Also, he was older than I, and I think he gave me some of the nurturing my own father never provided.

"One huge drawback, however. Michael was white. Far worse than that, from my parents' point of view, he was divorced and had a son from his previous marriage. To them, it was inconceivable that I would be interested in such a man. I was in a very difficult position. On the one hand, I was at a rebellious point in my life. My involvement with community issues helped me become more articulate, to speak out about justice and fairness. Michael fit the qualifications I was looking for. So I had the attitude, 'This is my life. This is the person I choose.' But on the other hand, I didn't want to disappoint my parents, to let them down. So ultimately, even if I made the decision to get married against my parents' wishes, part of me felt very bad, very guilty for bringing them so much pain.

"When I told my parents about getting married, they asked me to move away, to change my last name. They threw away all my clothes. I went ahead with the wedding, which only one sister attended, and I did move away—but not very far. The day after we were married, I asked my husband to bring a piece of cake to my family's house. At least they did not refuse it.

"This whole situation was very upsetting to me, but I always tried to keep the lines open. I never even considered breaking my ties to my family, leaving in anger. And slowly, my parents came to accept Michael. My sisters learned to tolerate our relationship.

"Unfortunately, Michael and I had a number of conflicts in our relationship, many related to cultural differences. In the beginning, I was very quiet but expected my husband to know what I was thinking. If we went to a restaurant, I'd want him to serve me, although I didn't tell him that. When he failed to do so, I'd get mad. We also had fights about money—he thought it was fine to borrow now and save later. For me, I didn't feel secure unless I saved and saved. I felt he was giving his son too much freedom. Even little things became an issue: if I went to bed without saying good night, he'd get upset. After a few years, we worked our way into an impasse and decided to separate. At this, my parents were overjoyed. They welcomed me back home with open arms.

"So now, here I am, back in my parent's good graces and then Michael and I decide to try to work out our differences. While we were apart, I started to understand how complicated marriages really are, how much work they take. You have to talk things through. If you go shopping, it's nice to think about your husband and his son as well as yourself. You say good morning in the morning and good night at night. We both realized we needed to work through our cultural conflicts and so we have been attending classes, going to therapy.

"I'm hopeful about my marriage now, but what can I possibly tell my parents this time? Maybe it will all come out right again. Maybe they'll get used to this situation as they learned to accept our marriage originally. But it's already been over a month and I still haven't worked up the courage to talk with them."

On the whole, parents (at least in my generation and older) prefer their children to marry Asian. Caucasian is considered a close second, provided that certain other requirements are met (education being the chief of these). Two reasons are usually cited: that the children of these marriages will have an easier time, and that the parents will have a basis on which to relate to their new son-in-law. For this reason especially, it is often desired that the daughter marry a man who speaks the parents' language.

On the other hand, pure racism and prejudice form the

shadow side of this desire that daughters not "marry out." It is clear that Latinos, Native Americans, or African Americans (listed in descending order of preference) are not considered good choices. My own parents, among others, would add Jews to the list, citing age-old stereotypes of the "Shylock" variety. Interracial marriage is also seen as a threat to the "purity of races."

Generally speaking, Asian American women tend to pick partners from the list of acceptable choices. Some would say that if the "right" black or Latino man showed up, they would certainly consider marriage, that racial considerations would not obscure their views. But in fact, the overwhelming preference is still for an Asian or a Caucasian husband. When Asian American women choose Caucasian men, it is occasionally for the same reasons that I did: a deep-seated belief that Asians are inferior to whites. But more likely, one of several explanations is given: (1) Many grew up in areas where there were very few Asian men to choose from in the first place. (2) Asian men are not physically attractive. (3) Asian men are more likely to be too traditional, or conversely, they will find me too liberal, too "Western." (4) I married for love, the man just happened to be white. And while the white partner may not have been the parents' first choice, the act of marriage is not, fundamentally, an act of *rebellion*.

When the daughter makes a union against her parents' wishes, it is sometimes possible that the transcendent power of love overcomes the objections. Even if the intended is a black man. Even if the intended is not a man at all, but a woman. Amy's story is told first.

"My mother has suffered two major traumas in her life as a result of what I've done. The first was when I got pregnant in my early twenties and was not married. My baby's father was black and I decided to raise her on my own. The second was when I married my husband, who is also black. In both cases, my mother was very hurt and we both endured a great deal of pain. But there was something in my life greater than the bad feelings and difficulties—the love and abiding support of my grandparents. Even though they are Issei, they never had a judgmental view about my life. They were truly wonderful people who accepted and loved me for who I am. Without their support, I think it's likely that the rest of my family would have condemned me, in a sense thrown me out.

"My parents are both Kibbei, born in the U.S. but educated in Japan. My mother was living in Hiroshima at the time of the bomb and still goes back to Japan every other year for physicals provided by the Japanese government. For a long time, she never said a word about her experience in the city or the fact that she was not allowed to return to the U.S. for several years afterwards even though she was a U.S. citizen. But about eight years ago, she suddenly became active in speaking out about the consequences of nuclear war. In broken English, she recounts her story and her feelings. I got the full brunt of her story one year when she found she had been scheduled to speak at two different peace rallies at the same time. She gave her notes to me and asked me to appear at one of them. I had a hard time with that one.

"I grew up in Colorado, where my parents owned a grocery store and a hotel. I spent a lot of time with my grandparents and in many ways was raised in traditional Japanese fashion. We went to the Buddhist temple, spoke Japanese at home, went to Japanese school. I don't remember learning English, but I'm sure that didn't happen until I got to school. I also don't remember feeling any sense of being different from my classmates. We lived in a primarily black neighborhood, and in addition to the white and black kids at school, there were also a few other Asians, whom I knew and liked. I was aware, however, of being Japanese and the fact that my parents considered Japanese to be superior.

"My mother's primary expectation of me was to get good grades. As long as I was doing well in school, I was pretty much free to do what I wanted with my life. We didn't have the usual teenage conflicts over makeup, etc. But things were different when I got to college. What I learned was how to party, cut classes, have a good time. In part, I was rebelling against the wishes of my parents, but in part I just didn't care. The only time I'd start to feel guilty was when tuition time rolled around. My mother would tell me to try to work harder, maybe take fewer classes. I'd resolve to get on track, but never quite managed. Eventually, I dropped out of school and went back home to live for a while.

"Looking back, I know that I would *never* have done the things for my children that my parents did for me. While I was at college, my mom used to come up every Sunday, take any dirty laundry, bring back clean clothes. Paid for my apartment. And when I lived at home that year, she even paid the fee at the employment agency so I could get a job. But I think she was driven by this Japanese belief that parents should do everything in their power to help their kids financially, especially when it comes to education. Now, however, I'm back in school and my mother does remind me that if I had completed my education when she originally sent me to college, she would have paid the whole bill. This time, I'm on my own.

"The other really important thing to my mother was that I marry Japanese. She always expected me to. So when I first started dating—whites, blacks, Hispanics (never an Asian man)—I simply didn't bring them home with me. I knew she could be mean to them and I just didn't want to subject anyone to that. One day I remember having this conversation with her. I told her that I would date who I wanted to. She couldn't expect to live her life through me. Mom got this sick look on her face, but all she said to me was, 'Oh well.'

"I didn't feel ashamed that I had had a child out of wedlock. But my mother had a very hard time with it and refused to have anything to do with my daughter after she was born. Not until Bochan and Chichan [grandparents] intervened. They invited my mother over to their house, not saying anything about the baby. I still remember my mom walking into the living room, quiet as a rock. She didn't move for a long time. Finally, she walked over and picked up my baby, held her, started crying. After that, they were always very close.

"I have always talked very openly with my daughter about her father, about her being half black. I have a cousin who also had a child by a black man she was not married to. She absolutely refuses to acknowledge the black part of her child, acts like it never happened. I think it's because she's more snobbish about being Japanese than I am.

"I think the biggest mistake I made with my daughter was not telling her the truth about her father. I never lied about him, but I also tried not to say derogatory things about him. And then, totally out of the blue, she ran into him when she was in eighth grade. He was probably very drunk, maybe using drugs, and my daughter was totally crushed. Devastated. All these years, unknown to me, she had been harboring these glorious fantasies about her father. That incident hurt her profoundly and she started directing all her anger at me. How could I pick such a man for her father? She became very rebellious, even tried to commit suicide. It was a terrible time, and I regret not having better prepared her to face the truth. I also used to have a great deal of regret for hooking up with her father in the first place. But over the years, I have learned to let go of that.

"I dated the black man who was to become my husband for many years. When we first got married, my mother refused to talk to or see me. If we showed up a family gathering, she'd leave. And she would punish my father if he tried to communicate with me. They have a very traditional marriage; she still runs his bathwater, gets his socks out, etc. So if he came to see me, she'd refuse to do anything for him and he wouldn't even be able to find any underwear. But once again, my grandparents supported me and let me know they cared. And painful as it was, I held on to the notion that my mother would eventually come around. I always believed that. I knew she was very hurt—here I had both given her an out-of-wedlock half-black grandchild and then married a black man—but I tried to explain that these were choices of *mine,* not things I was doing to hurt *her.*

"After our son was born, she did relent. Over the years, she and the rest of my family have gotten to know my husband, and really love him. In a sense, that exonerated me. Now, my mother is so close to my husband that she'll call him when she has a problem. Sometimes bypasses me altogether! My husband also feels very loved and accepted by them. I guess I knew he had been truly brought into the fold one family gathering when I saw my uncles plying him with sake and all of them sitting around loudly singing Japanese songs! The hurts have been forgiven. We have moved on."

Christine's story has a similar flavor. Her choice of a partner was unorthodox, and in another family might have caused deep divisions and animosity. But here, the underlying rule was that, lesbian or not, a beloved daughter is a person to be cherished, not scorned.

"Once you become a part of my family, you are a part forever. That's how I grew up with two fathers and considered it perfectly natural. My mother's first husband was welcome at our house, even after the divorce. He's the one who taught me to hunt and fish, he's the one who spoiled the hell out of me. At the same time, I see my real father as a very compassionate man, a hero. Growing up in this family has given me the encouragement and support to come to terms with my sexual preference and to pursue the kind of relationship I wanted for myself. It has been nothing short of miraculous.

"As a child, I had no sense of identity as an Asian. I was totally immersed in white middle-class culture, and the only real link to my parents' roots was the fact that we ate rice every time a starch was called for. No bread, no potatoes, only rice and more rice. I was a good student and an athlete and this is where the Chinese part comes in: I had the same inherent pressure to succeed that every other Asian kid in America experiences. In fifth grade, they put me in a class for gifted students, which was to my detriment. People were already asking, 'So, are you going to Stanford?' I made the honor roll, but for some reason, my name didn't get published in the paper with all the others. My mother popped a cork. I kept trying to explain that I really did get the grades, I swear I made the honor roll, but she wouldn't listen. It wasn't there in black and white, in print.

"By the time I got to high school, I was in a very rebellious phase. Typical teenager, I thought I knew everything. You've heard about the generation gap? Well, for me, it was more like the Grand Canyon. I lost interest in school, I couldn't do that anymore. Plus, I was pretty much unsupervised. My mother worked until 5:30 and by the time I was eleven or twelve, my older sisters had all moved out and it was just me at home. I tried wearing all these different hats—be a cool teenager, play sports, and still make it home every evening to cook dinner for my mom and dad.

"After high school, I got married to my high school sweetheart. My parents were against it, but not because he was Caucasian. They just thought I was too young. He was a very nice guy, but we were absolute opposites. And in the fifth year of our marriage, I discovered my sexuality. My first girlfriend was a woman I met through softball. Meeting and being with her was an affirmation, and I never went through the thing of trying to deny that part of myself. The first question was not, how do I tell my family, but how do I end this marriage? I just told my husband the truth. He had to accept it, there was no choice.

"None of my sisters had ever been divorced. I had to think about how to break the news to my family. I made a plan. I called my sister Belinda and said, 'I don't know how to tell you this, but Mark and I are getting a divorce. And by the way . . .' She and her husband and two kids came over to my girlfriend's house and we talked and talked. It took a huge weight off my shoulders. After that, I don't even remember telling my parents, it just wasn't that traumatic. But I did leave it to my mother to pass the word along to the aunts and cousins—whether through embarrassment or just plain being too tired, I don't know.

"I've never been around Asians much and I imagine that dating an Asian woman would feel almost like incest. I'm involved with a Caucasian woman who has two teenagers and I think this is probably the 'right one,' although I'm aware that we always tell ourselves this kind of shit. My partners get as much legitimacy as my siblings' spouses. In fact, the other day, my mother remarked to me. 'Now I have two more grandchildren.' I was dumbfounded. Did a double take—did those words really come from my mother's mouth? But I was also elated. However, the fact that I am a lesbian doesn't stop her from reminding me that my biological clock is ticking. She knows I love kids and wants me to have one of my own. She always mentions that at least I can adopt.

"One thing I have always let my partners know is that my family is very important to me. I expect her to come to family dinners, get-togethers, and if that's a problem for her, it will be a problem for me. My partner now is not as out to her family. We want to plan a traditional matrimonial ceremony of some kind, and the joke between us is who'll make the guest list. I know that I can always rely on my family. No matter what. This is what I'm telling the kids now—there is nothing so bad that you can't come home. You're always welcome.

"You could ask, how do I identify myself now? That's a good question. My dad is Filipino, my mom is Chinese, I'm gay, living with a white woman, and I have an Irish surname. (I kept my husband's name partly because I love to see the look on people's faces when they see me in person: 'Oh, uh, you don't look like a Bowers.') Sometimes I think it's kind of sad when my partner asks about my culture and I don't know a lot to tell her. Most likely, I'll always be searching for my identity to some extent. I'm not sure that's ever going to be entirely resolved."

Other women haven't had it quite so easy. The process of coming out is complicated by cultural issues that may influence an Asian American woman's ability to come to terms with her sexual orientation.

Lorie is the executive director of a nonprofit agency that provides services to disabled children. She speaks about her struggle to accept her own sexual orientation in a way that does not conflict with her family's values.

"Recently, I discovered that my mother has a set of my grandfather's diaries and a whole box of negatives for photos that he took. She isn't particularly interested in them, but I really want to get them translated and develop those pictures. My grandfather came here in the early 1900s, returning to China at the age of thirty to find a bride. That's all I know. My parents don't know a whole lot more than that. I think they were primarily concerned with being Americans, but I feel badly that I don't have a strong connection with my past.

"We grew up in a multicultural community because my parents wanted to move out of Chinatown. I had a great time there, but I do remember that my parents would never let any of my friends come to the house. I take that back. They allowed me to invite my Chinese friends over. If my parents socialized with any of the neighbors, it was the Chinese ones. In fact, we called them Auntie even though we were in no way related to them.

"My parents didn't care a lot about their heritage, but they did raise us with many Chinese values. Extended family was very important, still is. My cousins were my best friends. Every weekend we'd see our relatives: kids running around together, the adults drinking tea and gossiping. I'm very close with my parents and other relatives today. They mean a whole lot to me. And that is why I can't come out to my parents. I have lived with two different women for long periods of time. Both of my partners have been warmly welcomed into my family, but the fact of my sexual preference is never discussed. Part of me longs to be able to name it, to be open about who I am, but I can't bring myself to take that risk. I guess I respect my parents too much to do that to them, to make them face this 'hideous' relationship I am in. It's enough that they accept the woman I choose to share my life with. I don't ask for more.

"Another reason not to come out to my parents is my fear that I will lose my 'good girl' status. I have always been the responsible one, done right by my family. Even with an older and younger brother, I'm the one my parents turn to, I'm the one they count on. A lot of my identity is based on that fact, and I can't jeopardize it. I have tried to live my life the way I felt I should to the extent that I married a Chinese man. Our relationship lasted three years. I wasn't really aware of what I was at the time, but I knew I was trying to do the right thing.

"This is how my first romantic relationship with a woman came about. Diana was my roommate and things evolved over time. I don't think I was really out to myself. We had a relationship for eight years, but in my mind, it was always just that we 'were together.' We never talked about it. And then, she decided she wanted to be more out. I freaked. Family was a big part of the reason. Diana wasn't pressuring me to disclose to my parents, but what I realize now is that I couldn't acknowledge my sexuality to myself without also at some level admitting it to my family. As long as I never really identified myself as a lesbian, I wouldn't have to be concerned about their reaction. But my family is so much a part of myself that it is sometimes hard to make the distinction. Because of all this, I found excuses to separate myself from my partner, pull away from the relationship.

"After ending my relationship with Diana, I got involved with an Asian woman. It was nice to be able to share certain common experiences. Like the time we had crab, one of our first dinners together. My family always eats that stuff inside the shell and I wanted to go for it, but I was afraid she'd be grossed out. It turns out that her family also ate that part of the crab, so we ended up fighting over it! Unfortunately, that relationship also came to an end, and at a very difficult time in my life. I was changing jobs, experiencing health problems. I felt like I was going crazy. And then my cousin called. I had to talk to someone. She was so cool, so understanding. It was a tremendous relief to be that open with someone from my family.

"Even though we never talk about it, I think my parents do know what I am. And I think they are OK with it. But it doesn't stop them from trying. A few months ago, my father had heart surgery. A handsome Chinese cardiologist did the procedure. My mother couldn't help herself, she just had to say, 'Hey, I wonder if he's *married?*' I didn't answer, just rolled my eyes."

Emilie, born and raised in the Philippines, turned to a Western psychological approach to handle the issue of parental approval of her choice of husband. Murry Bowen, a preeminent marriage and family therapist, talks about the need for adult children to differentiate themselves from their family of origin. This can sometimes be a very painful process, requiring a systematic and rational approach. One clearly opposed to the Asian notion of continuous and continuing intergenerational interdependence.

But it is one that gave Emilie the confidence to go ahead with her own choice and also gave her some reassurance that she could create a space where her parents would feel OK with the situation.

"I grew up in the Philippines. Attending college in Manila was my first opportunity at unsupervised living, but even then, my parents made sure an adult cousin was nearby to keep an eye on me. I didn't need much watching, however; the concepts of sin, compliance, what it meant to be Catholic and to be a good girl were deeply ingrained.

"My parents were both educators, and therefore had a wider worldview than would have been typical for their generation. But they still retained some traditional Asian values, for example wanting all their children to become doctors. I was trained as a nurse and my two sisters were social workers, so we got close but I was still aware of my parents' disappointment. However, my niece recently graduated from medical school and in a sense absolved the rest of us. At least there *is* a doctor in the family now, no matter which generation.

"I broke a major barrier by marrying an American Jew. There was some concern about his not being Filipino, but the religious conflict was an even greater obstacle. Making my decision, I knew about the heartaches I could cause for both our families. I could anticipate my sister asking, "How *could* you marry a Jew?" But I was very clear in my head and in my heart what I was about. I attribute this clarity to the clinical training I received at the psychiatric hospital that sponsored me to come to the U.S. One of my supervisors told me that if I wanted to be a good family therapist, I would need to start out by doing work on my own family. That made sense to me.

"I ended up working with a member of Murry Bowen's team. My primary goal in therapy was to have a person-to-person relationship with my parents, a concept that is not exactly commonplace among Asians. I wanted the kind of relationship my sisters weren't able to achieve—one that would permit me to make personal choices such as who to marry without provoking antagonism. I didn't tell my parents about the coaching I was receiving from my therapist, but I knew inside the ways I was changing, even with respect to the letters I wrote home. As time went on, I revealed more and more of myself and my feelings.

"With my therapist's help, I made plans to take my father and mother back to my father's village of birth, some forty years after he had moved away. I knew how much this would mean to him. And I also knew that this pilgrimage would help clarify my role as an *adult* in the family who was capable of giving something back to her parents. My mother wasn't sure about going, so it didn't surprise me that two days before we planned to leave, she became 'sick.' I had anticipated this possibility and simply told her very calmly that she could stay behind, there were people to look after her. I didn't respond with the traditional and expected feelings of guilt. Just as we were about to take off, she felt better and we all had a wonderful time. Dad revisited his elementary school, saw the saplings he and his brothers had planted transformed into tall and majestic trees. It was a very moving experience.

"Seven years after we first started dating, my husband and I decided it was time to get married. I was very clear that I didn't want to be another statistic, one of the many divorces I as a family therapist had tried to help couples negotiate. Working through my family-of-origin issues was an important part of laying the groundwork. And so it was with a sense of quiet confidence that I announced my engagement at the annual family reunion. My father said, 'If you really love each other, we will support you. You're the one making this decision, you must know what you have chosen.' I couldn't have asked for anything more."

And then there are times when the daughter's ideas about marriage coincide with the desires of the parent. Cindy is twenty-one, a senior in college.

"The high school I went to in Maryland was 20 percent Asian. I'm at Stanford now and the percentage is just about the same, so I feel that all my life I have been surrounded by a community of fellow Asians. While I value my multicultural experience here (I have black, Jewish, and white friends here), I know that deep inside I'm more comfortable around Asians, especially Chinese.

I see my Chinese heritage as a very valuable part of who I am. Although I hated going to Chinese school when I was little and preferred McDonald's to any other restaurant, I now appreciate the fact that my parents kept alive the culture for me. I hate to admit it, but they were right! I see the value of learning Chinese and learning about the traditions. Even now, I try to keep up my language skills. And I know that it will be very important to me that my children be able to speak Chinese. That is one reason I feel almost 100 percent certain that I'm going to marry an ABC (American-born Chinese) like me. Asian men *are* attractive to me; I don't buy the stereotypes about them. If I see a cute Caucasian guy, I'm like, 'Well, he is good looking but only for aesthetic purposes.' I simply believe it will be easier for me to get along with a Chinese man who has a similar background. We would just understand each other better.

"That's one of the reasons I even think it would be hard to marry Korean or Japanese. We wouldn't have as much in common. And I know it's very unlikely I'd marry black or Jewish. My parents consider Caucasian to be at least no worse than Chinese, but they are definitely prejudiced against other minorities. Stanford's a pretty PC (politically correct) kind of place and I wouldn't want to admit it, but I'm sure I've been brainwashed into adopting some of my parents' attitudes.

"I like being Chinese and I like my Chinese connections. I appreciate the fact that I can speak two languages and I like knowing I have a separate community to feel part of. It's like extended family and very close knit. Sometimes I feel sorry for my Caucasian friends that they don't have that to fall back on. But sometimes, close is a little too close. I remember when my sister first got her period. We were going to some Chinese youth activity that night and all the other mothers came right up to her. They all knew already! They said something about, 'Oh, we should rub your feet.' (I'm not sure, some connection Chinese see between feet and all other parts of the body.) That part can be exasperating, but even so, I'd rather be part of this environment—and I'd want my husband and children to be part of it too—than any other place I can think of. On the whole, it's just fine."

For Asian American women, the act of choosing a partner not only invokes potential conflicts with traditional values, it also brings to the table the uninvited guest of racism. For myself, I never dated or even considered dating a single Asian man, never had any desire to do so. Most of the Chinese boys I knew as a child were sons of my parents' friends, and in my desire to discard my ethnicity, I spent many years trying to distance myself from what I saw as these studious, unathletic, conservative, and fundamentally uncool acquaintances. I found Asian men physically unattractive in the same manner that I considered my own Asian features to be undesirable. There is a way in which I imagined that physical intimacy would smack of incest—too much like finding yourself in the arms of your brother. And although I could not have articulated this thought at the time, I believed that if I married a white man, it would raise my self-esteem. A guy with blond hair, who had his pick of women with blond hair and Anglo last names, choosing me? Through the process of internalized racism, I had learned too well the lesson of the dominant culture: White is better than Asian. In all respects.

Racism clearly played a part in Maryanne's experience. Marriages between Asians and whites are an increasingly common occurrence, but it was not until 1948 that the California Supreme Court actually ruled antimiscegenation laws unconstitutional. Laws can change, but attitudes sometimes linger.

"I was actually born in Manila, but only lived there two years. My father was an army officer there for the liberation. He was English, with a last name of Farnell. At the time, my mother was in her late twenties and still not married, almost an 'old spinster woman.' However, she was a practicing physician and had been for several years. She came from a very well educated family; all seven of her brothers and sisters went to college, one got her Ph.D., and one became a judge.

"My mother experienced real hardships marrying my dad. His family was totally against the idea and threw a fit when they found out. They didn't disown him, but they came close. Later, when my parents moved to Virginia, my mother started writing letters to the editor about the miscegenation laws then in effect which made it illegal for a nonwhite to marry a white. My mother's not really an activist, but she felt she had to speak up about this issue. I've been reading some of those letters lately. I think these experiences have a lot to do with the person my mother became—quiet and shy, afraid that others would not accept her.

"Her pain around these issues was an important factor in how she raised her children. She never wanted us to endure the things she did, so she made it clear that the only thing she cared about in a husband for her daughters was whether or not we loved each other and that he treated us well. She didn't care if we married Filipino or white. She was very accepting and open when my sister Katie married a black man. For myself, I have to say I was a little surprised when I first saw Hobart's picture. I was thinking that their mixed-race children would have a hard time in Virginia, remembering back to the prejudice I had experienced there. What made me especially mad was that kids assumed I was Chinese, never bothering to learn the difference. I'm not even all Filipino; my dad is white and I have an Anglo last name.

"In Hawaii, I met a white man who was a lieutenant in the navy, and we became engaged. Hawaii was a very comfortable place to live, easy to fit in. Within just a few days of moving there, people were already asking me directions! Anyhow, the day of our engagement party, we called to tell his parents the news. They lived in northern California and I expected them to be cool, cosmopolitan. But instead, they were very upset that their son wanted to marry a Filipino. They said, 'But you don't even know her that well . . . etc. etc.' My next communication from them was a twelve-page letter absolutely seething with hate. Really vicious hate mail. In response to my fiancé telling them that my grandfather had been the mayor of his town in the Philippines, they said, 'Oh, that doesn't mean anything, corruption in that government being so rampant and all.' But the worst part of the letter was a line I will never forget. 'You know,'' they wrote, 'Filipinos most closely resemble monkeys of all the Asiatic tribe.' I cried that entire night.

"Still, we kept our engagement, although postponing our marriage for a while. My fiancé came out to meet my parents, that went well. But then he moved to San Francisco while I was in graduate school and I really think he fell back under his mother's influence. He didn't even have the guts to tell me in person he wanted to call off the marriage. He ended up marrying his secretary. She was very blond. How did I react? I was angry at him for being such a coward. I'm still a little frosted. But I didn't take it on myself, feel it had something really to do with me.

"After this experience, I certainly became gun-shy. I would always ask guys right away what their mothers were like, etc. Still, I got into another situation with a man that ended painfully. And this time, it wasn't his mother, it was *him*. She was very fond of me, walked right out of the car the first time we met and put her arms around me. But the problems came when we decided to move back to New Hampshire, where he was originally from. We lived in Berkeley at the time, where things were quite open and liberal. But when it came time to seriously consider what life would be like with a Filipino bride in the northeastern part of the country, he balked. Again, this guy didn't have the guts to tell me personally. He just kept talking about how I wouldn't like all that snow, etc., even though I assured him that I had grown up on the East Coast.

"So that brings us to Fred. I met him when he was still married; we all belonged to a tennis club and his ex was my doubles partner. One day, I asked if she and Fred were going to the banquet that night, and she responded, 'I don't know *where* Fred is going.' They were getting separated, having grown apart. She was into her music and tennis, he was spending more and more time in the basement building his computer and she found him boring. Anyhow, after their divorce was final, we got married. I have to say, I was a nervous wreck meeting his mom, but it turned out fine. We get along great.

"The really wonderful thing about Fred is that he has absolutely no prejudice of any kind. Even about weight. He doesn't care if I put on a few extra pounds. He doesn't care if I'm Filipino. And that is what I really love about him.''

7 MARRIAGE AND DIVORCE:
Coming Together, Coming Apart

My husband, Jim, and I still argue about the right way to eat dinner. He came from a very proper British family where dinner was served according to a fixed ritual each evening. No one picked up a fork until the hostess picked up hers. Improper use of silverware was not tolerated. I, on the other hand, suffer from cutlery dyslexia and still have to think about how to set the table correctly. (On a bad day, my husband accuses me of doing this deliberately.) In the Chinese meals I remember, large bowls of food were placed, steaming and fragrant, at the center of the table. My mother would pick a particularly tasty piece of chicken or tofu and let me sample it from the end of her chopsticks, right at the table. Food was to be enjoyed—slurped, chewed, shoveled into the mouth directly from the bowl.

This argument remained fairly benign until the children were born. Most of the time I agree with my husband about the importance of table manners and ask Rebecca to please cut her meat or tell Julian not to eat with his hands or risk being asked to leave the table. However, on this one particular evening, I was feeling particularly ornery, and a self-righteous howl of protest escaped my lips. I couldn't tolerate one more minute worrying about whether the children's manners would handicap them for life or be acceptable to my mother-in-law. I have enough trouble getting Rebecca to eat anything at all, let alone worrying if she is cutting her meat into bite-sized pieces.

Of course, the children thought this was wonderful and used the opportunity to slip some unwanted dinner to the dog. And once I'd had my say, I didn't feel particularly vindicated, only tired and a little sad. Because the issue isn't really the importance of table manners, it is whether or not my cultural traditions are as valid in this household as my husband's. Whether my children will be able to identify the salad fork but feel embarrassed when their great uncle lustily slurps a bowl of hot-and-sour soup and then belches heartily right in the middle of dinner. I am concerned about the message we are sending to our children. We can spend a lot of time worrying about manners and in the process miss the deeper connections that could be made at this shared meal.

When I married my husband some fifteen years ago, I did not believe my cultural background or my ethnic identity would play any real part in our life together. I had spent too many years feeling ashamed of who I was, and even though I had worked through a lot of these issues (or at least managed to thoroughly repress them), I did not give the fact of being Chinese much conscious thought. I was getting married because I loved this man and things "felt right." We would build a relationship based on trust, open communication, respect, and equal sharing of household chores including, but not limited to, cleaning the loathsome bathrooms.

But what I discovered is that the fact of being Chinese as well as American shows up in the mundane and intimate transactions of married life. It is not the most important issue, but neither is it inconsequential. Not when my mother comes to visit and lives with us more as a member of the immediate family than as a relative/guest. She and my husband have yet to work out the right balance of cordiality and familiarity, and sometimes I just find it easier to be my mother's daughter when she visits and to treat my husband as the outsider. As a marriage and family therapist trained in Western theories of healthy families, I know better than this: My marriage should take precedence over my "family of origin." I should grow up and take my place beside my husband. But in the kitchen, cutting up bok choy and listening to the subtext of displacement and abandonment in my mother's conversation, it's not so easy to practice what I preach.

Especially not when I am feeling vulnerable about my ethnic identity, and Jim says or does something that underlines my discomfort—such as insisting on table manners that I was never taught and feel awkward about already.

Most Asian American women, even if raised in traditional households, come to marriage with Western ideas. Their Asian mothers or grandmothers may believe in marriage as a formal, prescribed relationship with clear role divisions, and view divorce not as a question of incompatibility between individual partners but a challenge to the honor and integrity of the whole family. But my generation does not see things that way. We also tend to discount the role of culture or cultural differences in marriage. From this point of view, it should not be any more difficult to make a bicultural marriage work than one between partners of similar background. In fact, differences can add richness and depth to a relationship.

Where the rocks of cultural misunderstanding seem to lie is in the hidden, unexpected places. For example, an Asian woman marries a white man and finds out that he disapproves of her attachment to her aging parents. They fight about how much money she should be allowed to send to them. Even if culture is not the only reason for tensions in the marriage, it can magnify other problems and make things that much harder to resolve.

Lisa grew up in the shadow of traditional Chinese values, including the preference for males. Unfortunately, the imprint of these early experiences made their painful consequences known in her marriage to a white man. This is a difficult place to be: raised in the old ways but hoping to make a life for yourself in the new world.

"I am the oldest daughter and also, I think, the most Chinese. Certainly, in terms of language. I came when I was nine and had the hardest time learning English. My values are more Chinese, and I'm the one who always went around serving tea when my parents had guests.

"Now, I look back on my childhood and I feel angry about a lot of things. I was angry then too, but I didn't realize it, and I had no way to express it. My parents never paid much attention to the three of us girls, but they were attentive when my brother (twelve years younger) was born. They didn't even talk to us much, and I think this is part of the reason I'm not as fluent in English as I'd like to be. My mother had this idea, I don't know if it's Chinese or not, that there is something wrong with getting sick, it shows you don't take care of yourself. So, as a child, I would try not to sneeze or cough in order to avoid getting 'the look' from her. By the age of twelve, I developed a kind of chronic pneumonia that I still suffer from today. I would have these high fevers every other day and have to stay in bed, and I think this is a direct consequence of having forced myself to stifle natural body defenses for so many years. What also hurt at the time—my father was and still is a practicing physician. But he never took care of me—he was too tired when he came home from treating his patients all day. Now I am working in a biotech firm to develop a new vaccine for pertussis. I know that viruses cause illness, not lack of willpower, and I'm trying to turn those early hurtful experiences into something positive through my career.

"By the age of fifteen, I was turning into a rebel. I had a boyfriend who truly loved me and treated me well. It was such a good feeling to have that kind of caring that I stayed out late with him, risking my parents' wrath. I wasn't doing it to try to defy them, I just cherished that sense of being loved.

"Unfortunately, I ended up marrying a man who put me down, who never allowed me to express myself, to feel something and acknowledge it. I guess I grew up in that environment and felt comfortable with the treatment. Gregory is white, and cultural differences were part of our problem. One of the first times I took him home to meet my parents, my mother had made a wonderful dinner. Greg ate almost nothing, then asked me to take him to McDonald's so he could get a meal. It was very embarrassing. But as a Chinese daughter, I was brought up to put others' feelings first, so I ignored my own reaction and hurt. His family was also very negative. I was raised as a 'good girl.' I felt it was wrong to talk behind people's backs. Something they did continuously.

"Things between us went from bad to worse. He was emotionally abusive to me and we fought a lot. The only thing that was working for us was sex, but that wasn't enough. The Chinese part of me said not to give up, to keep working until it comes out right. Things escalated to the point where one time I hit him and he decided we would have to separate. He pushed me away for a year, and during that time, I felt so repentant, so guilty. I felt I deserved everything that happened to me. After that, I kept putting off filing papers. I asked him to go to counseling so we could try to work things out, but he refused. I finally did file, and then all of a sudden he said he wanted me back. Again, I felt remorseful, guilty, but this time I'm sticking with my decision. Surprisingly, my parents have been supportive and don't act like this is a big shame to the family, but *I* feel like a failure. I don't know where I'm going anymore.

"At about the time I filed, I met this guy who is half Chinese. I've never dated an Asian before. Somehow, I'm more interested in men who are different from me. This guy is exuberant, full of life, and when I look at him from a certain angle, more of his Arabic and Persian features show up. That makes it easier for me to think about dating him. I'm attracted and I'm not, and I guess the biggest reason I hesitate is that being with someone Chinese reminds me of what my parents represent that has been so hurtful to me."

Theoretically, one way to avoid multicultural conflict is to marry Asian. Shared background and a similar upbringing should be able to bridge the differences in personality and temperament we are all heir to. But sometimes, this is no guarantee of marital satisfaction. Generally, women acculturate more quickly than men, so even if a woman marries a man from her own generation, the differences in philosophy and exposure to Western ideas—particularly those regarding the place of women—can create an insurmountable barrier. Asian American women sometimes describe their Asian American husbands as a kind of unwelcome surprise package: prettily wrapped on the outside, same old unregenerate traditional man on the inside.

Kathy has traveled around the world and been exposed to many different points of view. But that old pull of Chinese tradition and roots led her into an unsuccessful union. Ultimately, she found a novel solution to the age-old dilemma of what to do with a marriage that isn't working.

"The world is my village. I left mainland China at the age of five and traveled around the world with my mother and father, a physician for the UN. During my childhood, I lived in the Philippines, where I learned Tagalog (my second language after Chinese); moved to Germany, where I was given a bike and pointed in the general direction of the German school; moved to Switzerland, where I was thrown into the International School in Geneva and had to learn French; and finally landed in Egypt, where I attended a very elite girls' school. No one there paid any particular attention to the fact that I was Chinese because Alexandria was such a cosmopolitan city.

"But *I* knew I was Chinese. My father had a very grand vision of life, but he was also authoritarian and traditional. He forced us to speak only Chinese to my mother. In the summer, we were not allowed to go to the beach with other children, we had to sit down and learn Chinese. My father was a Chinese gourmet cook, and we learned to make our own tofu, even when we lived in parts of the world far removed from Asia. And then there were the lectures on Confucius, the stories of Lao-tzu. Small birds live in their nests. The old ravens fly off and bring back worms to feed them. When these birds grow up, it will be their turn to care for the old, decrepit parents. Filial piety was very strongly stressed, and to this day I value older people and respect them.

"I went to high school in Ethiopia. By this point, Dad started to worry that I wasn't dating any Chinese boys. So he sent me to Hong Kong. I looked around and thought, 'These people are all colonialists!' Plus, there was no air-conditioning, and water was rationed. People suggested I go out to the new territories where there would be real Chinese and no rationing. I went, and for the first time in my life, *I* felt different. There were six girls to a room. Changing a blouse required locking yourself up in the bathroom. No one spoke with their hands the way I did (I learned to sit on my hands to keep them still). I go to class. I sit in the front row. They sit in the back. They don't answer teachers' questions even if they know the answer. I do. The girls do not like me and call me the 'African girl.'

"This was a very difficult time for me. I had never before experienced the feeling of not belonging. Of being considered inferior because I used my hands to talk. Until then, I had always been just me. It was a moment of epiphany for me, and I realized I had to lose myself for a while before I regained my serenity. I got to the point where I realized I had to be myself. I was never going to be like those girls in Hong Kong. And then my life was hunky-dory again.

"When I learned everything I could in Hong Kong, I returned to Ethiopia and Haile Selassie University. I fell in love with an Ethiopian man, which was a big problem for my father. So I was off again, this time to the U.S. with a scholarship to Bryn Mawr University. For the second time in my life, I realized I was different, but this time because I was British educated and discovered that speaking English didn't necessarily prepare me for living in America. I got involved with the Chinese student organization, but realized I didn't fit in there either. All the women wanted to talk about was their children. I preferred to discuss politics and world affairs with their husbands.

"At about the age of twenty-three or twenty-four, I started feeling the pressure of 'marrying someone of my own kind' strongly enough that I succumbed. So when Robert proposed, I accepted. He fit all the criteria a Chinese mother in America could possibly have: a nice boy from a wealthy family who attended RPI (Rensselaer Polytechnic Institute). In every way, a most appropriate young man. The night he made his proposal I returned to my place and found a Valentine's card waiting for me. From the White Russian man I had truly loved all my life.

He was finally ready for marriage, but I could not go back on my word. My father had taught me well. My word is my honor, and it will be passed on and on for generations to come.

"The marriage did not work. He was more Chinese than I. Actually, he was Chinese when it suited his purposes and American when it was to his benefit. He liked the Western idea that we both work, split the expenses. But he also wanted three courses and rice and soup for dinner every day, which I had to prepare when I got home at 7:00, after having left at 7:00 in the morning. Things went from bad to worse, and finally I left him.

"My parents were supportive and suggested I return to Ethiopia with my young son. Then ensued some of the most exciting years of my life. I flew to Rome to buy shoes and flew back in a single day. I was fully challenged. But then the revolution came, and I had to go back to the U.S. I decided to give my marriage to Robert another chance. I tried to be the good wife. I vacuumed the living room. One day, I was doing the laundry and went down to the basement, where I found my husband serenading his girlfriend. That was it. I threw up my hands and went back to Ethiopia. Dad was OK with me returning, but he didn't want me to pick up with my old activities. Mom said to him, 'Well, then, what should she be doing?' His honest-to-goodness answer: 'She should be home embroidering.'

"I came back to the U.S. again, poor this time, and ended up working with Vietnamese refugee issues. In fact, I'm the one who helped the shrimpers resettle in the Gulf of Texas. A friend of mine suggested moving to Washington, D.C., so I did. I also decided my son needed a father, so I met a Caucasian man and got married. Unfortunately, he became ill and somebody had to work, pay the bills. I got a job as a Peace Corps director in the Cameroons. When I returned three years later, my husband felt I had neglected him, so he asked for a divorce. I said, 'Fine! But this is not the most propitious moment to sell the house. Let's just share it. You do your thing, I'll do mine. Let's just be polite.' So we did. And we're still together eighteen years later. Like an old married couple, most cordial to each other. And you know something, I'm content with that. My life is just fine.'"

Fairy tale stories are supposed to have happily-ever-after endings. But even being a real, live princess was not enough to save Yem Han from the rigors of a traditional marriage. She is the first to acknowledge that her husband and mother-in-law are not bad people; it is simply that their views on marriage are about as similar to hers as black is to white. Then, there is the question of divorce, an act that parents of Asian American daughters generally discourage. Sometimes quite vocally. But Yem Han found her own way to get around that barrier.

"When I was studying the ancient art of calligraphy in Taiwan, I discovered that I was a flesh-and-blood princess—a direct descendant of the Sung dynasty, twelfth century A.D. Now, I am married to a retired Norwegian physician whose cousin is related to Laura Ingalls Wilder (of *Little House on the Prairie* fame) and we live in Pepin, Wisconsin, which is Laura's birthplace. What a long, strange, wondrous journey it has been!

"Growing up in Sacramento, California, I remember my father demanding that I stay inside and learn to write my name in Chinese when I would much rather be out playing with friends. I went to kindergarten not speaking a word of English but over the years introduced more and more of the language at home. I wanted to shed my Chinese identity, and I knew how to do it: 'Yeah, yeah, Mom, what's that you said?' when she asked me questions in the Chinese she wanted me to retain.

"My father told me he thought it would be a good idea for me to go to college, get a job as a secretary, marry a nice Chinese man, and then have some kids. I, however, wanted to be an artist, something my father just could not comprehend. Worse still, I had harbored hopes of becoming an actress, a career he considered disreputable. Once, I discovered that his distant cousin was in Hollywood, played a role in *Flower Drum Song*. I wanted to go meet him, but my father threatened to disown me if I did. So we compromised. I agreed to become an art educator. The teaching part salvaged what otherwise would have been an unacceptable career.

"After college, I got selected as a foreign exchange student to go to Taipei. Something in me was drawing me to the Orient. A spirit pulling me back to my roots. There I had this incredible experience of sitting in an auditorium and finding out that the man sitting three rows in front of me, blocking my view actually, was a descendant of Confucius. The royal empress I was related to had done calligraphy of Confucius's sayings. He was introduced to me and told me that he was glad I had come to Taiwan. Wow! What karma!

"Then it was back to the U.S. to get that teaching credential, the promise extracted from me in exchange for the opportunity to study in the Orient. My mother started dropping hints. 'You are *twenty-four!*' 'No getting any younger!' 'That's an awfully nice *Chinese engineer* you've been dating.'

"So, I marry the guy. He's good looking (for Asian). He's Mr. Jock. *Financially stable!* Tall! I had dated other guys before, but I knew that was just for fun. I always knew I'd end up with the type of man my parents wanted.

"Our marriage lasted ten years. He was too traditional for me. I used to get terrible migraines as the weekends approached because we'd be expected to spend the entire time with his mother. If I wanted to go home to visit my family, my husband would say, 'OK. Half an hour.' And he'd sit there that whole time with his arms crossed over his chest. It's not that I didn't like his mother. Despite the fact that my husband and I fought about her. 'You don't like my mother?' 'No, I didn't say that.' 'You *hate* her!' My mother tried to prepare me for this. 'You're getting married,' she said. 'You're now a Lee. Not a Fong anymore.' But I had hoped we'd be starting our own new family. I wasn't cut out for this type of life.

"Plus, there was the matter of sons. I had two daughters, which made my mother-in-law unhappy because I had married her favorite son. This was something I already had my fill of, remembering back to the days when my mother would make me watch after my brother, even to the point of going to 'wipe off his butt.' Also, my father had already informed me that all the inheritance was going to that same kid. This doesn't make me bitter. I understand where my father is coming from, even if I don't agree. Sometimes it makes me sad, however, to know that my daughters (who now live with their father and the very nice, very traditional Chinese wife his family found for him soon after we parted) sense the difference between how he treated his granddaughters and his grandsons. Still they both know that they want to marry Chinese.

"My parents weren't too thrilled about my divorce, but they learned to accept it. Then, I came home with this white guy I was planning to marry. 'Huh, you gonna marry white guy?' 'Mom, Dad, he's a *doctor*.' 'Oh, in that case, welcome to our family!' My husband's name is Larry, which my mother can't quite pronounce. But she loves to cook for him. 'Lally! What you like eat? I make you some mash potatoes!'

"So here I am now, the Princess of Lake Pepin. I have a gallery and shop called East Meets West. I miss my Asian friends and I miss Chinese food. But on the whole, this royal descendant of the empress, who is also the first Asian elected official in these parts, is pretty content!"

In traditional times, Asian men were accorded the *right* to concubines. In fact, the number of concubines indicated a man's status and position. Wives had to tolerate this situation and keep their feelings to themselves. They had no recourse. But even if this behavior on the part of husbands was socially condoned, it sometimes caused great private pain for the wife. In my own family, there is still unresolved bitterness over the young woman—prostitute, actually—that my grandfather rescued and took as his lover. Over the years, the feelings of abandonment and betrayal linger like unaired linens in the back of the family closet. Coming out of this tradition and into the Western belief that unfaithfulness is unacceptable—grounds for divorce—can put an Asian American woman in a quandary. How should a woman today view her husband's infidelity? And more important, what response should she have? Her white friends may counsel separation. But Michelle, after a time of great personal anguish, returned to her philosophical roots and found a way to keep her marriage intact.

"The last ten years of my life have been very hard, a lot of suffering. For a long time, I was pretty depressed, pretty sad about things. But now, I look at things from a Chinese way of thinking and I say, it's my fate. I can't really change that. At the same time, I don't have to live like this forever. Maybe what I am doing now is making something else possible for myself in the future. This philosophy is very comforting to me. I feel a lot better, more at peace now.

"I came to this country in 1979 to study. I was nineteen, but very young compared to girls here. However, I was also very ambitious. I wanted to get an education and then go back to Taiwan and really make something of my life. I had high hopes for myself. But things didn't really go the way I planned. While I was attending City College, I lived in an apartment nearby. I didn't really know anyone or even how to act, so it was nice to have an older Chinese couple living next door. Turns out their son is the man I wound up marrying. I actually didn't like him the first time I met him. He wasn't stylish, and he looked like an old-fashioned Chinese-style man. But we became friends, like brother and sister (he's eight years older than I). I think this is very different from American couples. He helped me to grow up.

"We started a restaurant together. It wasn't really what I wanted to do with my life. I consider it the lowest kind of business. But it was a good way to become financially secure. So I was working hard at the restaurant and going to school when we married, and then I got pregnant. I wanted to finish my education but I just couldn't manage it. I feel very sad about that. I know my mother is also disappointed, but she doesn't actually say it.

"Then, the problems started. When I was four months pregnant, I found out my husband was having an affair with a friend of my brother's. My husband acted like nothing was going on when I confronted him. My brother was pressing me to decide what I wanted to do about the marriage, and my mother kept

saying I should get an abortion. You see, she had been through
the same thing numerous times with my father. They were married by a matchmaker, and I think if they had been brought up
here, they would already have been divorced fifty times! He was
unfaithful many times, but she had enough control to be able to
persuade each of those girls to have an abortion and then for
him to return to her. She was very unhappy, but she did it for
us—to keep the family going, and I have benefited from that, so
I am grateful to her.

"Anyhow, I knew deep down in my heart that I didn't want
a divorce, I loved my husband. But at that moment, I also hated
him. Here I was, working almost like seven days a week to make
the restaurant successful, and he does *this*? But when I mentioned the abortion, he says to me, 'This child is mine too, I have
a right to the child.' So I reconsidered. I don't know why, but
he made me feel guilty, even though he's the one who had the
affair.

"Now I guess I kind of look back and say he was probably
having a hard time then too. I was depressed, morning sick and
so on, living with my mom. He was at the restaurant most of the
time. I just accepted it. Yet, I also remember what my sister-in-
law said when she was in the same situation. She did have an
abortion and she didn't leave her husband. She already had three
kids. What could she have done? She stayed, but for her, it was
a feeling that once the mirror has been cracked, it can never be
fully repaired. You just try to put things back the best way you
can. You think about the kids. You stay married because it's the
right thing to do.

"Since then, I have tried to make the marriage work. In the
business, for example, my husband treats me more like an employee than a partner. That's OK. In the beginning, we fought a
lot. One time, his brother was over, they got into a big argument.
My husband has a bad temper. His brother started throwing
dishes, food around in front of customers. It was very embarrassing. I tried to break up the fight and pulled my husband outside.
He got really mad and pushed me. Just happened that at that
moment, a car was driving by and a man in there watched what
was happening between us. He was a customer and he wrote a

letter to my husband saying he had witnessed an employee being abused. He suggested that my husband, as the owner, should do something about it. Obviously, he hadn't recognized my husband. Even then, Joe blamed his brother for the whole thing, but he did learn to control his temper better after that, walk away from me when he was really mad.

"Recently, I went back to Taiwan to visit old friends and relations. That was a hard trip for me in some ways. Many of my friends were still single, had gone on for an MBA, become a professor, etc. I couldn't really talk about the restaurant or even having little children. I saw them all making a path for themselves and I felt sorry for myself. I should have been one of them, but I was not. I thought a lot about how my life would have been different if I had stayed there. I think I would have had more the life I wanted for myself.

"My mother too was hoping that my life wouldn't turn out like hers, that the infidelity wouldn't come full circle back to me. I know she gets depressed for me. I've very close to her, but now I don't tell her as much about my life. I still hope to have my own career someday. Is that crazy? I used to be good at computer science. I want something different from the restaurant. It's OK to help my husband, but I really want to do something I can feel proud of. And we both agree, we don't want the restaurant business for our children.

"And yet, today I see myself as lucky. We each have our own fate. This is mine. It's all right."

All things considered, the majority of Asian American women today seek partners and attempt to make marriages work based on Western models, where the negotiations of daily life are tempered to individual needs and personalities rather than to the larger social expectations. In the end, it is the strength of the human connection between partners that speaks to the ultimate success of the marriage. For Sheila, who was married twice, each time to a Filipino man, the issue was not one of marrying in the right culture but rather marrying a man with the right attitude and personality. Marrying someone who truly loved and respected her.

"Growing up in the Philippines, everyone had the fantasy of coming to the U.S. That was the big thing. We knew our chances would be better if we were well educated, so my parents kept telling us, 'We have no fortune to pass on to you, but we can give you the gift of a good education.' I had always wanted to be a nurse, maybe in part because that was my mother's dream for herself. Her mother had discouraged such ideas, saying that girls were supposed to stay home.

"I met Danny when I was seventeen, and we fell in love. At that time in my country, it was OK to date, but physical affection of any kind was a big no. Even walking down the street holding hands was something that concerned my mother. What would the neighbors say? 'Oh, did you see that daughter of so-and-so?' She would get really mad until one day I decided to sit down with her and make this promise: 'Mom, I'm not going to let anything stop me from finishing my nursing degree. You don't have to worry about that. But I don't care what people say about me and Danny, let them think whatever they want to.' She never brought up the subject again.

"Then came the opportunity to emigrate. My sister was already in the U.S. and established. Three weeks before we left, I secretly married Danny for reasons of security, to keep the relationship alive. A year later, I returned to the Philippines for a church wedding, but had to leave him again after a month. In April, just six months later, I got a call from my sister. The phone rang, but first there was just silence on the other end. My sister could not utter a word. Then she started crying, didn't know what to say. Finally, she got up the nerve to tell us, 'Sheila, don't cry. I have to tell you something.' By this point, I suspected what her news was going to be. 'Danny has eloped with someone. He's been gone a month. We can't even reach him.' That 'someone' turned out to be a younger neighbor of ours back home. Someone I remembered only as a little girl. After I hung up the phone, everyone was very quiet. Dad broke the silence when he proclaimed, 'I knew it.' My parents hadn't really liked him from the start. But for me, it was terrible. I didn't know what to do. I just kept saying to myself over and over, 'I can't believe this. Seven years down the drain.' If it wasn't for my family's support, I don't really know what would have happened to me.

"Even after the phone call, I still had to go back and confront Danny myself. Seeing is believing. I said, 'Level with me. What's the score?' I went to see his mom, his relatives. They all told him he had made a bad decision. 'You were sleeping on a nice soft bed—now you'll have to go back to the hard one.' Finally, he just told me, 'I don't love you anymore.' When I got back to San Francisco, I tried to kill myself. I was scared, feeling betrayed. Saw no future for myself. And on my twenty-seventh birthday, I got a letter from him with the divorce papers.

"Now, I look back, and I don't feel much anger for him. I just pity the guy.

"I met my second husband through his mother. We were both working at the same hospital and she kept telling me about this great son of hers who was so busy working two or three jobs that he never had any time to meet someone. One day, I said to her, 'OK, Manang [a term of respect for an older woman], I'll meet this son of yours.' So we arranged a date. I was twenty-nine by this point, antsy to get married and have kids. There's this big glass window in the living room, and my mom and sisters were all eagerly awaiting his arrival. 'Oh, this must be him. He's tall! He's OK looking!' He was also driving his brother's red MG.

"William had never been married but he already owned his own home. His mother kept trying to push us together. 'Go on over to his place! You're both adults. It's OK!' So, two months later we moved in together. My mother was very concerned, very upset. Not because she didn't like him, but her belief was that you do whatever you want after Holy Matrimony. Not before. I tried to explain to her that I didn't want to go through the same thing I did before. This time, I wanted to give the relationship a trial first. She couldn't see that.

"Then, one hot August day, I found out that I was pregnant. I was very worried about Mom's reaction, but I was also very happy for myself to be having a baby. Married or not. Anyhow, I knew we'd make it legal sooner or later, and in fact, we drove out to Las Vegas three months later.

"We lost that baby. Our little girl, Catherine, had the umbilical cord wrapped around her neck seven times. Why? What did I do wrong? What was I being punished for? I had all these hard questions and no answers, but again, my family was there for me. In the Philippines, we grieve for a lost baby but we also believe that maybe it is a blessing too. Maybe that child was destined for real hardships later in life. Today, I still think about her. Would she be as tall as my husband by now? We talk to our kids about their sister. Probably she and my twelve-year-old would be at each other's throat all day long.

"This marriage has worked out well. Never a dull moment! We share responsibilities around the house. We've also sacrificed our relationship to some extent in order to have one parent at home with the children at all times, meaning we work different hours and don't see much of each other. But on weekends we take time to be together. I think one important fact is that we are both Filipino. You know, we really believe in the concept of extended family, and I've known some Filipino women who married Caucasians. They fight a lot about in-laws staying with them, or sending money back home. That is never an issue for us. We understand each other."

8 HOW WE WERE RAISED, HOW WE ARE RAISING OUR CHILDREN

My nine-year-old is at the computer, working on his math program, an accelerated course developed by Stanford University for "gifted youth." I am doing some paperwork in the other room, but with one ear, I can monitor his progress. Every time he types in the correct answer, an upbeat little "tah-dah!" issues forth from the sound card. Wrong answers produce an altogether less pleasant response. As long as the sounds I hear are chirpy, I go on with my own work contentedly. But if I hear too many of the other kind, I get up from my chair and go find out what the problem is. I don't want him to get any wrong answers if I can help it. At the end of each session is a small report, listing his grade level for each of several categories, for example, sets and probability, geometry. I am only interested in watching those numbers increase. If Julian seems to be losing interest, I have no hesitation in mentioning that his good buddy Steven is "already on *sixth* grade math."

The whole time I am doing this, however, the Western therapist part of me disapproves of my own behavior. I should know better. I believe that children should be nurtured in developing their own potential, not pushed in the direction parents think they should go. I believe there are other yardsticks to measure success than academic achievement. I am certainly aware of the dangers of comparing children. And I remember all too well feeling pressured by my own parents to succeed in math and science, fearful that these were subjects I just would never "get," no matter how hard I tried.

And yet now, do I expect all A's from my daughter? In the parent-teacher conference, do I focus on her one B+ in the midst of otherwise straight A's and wonder aloud how that could be turned into an A next quarter? Would I be disappointed if my children went to state college instead of a top university like Berkeley or Stanford? Would I flinch if my daughter wanted to marry a plumber, or if my son wanted to *be* one? You bet your bottom dollar.

For me, it is in the decisions I make as a parent each day that I am most aware of being from two different cultures. Parenting, in its most immediate moments, is a matter of instinct. Unless we make a conscious effort to do otherwise, we tend to parent as we were parented. For example, I take a limited view of the notion that children have a "right" to privacy, not exactly an Asian concept. I don't knock before I enter my daughter's bedroom to check whether she is actually doing the homework she promised to complete. I don't ever remember my mother knocking on my door; to this day, she is still apt to walk right in. My gut reaction is to insist on academic achievement and to insist that it be done my way, or at least the teacher's way. But when I take the time to think about it, to move beyond the instinctual reaction, I feel very different. I worry about my son's self-esteem, about the message I am sending my daughter when I ask if she has done her homework but don't take the time to inquire about her day. I feel torn, struggling to find some middle ground between what can be two very different styles of parenting.

Traditional Asian families are run more like monarchies than democracies. A woman I spoke to admitted that she had a hard time adjusting to the notion that here, parents are supposed to "listen to their children." Take into consideration a *child's* point of view. Back home, parents made decisions for their kids, who were expected to obey without question or hesitation. Parents did not see it as their primary role to help their children move toward self-reliance, independent thinking. But in this culture, of course, that is precisely the goal.

Traditional Asian families also do not believe in praising children, discussing feelings, talking about subjects such as sex, showing affection, or even telling children that they are loved. Parents do not think it is important to play with their kids. The value of play itself is questionable, but if you must entertain yourself, find a cousin. Parents do not worry about whether their children have friends. Childhood friends, outside of extended family, are not emphasized.

But parents do believe their children must be taught the value of modesty. And they reserve the right to discipline children as they see fit, screaming at them if necessary, resorting to physical violence if the need arises. That need might arise on a regular basis because Asian parents believe that children are born bad—naughty, uncivilized, wild. It is therefore up to the family to instill in children prosocial behavior or run the risk of bad children automatically growing up to be bad adults.

I believe that Asian parents would tell you they handle children this way because it is the proper thing to do, and ultimately in the child's best interests. For example, on the issue of praise, it was considered unlucky to be too positive about your children. The gods might get jealous and snatch a precious baby away. So sons, especially, were given derogatory names like "little dog," or "pig" in order not to provoke heavenly wrath. On a more practical level, it was believed that if you praised them, your children would grow lazy and stop trying. Also, the thing about modesty: Just as it is shameful to "boast" about yourself or your accomplishments, it is equally incorrect to speak highly of your children. So, if your daughter wins a full scholarship to Harvard, you are expected to say, "Well, it's nothing really. She should try harder next time."

The problem comes when you are a child of America, not China, and your next-door neighbor gets a buck for a good math test while you get berated for a score of 97 percent. In Western culture, the emphasis in parenting is on building and preserving the self-esteem of the child. So praise is freely and abundantly given. But Asians do not share these views. In my life today as a parent, I run into this conflict. Sometimes I want to say to my son, "Well, be proud of yourself! You did the best job you could!"

But at other times, I am more inclined to admonish, "Maybe you could have tried such-and-such . . ." Bear in mind this is a *basketball* game we're talking about. I don't know the right answer, so I commit a cardinal sin of parenting: I vacillate. I am not consistent. Sometimes I praise and sometimes I goad. Either my children will get the best of both worlds or the full benefit of neither.

Meg, a social worker, talks about how growing up in America with traditionally Japanese parents influenced her life.

"You know this thing you hear about how important it is to praise your children? Well, looking back, I realize that my parents *never* praised me. They were both born here, but raised in Japan, so I grew up in a traditional Japanese household. I remember getting straight A's on my report card, with maybe one A−. That minus sign was the only thing my mother paid any attention to. Then, I'd go over to a friend's house and his parents would be so positive about him. I'd think to myself, 'Why is his mother so happy? He gets B's and C's!' And then, the thought would inevitably follow, 'What's the matter with me that my mother can't feel good about me? She must not love me.'

"We visit Mrs. Sasaki. 'Oh,' exclaims my mother, 'your son is so smart, such a good student! Too bad my daughter can't be more like your son.' And I'm standing next to her, getting madder and madder. Once, I tried to whisper, 'But how can you say that, Mom? You *know* Larry doesn't do well at school.' She glared at me, and I knew enough to shut my mouth. But inside, I couldn't stop feeling that she was very two-faced, and wondering what I could possibly do to merit the compliments she so freely handed out to Larry's mother."

Addressing the issue of how Asian families avoid discussion of feelings, Meg continues her story.

"I went to Berkeley in the sixties and it was a real culture shock. I came from a small Central Valley town where we lived in the poor part with Japanese and other minorities. Here at Berkeley, most of the students were white. I thought, 'They're all smarter than me! I'm going to fail.' And I knew I just could not fail because my parents had scraped together a lot of hard-earned dollars and cents to send me to school, and because I felt that what I did reflected not only on me as an individual, but also on my family and on the whole Japanese American community. I simply could not *afford* to fail. So I'd call my mother a lot, nearly in tears. 'I'm scared, Mom,' I'd tell her, my voice quavering. 'I'm not going to make it here.' The only thing she ever said to me was, 'But you speak English, don't you?' She never acknowledged what I was feeling. Finally, I just gave up. I'd go to the bathroom instead, turn on the shower, and start crying. Then I'd stumble back to my dorm room and fall asleep, exhausted."

For myself, I find that, even as a psychotherapist, I have a hard time identifying my feelings. Growing up, the only time feelings were ever mentioned would be in the context of something like "Don't be sad!" (after discovering that a dog had just dispatched the pet rabbit I carelessly left unattended). So, instead, I ask a friend, "How would you feel if you called someone long distance and they wanted to get back to you because there was something they just had to see on TV?" If my friend's response strikes some inchoate but resonant chord within me, then I assume I am also feeling hurt, or angry, or extremely angry. With my children, this is one area where I am trying to do things differently. I am trying my best to help them name and acknowledge their feelings.

Other women experience similar conflicts between the way they were raised and the way they want to raise their children. Of course, this is not a dilemma limited to Asian Americans. But it may be more difficult for us to resolve because one of the hallmarks of Asian culture is respect for parents and for established ways of doing things. If I fail to chastise my daughter for lying on the floor and doing her homework in a dimly lit room, my mother will take it that not only do we differ about the relative importance of posture and good lighting, but she will feel personally rebuked. She will feel that I don't care about her or value her position as the eldest member of our household.

Terry reflects on the contrasts between her own Chinese upbringing and the way she wants to raise her children.

"Several years ago, my husband (who is also Chinese) and I took our kids out for ice cream. There was another Chinese family sitting nearby, speaking Cantonese. All of a sudden, my six-year-old son points to them and says, 'Look! There are *Chinese* people over there!' He said it as if the concept didn't apply to him at all. Ironically enough, we had just returned from a daylong outing to Angel Island, hoping to educate our children about their own grandfather's immigration experience.

"I had no such confusion about being Chinese. I grew up in a suburban neighborhood in Sacramento, but there were at least four or five other Asian families on our block. In fact, one woman ran a Chinese school out of her garage. We played with Chinese and white children, it didn't matter. But one day, I learned that in my family, things were a little different. I remember a white girlfriend and I sitting around, getting bored. She suggested we watch TV and I said, 'I'll see if my mom things it's OK.' My friend was astounded. 'You mean you have to *ask* her?' I was equally astounded that this would be such a big deal.

"We grew up with many traditional values, including the emphasis on education—even being excused from chores to study on weekdays—the Chinese preference for boys, the celebrations, and what my brothers and sisters called the 'superstitions.' Don't wash your hair on someone's birthday. Don't eat shrimp or crab when you're pregnant—they have too many legs and will produce for you an overactive child. After my husband and I were married, my parents handed me a box of chopsticks, which is a symbolic way of saying, 'Hurry up and have a boy!'

"College was a real struggle for me. I mean, I wasn't the type with 800 SAT scores. At one point, I thought, 'Do I really want to do this? Compete with all these other good students?' But then, my immediate next thought would be, 'If I don't do this, what will I do?' I couldn't figure that one out. I didn't even feel that I had the option to take five years to graduate, as some of my friends were doing.

"Parental approval has always been important to me. So is respect for authority. And although I feel I've grown in many ways, taken on challenges that go beyond what my parents expect of me (i.e., my present position as a branch leader for my chapter of AAUW), I know that my fundamental relationship with them will probably never change. There just isn't that same progression as in Western families, where you go from being a parent and child to being adult and adult. I'll always be the kid. So when my mother tells me I can't possibly let my daughter out of the house in that T-shirt, I plead with the child to put on more clothes. 'Do it for me,' I beg, 'or I'll get in trouble with your grandmother.'

"I'm raising my children to feel that they have options, to be able to tell me if I've done something they don't like. Very different from my own childhood, and something my parents just don't understand. Their attitude is, 'Why tell her she can have milk or juice for dinner? Just *give* her the milk!' I feel that, in some ways, my life has been too much directed by my parents and sometimes I have trouble making my own choices. So I want life to be different for my children."

Marjorie grew up in Taiwan, but is raising her children here. The conflicts between her upbringing and the style of parenting promoted here are very obvious to her.

"I grew up in Taiwan. My parents moved from the mainland. My dad was a soldier and follower of Chiang Kai-shek. Living in Taiwan was difficult in some ways, there was discrimination against us for being from the mainland. The Taiwanese believed we got all the good jobs, had a better life. My own thinking is that mainland Chinese are more smart, so that's why they had higher positions.

"After school, I got a job with a steamship line doing inside sales. Some people would speak to you in Taiwanese, and if you didn't answer in that language, they just wouldn't talk to you at all. After my son was born, we started to worry that it wasn't safe in Taiwan. We had relatives in the U.S. who said we should move. That's how we came here.

"When we first arrived, my parents were with us. They stayed a few years, but then my dad got lonely, so they went back. I believe old people should have an easy life—work in the garden, play with grandchildren. But my dad is very social. He doesn't speak English and doesn't drive, so he would take BART to Chinatown. He'd complain he's lonely. In my heart I think I should take care of him. I feel guilty they are in Taiwan and it's not possible for us to go back now.

"My daughter, Marsha, was born here. She's very American. She doesn't speak Chinese, and I don't make her. But I also can't always explain everything to her like I want to. When I grew up, I always knew I had to obey my parents, follow all the rules. Sometimes I didn't like that, for example my mother saying reading novels is a waste of time, only schoolbooks are important. But I didn't say anything and I did as I was told. By fifth grade, I would study every night until 10:00, and still had a hard time finishing my homework. Now, I watch my daughter. She doesn't have much homework. It makes me nervous. Then I tell myself, 'Don't be too much like your parents were to you.' Sometimes I fight with her, and sometimes I give up. Like the time my mother sent her some formal dresses. Marsha says she won't wear them, too uncomfortable. I say you don't have to wear them to school, but for formal occasions like Chinese New Year's, you have to. I try to make you happy, you should try to make me happy too. Then she does. She's a good girl.

"My son is fourteen and he loves to cook. Actually, he eats too much, but he would like to be a chef. My husband says to me, 'Restaurant work is too low.' He tells me that he works hard so our children can go to a good college. If they don't do well, he threatens they will end up with a low job. My attitude is different: We're in America now, we just have to accept how things are here. Sometimes we argue with each other.

"I wouldn't really care if my children didn't carry on Chinese traditions, and I don't care if the don't marry Chinese. (Just as long as they don't marry black.) But the other day, Marsha all of a sudden says, 'Mom, will you teach my children Chinese?' I said, 'Well, how about *you*? How about you learn Chinese?' She just laughs and says, 'It's too late!' "

Another dilemma for Asian American parents is whether or not to pass on the language and traditions of their heritage. Ask a mother if her kids speak Chinese (Japanese, Tagalog, etc.) and you'll most likely get a rueful look and the explanation, "It would be nice, but it's too hard to do." This, even from women who speak the language fluently themselves. First-generation immigrants tend to believe that they will handicap their children if they do not push them to assimilate. So success is purchased at the price of culture loss. But over time, the question of tradition becomes more problematic.

Many women share my experience of coming to an appreciation of culture only after resolving identity issues. In my twenties, I took time away from a busy graduate school schedule to try to learn a language I had been able to speak more or less fluently at age three. (It was a whole lot easier as a toddler.) I never did master Mandarin, but I noticed a sense of calm welling up in me as I heard the language spoken. Comfort food for the soul. And yet, I realize that, if I am only now beginning to reclaim my heritage, how much of it can I pass on to my children? But if I do not pass it on, who will? Sometime I wonder if the whole Chinese half of their lineage—centuries of richly textured history and tradition—will register as nothing more than a blip on the radar screen of their life experience.

Other women too have struggled with these questions. Jan is married to a Caucasian man. She is starting to understand that if she doesn't pass on her culture to her son, it won't happen.

The customs will fade away, a victim not so much of conscious choice but of benign neglect.

"I am a Sansei. I don't know a lot about how my grandparents came here, just some of the stories that have been passed on. I think one of my grandmothers was a 'mail-order bride.' And I do remember hearing about how Grandfather came here knowing only a few words of English, 'Ham and eggs, please,' to be precise. He traveled to Colorado on the train and, by the time he arrived, was pretty sick of eating just that one meal. Although he lived here the rest of his life, he never spoke the language well.

"My mother learned Japanese by attending Japanese school in the summer. Now, however, she feels more comfortable with English. I, like many other Sansei, don't speak much Japanese. My mother tried to send us to Japanese school, but it was too late. I can't say I regret not knowing how to speak Japanese; I don't have the opportunity to use it anyhow.

"I grew up surrounded by extended family. We celebrated all the holidays together, Western ones primarily, but also Obon in the summer and Hanamatsuri in the spring. I went to a high school that was mostly white and had a few friends there, but mostly hung around with Japanese friends from the Buddhist temple we attended. Interestingly enough, my brother was better friends with his white classmates in school, but now he's married to a Japanese woman, while I am married to a white man.

"I know my mother didn't have strong preferences about whom I married, although she wouldn't have been happy with a black son-in-law. I didn't think my father cared, either. But I remember coming home one evening from a date with this white guy I was seeing. We were a little later than usual, and Dad started asking me about Rick. I told him we weren't all that serious. That's when my father told me he would really prefer me to marry someone Japanese. I was really shocked! I had never imagined that it would matter to him. I remember saying, 'I don't care what nationality he is. *I'm* going to live with him, not you.' I had always just assumed that if I really loved a man, my parents would accept him. But I have to admit that learning how my dad felt, surprising as it was to me, did not change my views. I would marry who I wanted to marry, regardless of their opinion.

"By the time I met Dave, I was already in my early thirties, and I'm sure my parents were wondering if I would ever settle down. So even though Dave was white, they had no reservations.

"Things have worked out very well for us. But I am reminded of the fact that we are from different cultures through my six-year-old son, Christopher. The other day, he came home from school reciting some playground jingle about "Chinese . . . Japanese . . . Dirty knees . . . Look at these!" (with accompanying hand motions to indicate slanted eyes, etc.). We started talking about race, and I explained to Chris that he was half Japanese. I was totally unprepared for his reaction. Chris got really upset, and I just couldn't figure out why. Finally, I realized that he thought you could only be Japanese if you spoke Japanese. He had also heard derogatory comments about Asians at school, although I don't believe these had particularly been directed at him.

"Finally, we got things straightened out, but the incident made me really think about how much of his Japanese heritage I want to pass on to him. For me, growing up around all the relatives really reinforced the culture, made it meaningful to me. I still remember my uncles pounding the mochi (a steamed glutinous rice cake symbolizing longevity) every December in preparation for Japanese New Year. They did it the old traditional way, with long wooden mallets. My parents kept up this custom although they did use electricity. When we moved to California, I made the mochi for a while, but then a few years ago, I just kind of stopped. Dave doesn't really like it anyhow. But I realize now that if I don't carry on the tradition, Chris will never have it as part of his life. I don't want to get to the point, whether through laziness or oversight, that I fail to put him in touch with his Japanese roots. At this age, he doesn't really understand what it means to be Japanese. I see it as my *responsibility* to teach him."

Daphne grew up in Taiwan, but is aware that certain aspects of her childhood made life difficult, for example, her father's traditional authoritarian stance. Yet she also very much values the culture and traditions in which she was raised. So here in the United States, she is trying to raise her children with knowledge and appreciation of their heritage, but without certain of its beliefs about the proper relationship between parent and child.

"My parents were both well educated and very successful in their careers. Each, in turn, came to the U.S. to study and then returned to Taiwan. I was only one year old when my father left; by the time he returned, he was a stranger to me. But then it came time for my mother to complete her education, so Dad took on many of the responsibilities mothers usually have. One day, my father decided that my sisters and I needed haircuts, so he took us to the barbershop. My father was very strict, expected us to agree with everything he did. In this case, he got us all these very short haircuts, and I remember sitting there crying and crying, but not able to say anything to him. I also remember him taking us out to eat once a week for the sole purpose of lecturing us on all our faults. Not behavior problems, but academic weaknesses.

"For high school, I went to a boarding school. Even before that, my parents were both consumed by their careers, and so I mainly lived with my nanny and our maid. I didn't resent it. School did a lot of parenting: I don't think we needed our parents the same way that my children need me. Also, I didn't feel abandoned when my parents left Taiwan when I was very young. We just accepted that's how things were.

"I was a very obedient child. My father intimidated me, I always did as I was told. Not so with my sister, who was only one and a half years older. One day she decided she didn't want to practice piano anymore, so she simply quit. Then, much later, she wanted to marry a white man. When her fiancé asked my father's permission to marry his daughter, my dad's reply was, 'You must be *out* of your mind!' He did not attend the wedding, and he did not permit my mother to go.

"I, on the other hand, married a Chinese man that my parents were very happy with. I wouldn't consider him very traditional, however. Even compared to other men of his generation. He's my partner, not my boss. My husband is very involved with the children. When my daughter was trying to learn a ballet routine, he was the one who watched the whole practice and then tried to help her learn the steps. Something my friends' husbands would consider stuff for the mother to do.

"My parents fought a lot because he thought she didn't need to work. My mother had made a very high position for herself, as the vice president of a bank, and her career was important. I also value my career. Sometimes I wish I could spend more time with my kids, but I know that my job adds to our financial security and gives me added confidence. My parents didn't send me to college to be a housewife. Now, for my own daughter, I'd like her to make her own choice about whether or not to work. And I keep telling myself I don't care who she marries. At least that's how I *think* I should feel.

"One thing I do feel strongly about: I would like my children to keep up with the language and the cultural traditions. That's why I'm the principal of a Chinese school that meets on Saturday. The whole family is involved. I also hired a Chinese baby-sitter who doesn't even speak English, so my kids would have to talk Chinese to her. I know I will feel sad if my children drift away from their culture, but at least I am doing what I can to help them retain it."

Moy is married to a Caucasian man, but she has definite ideas about what role her heritage should play in the lives of her children. Newly arrived immigrants tend to push their children to assimilate, one of the consequences of which is an emphasis on learning English, perhaps at the expense of the original language. You have to have a certain amount of security in your ability to navigate the American culture in order to make the choices that Moy did.

"The moment my first child emerged from my body, I took one look at her as I held her in my arms and, in that instant, decided she would grow up speaking Chinese. Toishan dialect, to be precise. Although I was raised in a traditional Chinese family that owned a laundry, I hadn't really spoken Toishan on any regular basis for at least ten years. In making this decision, I literally had to piece the language back together for myself, phrase by phrase. Now my two daughters, at six and two, speak only Chinese at home. School is obviously a different matter, and they do speak English to their father. But otherwise, the rule at home is Chinese only. When my oldest was two, she threw a hissy fit about not wanting to speak Chinese. 'Fine,' I said calmly. 'If you don't want to speak Chinese, you'll have to have Daddy take care of you. You won't be able to talk to Po Po or Gong Gong. And your great grandmother won't be able to understand a single word you say.' Emotional blackmail . . . I know. But I strongly believe that being fluent in Chinese is the key to introducing and sustaining Chinese values as well as to firsthand communication with my children's Chinese relatives.

"My upbringing was very Chinese in many typical ways. Never any discussion of physical or emotional intimacy whatsoever. Strict pecking order about desirable spouses: Chinese first, non-Chinese Asian a distant second, no intermarrying, and definitely no blacks or Puerto Ricans. My father never told me directly what he thought of me, I only learned through the family grapevine. Nor did he ever tell me he was proud of me. The closest he came was the time when I got the job as development director for the Alvin Ailey American Dance Theater and my promotion was mentioned in a *New York Times* article. He went out and bought up an armload of newspapers and passed them around to all the relatives and friends. My parents also had the 'divide and conquer' thing down pat: telling each sibling what they didn't like about the others, but never saying anything directly to your face. My mother and father are wonderful, loving parents as well as skilled manipulators at indirect personal communication.

"By the time I was twelve, I was absolutely torn apart being bicultural. I felt ripped open, unable to merge the traditional Chinese expectations of my family and home life with the other parts of me: the part that was deeply affected by feminism and the civil rights movement, that loved jazz, rhythm and blues as well as opera, that eventually majored in theater arts to the horror of my parents who believed that only 'women of the night' would choose that career. I used to have to come straight home from school, study, and then help out in the laundry and other family businesses. This responsibility was nonnegotiable. But having taught myself to read at the age of four, I knew there was a whole other world out there, and I longed to be a part of it.

"In order to become an adult, and in order to save my sanity, I had to leave home. In Trenton, my parents could—and would—call at any time and say, 'We've got dinner with us. We'll be over in ten minutes.' So I spent ten years running away from home, from being Chinese. In that decade, I married a classical musician, developed a successful career in fund-raising and nonprofit management, and finally, I made peace with myself and my ethnicity. Now, I'm actually emotionally closer to my parents because I can relate to them as an adult.

"My father, who deeply believed that my marriage to a Caucasian meant I was no longer Chinese, recently complimented me when he commented that my two children spoke beautiful Chinese—the best of all his eight grandchildren. I felt that I had finally come back home."

In conclusion, a story from Ching, who is now in her mid-seventies. She has three adult children, one of whom was awarded a share of the 1997 Nobel prize for physics. She remembers the way she was raised, and talks about how she wanted to raise her own children differently.

"The worst thing about how I was raised in China is that my mother *taught* me to be dependent, full of fear. When I was getting ready to go away to college, she cried and cried. 'How will you survive? You can't even take care of yourself!' This is dangerous. This is not a good way to bring up children. In my mother's mind, since I was a girl, I should only worry about getting married anyhow. But I went away and I learned to survive on my own.

"Real Chinese people are always worrying about the future. They have a hard time making a decision because there is always so much to consider. For example, 'Should I go on this trip to Las Vegas? Well maybe I won't be able to get any sleep. Well, maybe I won't get anything out of it. Well, maybe I just shouldn't spend the money.' That's what I like about Americans. They can live for today, enjoy life. Chinese live for the future, not for today. The future you're going to be dead.

"When I was a little girl, I was primarily raised by servants. That's how it was for many families. The mother gets up, gets dressed and then goes out to play mah-jongg. Sometimes all day and all night. My mother didn't play mah-jongg, but still she was gone a lot. I think in early childhood that mother-child feeling is very important, nothing can replace it. But it was uneducated servants who put me to bed, and every evening they told me scary stories about ghosts and other superstitious things. And my father? He didn't even know what I was doing. Or care.

"So when it came to my kids, I wanted to do things in a different way. For one thing, I came from China, I didn't understand real American culture. They were going to have to live here, so they should mix with the Americans. When they were younger, their friends, who were mostly white, came to our house all the time. And that's the way I wanted it. The most important thing for me was that my children be happy and independent. I wouldn't like it if they were the kind who could never hold a job, always borrowing money, owing here, owing there. I would rather they were a janitor or a garbageman.

"I have gotten to the point in my life where I don't really give them my opinions anymore. They wouldn't listen anyhow, they do what they want to do. And that's fine with me. They can run their own life. So when they were getting ready to go to college, I didn't give them any advice. I just said, 'You have to choose what you want to do, you're going to have to live with it.'

"As far as passing on my culture, well I did have a Chinese school on Saturday morning where other parents and I taught our kids to read and speak. But by high school, they forgot all that anyhow. I don't feel sad they didn't retain the language. Sure it would be useful to them, but it doesn't really matter. As far as holidays and other customs go, the fact is, I've been here fifty years myself, and I really don't know which day is Chinese New Year's. Yes, my kids are Chinese, they have yellow skin, but the *important* thing is that they live here and feel comfortable here.

"Today I look at my grandchildren and think they are happier than Chinese children. They are not fearful, they say what they really feel. I have a good friend who was even scared to tell her parents that her servants were mistreating her. But as for me, I called my thirteen-year-old grandson the other day and asked if he thought about me. He said, 'I'll tell you the truth. I'm so busy I don't have much time to think about you.' Now a Chinese child would never talk to a grandparent that way. But I don't mind; I don't see it as disrespectful. Besides, the respect Chinese people give to elders is not really from the bottom of their heart anyhow. It's just to fulfill their obligation. Maybe the best thing about my children and grandchildren is that they know how they feel and what they want. I can't say as much for myself. That same friend of mine, I asked her if she was going to visit her children. She says, 'If they ask me, I come. If someone says go, I go.' At least I know this much, my kids don't feel this way. They *know* where they're going."

Finally, being a parent brings up for me the old issue of ethnic identity. I know that a certain amount of what is unresolved in my life enters into my relationship with my children. That is one reason I emphasize the need for them to feel positive about the Asian half of their heritage. Rebecca and Julian's Anglo-Saxon roots do not concern me as much. I want my children to feel proud of being 'half Chinese' for their sake, but also because it is a way of validating *me*. I have worked though much of the shame I felt about my ethnicity, but I have not been able to erase all of those feelings. They lie close to the surface. That is why my sister and I have this ongoing debate about which of us said to the other, "Gee, I'm sure glad my child doesn't look all that Chinese." Both of us are intimately acquainted with the little girl inside who hated her Asian features. We hate to admit it, but perhaps at some level we'd just as soon our children resemble the blond-haired, blue-eyed kid we longed to be.

How we were raised, how we are raising our own children . . . many of us who grew up as the first generation compared our family life to that of neighbors and friends. Almost invariably, life at home would appear less attractive, more restrictive. But now, as a parent, I know that I am a product of my upbringing. If I like the person I am today, if I am satisfied with the success I have been able to achieve, I have to give credit to my Chinese parents and the choices they made in raising me. My job as a mother is complicated, but it is also enhanced by being both Asian and American. In the best of all possible worlds, I can pass on what worked, but I can also explore new options to modify what did not.

9 ON THE JOB

How does our ethnicity intersect with our careers/jobs? What do we, as Asian American women, bring to our work that might be different from others? How do colleagues, supervisors, employees see us? Or perhaps the question could be asked in reverse: Does the fact that we are Asian American have anything to do with work at all?

I went to graduate school in English literature, in part because I loved to read, but probably just as much because it was my mother's dream for me. My extracurricular pursuits in high school tended toward the social welfare side, volunteering at state prisons, convalescent homes, and institutions for handicapped children. But as much as I was gratified by the sight of a little boy slowly learning to tie his own shoes, I knew that this was just a sideline, not my "real calling." Always, I had it in the back of my mind that I would get a Ph.D., write books, and teach. That was where my mother thought I should be headed, and that is where I wanted to go. When I was rejected by the University of Chicago's Ph.D. program, it was a real blow. It was like being on a train that had derailed; I no longer had any sense of destination.

After that, I did not try to pursue an academic career. I took the rejection as an omen, a portent of things to come. But I found jobs that were at least peripherally involved with writing: proof-

150

reading copy for the *Encyclopaedia Britannica,* writing or editing publications on subjects such as coal gasification, fitness, and gastrointestinal disease, of all things. I finally managed to find a job with the Arthritis Foundation that required some writing skills but also gave me the opportunity to provide direct patient services. And I loved it there until the Friday afternoon in late October when I was abruptly fired, with no warning and no tangible grounds.

At the time, I was devastated. I had a sense of personal failure and shame, and there were moments when I felt suicidal. It never occurred to me that my ethnicity might have anything to do with the termination. Now I wonder. I don't believe that the pink slip was a result of conscious racism on the part of my boss. But I am left holding the only explanation my boss was willing to give me: that I didn't fit in, that I wasn't part of the team, that my attitude was not conducive to the work environment. The quality of my work was never questioned. My dedication or ability to do the job was not the issue.

This sequence of events was particularly difficult for me to cope with. As a Chinese American, I grew up believing that good work would be rewarded and merit recognized. Playing the game of politics and learning to read between the lines of social banter were never part of the picture. So when my boss fired me, she also killed off something inside, my belief that I could rise as high as my potential would allow, my faith that the rules of the game were fair and would be enforced. The only bit of redemption in this incident occurred during an otherwise humiliating trip to the unemployment office. The guy took one look at me and said, "I know you Asians. *You* didn't do anything to deserve this. That boss of yours must be crazy." A glossy stereotype, but one that I embraced as a parched traveler might a desert mirage.

Eventually, I found the inner resources to pursue the career I had dreamed about. I studied for a master's degree in counseling and, several years ago, got my license. But I did so with the knowledge that not only would I disappoint my mother, I would also be entering a profession that Asians generally regard with suspicion. My parents had passed down a cultural imperative that strongly discouraged exposing personal or family matters to public scrutiny. For example, even when I decided to take advantage of the free group therapy my health plan offered, I found myself much more comfortable sagely commenting week after week about the behavior of others instead of sharing the real reason I had come: to try to cope with the painful end of a long-term relationship. For Asians, the idea of paying a stranger for the purpose of revealing deeply held concerns and emotions is illogical if not ludicrous.

When I became a licensed therapist, I entered the profession the same way that I had tried to blend into the neighborhoods of my childhood. I looked and acted as much like a white therapist as possible, even to the point of imitating the style of clothes I saw my colleagues wearing. And when one of my clients told me after a long and successful therapy that she initially had real doubts about working with a Chinese therapist, I remained silent. It was too disturbing to consider that a Chinese therapist might not be as effective with white clients as a white therapist, especially since most of my clients are white. I never asked subsequent clients whether this was also a concern for them, because I didn't want to deal with the consequences if they said yes. Once, my psychiatrist brother-in-law suggested I consider working with Asian families because he thought it would be "a good niche." I felt almost demeaned by the remark. "I'm a grief therapist with very specialized training," I told myself. "What does being Chinese have to do with that?"

Unsure of myself, and surrounded by white colleagues who, for the most part, treated me as if there was nothing different about me, I did not see myself as consciously denying my ethnicity (as I had as a child), but neither did I make any effort whatsoever to embrace it.

Today I am in a different place. Whether my clients or colleagues care about the fact that I am Chinese, I know it makes a difference to me. I believe that drawing on my strengths from a bicultural perspective makes me a better therapist. I can be sensitive in a new way, not only to the part that culture and ethnicity play in the lives of minorities, but also to the place that all of us at least occasionally encounter, the place of being different, of being the outsider. I am in a position to challenge the assumptions of a largely Eurocentric profession, designed primarily to address the needs of the dominant culture. In so doing, I achieve a measure of freedom for myself, a new way to look at my life and my experiences. Maybe it isn't entirely that I have been lacking in self-esteem and self-confidence, maybe it's the way some of us Chinese Americans just *are*.

How is it for other Asian American women? Those in traditional, those in "nontraditional" jobs? Those who are struggling to balance parental expectations against personal desires? How do certain culturally sanctioned behaviors (e.g., modesty, lack of aggressiveness) help or hinder our careers? Complicated questions without easy answers.

Nancy is a police officer, a job that is nontraditional for women, but even more so for Asian American women. She has had to contend with her family's reaction to her choice, but it did not deter her from pursuing her dream.

"Two years ago, I gave up my job as an attorney and went into law enforcement. I'm a police officer now, the only Asian woman in my department. Police work is generally too macho for most women, you have to be very assertive and very physical. Asian women are even less likely candidates. At first, my parents' reaction was, why throw away a perfectly good job, go into *blue-collar* work? They're also very protective worry-warts, so they were concerned about my safety. At the same time, they're really cool and they want me to do what makes me happy. I tried law, thought I'd give the civil part of it a shot. But it just didn't, you know, light my fire. Now I love going to work! This is the job I've always wanted and I love that adrenaline rush it gives me.

"My parents are cool, but we haven't said a word about this to my grandparents. They still think I'm a lawyer. It would kill them if they found out the truth. So that's kind of stressful, trying to hide it. Last time we were in San Diego, we had dinner with them. I let something slip and my mom's under the table kicking me. Still, I agree it's better to play these games. There's no point in upsetting them unnecessarily. I guess one of the main influences being Japanese has had on me is the closeness of family. My grandparents lived with us and they're important to me. I don't want to hurt them by telling them what I really do for a living. I'll live with the lie.

"I'm a Sansei on my mother's side, Yonsei on my father's. I grew up in Indiana, and it was horrible there—daily taunts, even having things thrown at me because I was Japanese. At first it pissed me off, but eventually I learned to ignore it. My mom would say things like, 'Sticks and stones . . .' In junior high, I remember this one group of girls who really had it out for me, saying things behind my back and so on. And dodgeball was a real trial—guess who was always the one being hit? Bad as it was, I didn't feel like something was wrong with me. They were the ones with the major problem.

"My parents made a deliberate effort to raise us to be proud of our heritage. They had a hard time with the treatment they got, so they didn't want us to experience the same thing. I remember being shown the family crest—that was pretty impressive. They even took us to Japan to visit distant relatives and see where our ancestors were buried. The trip was a revelation to me. I was thinking, 'OK, here we're going to Japan, we'll be seeing our home boys.' People in this country were always saying things about my being Japanese, so I figured when I got to Japan, I'd fit right in. In fact, they could tell immediately we weren't Japanese.

"When I was fifteen, we moved to Virginia. Major Relief. It's like, in the South, people may hate your guts, but at least outwardly, they're polite. They still look at you funny, you know they're thinking, 'What's with these people?' but since they didn't say it to my face, I was much happier.

"Something else about me that's out of the ordinary: I'm dating this guy who's half Puerto Rican. We've been together twelve years and have no immediate intentions to get married. The thing is, he's from a culture where the women are expected to listen to their man. His mom is like this quintessential Puerto Rican woman, always running around making food and then she'll stay in the kitchen while everyone else eats. All the women in his family act like that, so he's used to it. At the same time, he's a realist and he knows that there's no way on God's green earth that he can expect me to behave like that. Still we have differences when it comes to considering children. We joke around about having a double standard when it comes to raising girls, but I'm not 100 percent sure how it would really be if we did become parents."

What about being an Asian American in the fine arts? Traditional Asian painting is taught by having students come to study with and imitate the master. Imitation is the sincerest form of flattery, but here, the emphasis is on the strikingly original, the innovative. Here also, the highest calling for an artist is to do the work she feels driven to do, regardless of commercial viability or recognition.

For Jennifer, a nationally recognized and prolific painter, these questions are important, and she has struggled to come to terms with them. Her cultural identity is definitely a factor in her approach to her work.

"One time, I was giving a lecture to some children at a Chinese school. I was explaining the kind of art I do, and this little girl raised her hand. 'Do you do your art for yourself or do you do it for others?' This was a very good question. To be entirely truthful, I can't say my art *is* just for myself. But in this country, producing art for others is not considered the work of a 'real artist.'

"Someday, I would like to paint only flowers. Use my hand to record all the flowers of the world, each flower the way I want to present it. This is my dream. I believe we all come into the world for some reason, and this is mine. If you're not Picasso, you'll never be Picasso. But I know I do flowers well.

"Someday, maybe I will paint only for myself. But for now I am very content to work for others, to do my art work through commissions and contracts. If I am asked to paint a butterfly, I have to find out what American butterflies look like. I had to learn to work in a round format to satisfy one customer. Others find this restrictive and limiting, but whether it's Chinese or just me, I have a different attitude. I see it as a challenge, a problem to be solved, something I can learn from.

"I am also aware that my work ethic is very different from many artists here, who are often free-spirited individuals. If something doesn't work, they are likely to take the attitude, 'Well, it's just not going to happen, I'm not going to kill myself over it.' The way I've been raised, I don't feel I have the luxury just to walk away. I will glue myself to the chair until I finish it! You have to keep trying until it comes to you. It's not always fun. My American friends say to me, 'Relax! You don't know how to enjoy life.' But for myself, I feel guilty if I don't push myself to achieve.

"Perhaps this comes in part from being raised in a family where boys were seen as more valuable. I am the second daughter, one year younger than my older sister. I remember hearing my mother say that if her next child was also a daughter, she'd give her to my childless aunt to raise. As it happened, the next child was a son. So, no problem. I also used to get mad hearing the story of how my father, as the only son in his family, would be sitting there eating a snack. His sisters all had to stand aside and watch him eat, expecting nothing for themselves. I remember feeling I wanted to be more like a boy, so my parents would love me more.

"I have been very successful with my art, but it still never ceases to amaze me. When I get a new job, I still think to myself, 'Gee whiz, they want *me*!' I don't know if it's being Chinese or being a woman, but I also feel a little guilty when I get my check. 'So much for *this*!' Luckily, my husband, Hong Kong–born, is good with contracts. He handles the business matters. I just do the painting."

Laura is the principal ballerina of a well-regarded dance company. Working with an ethnically diverse troupe has made it easy to take on such lead roles as the Sugar Plum Fairy. Her skin

coloring and hair have not prevented her from dancing the roles
she wants. But she has given thought to the ways that growing up in a Chinese household has influenced her approach to
her art.

"Right now, I'm in the middle of a huge career transition.
What lies ahead, I don't know, and that's kind of scary. But I am
certain that I'm ready to leave ballet, do something else with my
life besides dance. I've been with this company for fifteen years,
since I was seventeen. I never went to college, and, in a sense,
grew up with the director, who has trained me from the time I
was a little girl. I've had extraordinary opportunities: I've toured
in almost fifty states, I've danced the Sugar Plum Fairy. But it's
time to move on.

"I grew up in a largely white environment and, until junior
high, never thought of myself as Chinese, or different. In junior
high, I met my first Chinese friend, and we talked a lot about
our lives, 'Oh, you do that too!' kind of thing. That's when I
started to see myself differently, to identify more with being
Asian. But it was never a negative thing.

"My parents spoke some Chinese, but we never learned a
word. We celebrated Chinese New Year's and did the red money
envelopes, but not much else. Still, I'd say, my dad was pretty
traditional. He fits the Asian stereotype of being passive and accepting. We'll go to the store and something will be wrong, but
he never says a word, never complains. I get irritated, but I guess
that's something that never will change. He also would have
liked me to do things the way all my cousins did: go to college,
get the good job, get married. I too want those things and want
to please him, but I felt I had to go where my heart led me. If I
was really worried about his approval, I would never have
danced at all. Recently, however, I realized that my dad was
proud of me. In '88, I danced my first Sugar Plum Fairy, and
then he started telling all the relatives. It was a very nice feeling,
but not one I live for, or cannot live without.

"Dancing with the ballet has helped me to overcome some of
the stereotypes about Asians in my own life. For example, our
family is not very affectionate with each other. But dance is such

a physical thing that I've learned to be much more comfortable with my body. Now, after I've been away for a while, I'll get a hug when I go home. But it's always very stiff, very formal, and that's something I'm really aware of. I also used to be very shy, very uncomfortable about meeting other people. Dancing has changed that too. I've had to learn to be more extroverted, to 'schmooze.' And I think the changes have been positive. Being with the company and having to deal with the inevitable politics has also helped me to learn to stand up for myself. I'm not the one who goes around complaining at the drop of a hat, but I will speak up if necessary.

"Today, I clearly identify myself as Asian American, but do I feel my ethnicity affects the way I dance? I guess I can only say I've observed other Asian dancers and see some similarities among us. We tend not to be as showy, as 'out there.' More subtle, more interested in creating a line than in creating the effect of 'Look at *me*!' On the less positive side, we also get less recognition, less positive feedback because we don't demand it. This is bothering me more and more, and plays into my decision to want to leave the company. Recently, a dancer in our company retired. 'You've given me everything I have ever wanted!' the director exulted. Never a similar word of praise to me. I can't say it doesn't hurt, that I wouldn't like to hear that kind of thing myself.

"I feel like I'm closing a chapter in my life. I believe dance will always be a part of who I am, but I'm ready for something else. Frankly, I'm ready for a more stable income, time to develop a real social life. Maybe finally get married and start having those grandchildren my parents are longing for."

Connie Chung paved the way for Asian American women to enter the field of broadcast journalism. There are now a number of Asian faces on the evening news. But the assumption of television viewers may be that these women stepped up to the camera and took their places simply by virtue of being in the right place at the right time. The struggles, the hard work and perseverance, are not as evident.

Janet is a reporter for a TV station in a midsized market. She, for one, is clear that having black hair and "almond"-shaped eyes is no guarantee when it comes to this profession.

"I lived in both the U.S. and Hong Kong until I was six, when we settled here permanently. Until that age, I didn't really think much about being Chinese, about being the same or different. But by the time I got to grade school and they started that whole thing with the slanted eyes, it made me very angry. I knew I could never be fully accepted. For one thing, I was a good student, in many ways a better student than the kids who made fun of me, but still they excluded me. One I was Chinese, and two, I was smart. Two strikes against me from the start.

"I did very well in school, but not because my parents particularly pressured me. In fact, they decided not to raise their children in Hong Kong precisely because of the academic competitiveness—which sometimes drove kids to suicide. I did it for me. I also did it as a way to deal with not being accepted. And my sense of responsibility, my work ethic: Is it nature or nurture? I think I have always been extremely responsible. Even at the age of two, when I noticed my brother's tricycle sitting in the rain, I ran outside to go drag it home.

"Now, as a TV reporter, I'm having a very difficult time with my current station. I can't say if it's because I am Asian, but I do know that I was originally hired with a Latino woman and received a very cool reception when I came on board. I believe I have gone above and beyond what was expected of me. I think I'm the only reporter here who actually got someone arrested as a result of my work. I am always nice and always courteous. But my last performance evaluation did not reflect my effort at all. My boss suggested that 'I should not let my lack of interest in my work deter me.' *What* lack of interest?

"The fact is, I am not accepted here. It's to the point where I hear that people are saying things about me at parties they never invite me to. I guess if I really wanted to make it in this field, I'd have to be a different person. An insincere person. And I've never wanted to be someone that I am not."

Asian Americans generally have not made their voices heard in political debate. The recognition is growing that, in order to influence national policy on issues that affect the daily lives of Asian Americans, we need political power. But embarking on a career in politics may pose internal conflicts for Asian American women. Certain attributes that contribute to political success run counter to traditional notions of what is proper for a woman. The Japanese have a saying, "The nail that sticks up gets hammered down." Sticking your neck out in Washington may give you clout and recognition, but it will also make you a visible target to the hammers of the opposition.

Doris is a Japanese American woman who grew up in California's Central Valley. She reflects on the relationship between that upbringing and her work today, work that places her in a position of high visibility and political influence. Perhaps it is that her parents, despite being traditionally Japanese in some ways, were still successful in passing on to Doris the message that it was OK for her to make her own choices, to "stick her neck out." And the assurance that she would be supported if she did.

"Many people think I got this position because I'm Hillary's friend or because I'm Bob's wife. The explanations I've heard run the gamut. Those who know me well know that I got the job on my own merit. But either way, I let it go. It doesn't matter what others think. I have confidence in my own abilities. I know I'm good.

"I grew up with self-esteem. I was the firstborn granddaughter and always felt cherished. Maybe I have an unusual family, but my parents and grandparents never made me feel guilty, never gave me the sense that I owed them anything. They truly exemplified the child-rearing philosophy that 'if you let them go, they will come back to you.'

"My mother and father met in internment camp, and I was

born there. I believe that experience had a lot to do with my parents' desire to have us assimilate as much as possible. We felt we needed to be American to the extent that now, looking back, I see it was somewhat to our detriment. For one thing, we never learned Japanese. At school, we did not have Japanese American friends, but we were very comfortable in the small farming town where we grew up. I felt different only because the other children saw me as very smart. But this didn't isolate me; my friends valued intellectual achievement.

"They weren't overt about it, but I knew my parents wanted me to do my best, to set an example for my younger siblings, and it was important to be successful in the American way, which in my case ultimately meant the political arena. My parents were 100 percent behind me. They didn't pressure me to date Japanese Americans, but, at the same time, they always gave me very positive messages about my heritage.

"When I went away to college, I met more Asians and, over time, sensed a growing desire within myself to marry one. I had a greater appreciation for my culture and I was looking for someone like me. I met Bob in college; we had a lot in common besides our ethnicity. Our family backgrounds were similar and we both had almost exclusively Caucasian friends.

"When I was thinking about whether to take the job I have today with the current administration, I considered the fact that it might change me in ways I wouldn't like. That has not happened. I'm tougher than I was before, but in a way that I think will hold me in good stead for the rest of my life, help me face whatever comes my way. Over the years, working for many nonprofits and now for the President, I've had to do things the 'Washingtonian way,' i.e., make myself known, sell myself or the cause I was representing. What I've found is that I can be effective and still be myself. I can get what I want, but not by being 'in their face.' I don't get angry often, but when I do, people stand up and take notice. I value my Japanese culture, the emphasis on the family, the value of cooperation as a way to gain the greater good, but I can also pull out parts of myself that are more Western when I need to. For example, I've learned that, while it's nice to make sure everyone around you gets the credit they deserve, it's also important for you to receive the credit *you* have earned."

Diana talks about how she has had to adjust to a work environment that doesn't always feel comfortable. Moving to take her present job meant relocating to an area where there are fewer Asians. She is aware of missing that bond with women like herself, the feeling that you will be accepted, not judged.

"My current position is as executive director of a thriving nonprofit counseling center. I like the status, the variety, the challenge of the job. But sometimes, I wonder if it's the right place for me. And this has to do with being Asian. For one thing, I grew up believing that if you work hard, you will be rewarded. This isn't necessarily true in an agency like this, where not everyone sees things in the same light. More important is that I like peace, I like harmony. I want people to get along and I want them to like me. Previously, as clinical director of an agency providing services to an Asian population, it was easier to promote that working environment. The staff didn't directly challenge you, confront you whenever they felt like it. In this job, I have had to learn to be assertive, to set limits, to say no. To please people sometimes knowing that I'd displease others."

Sue worked for many years as a CPA and is now making a mid-life career transition, hoping to get licensed as a psychotherapist. She reflects on her Chinese upbringing and the ways in which those values have shaped her personal and professional life.

"In some ways, I'm probably so acculturated now that I don't really see myself as different. In my work today, the only time it consciously hits me that I'm Chinese American is when I'm seeing a client of color or another Asian. Then, there is a bond, a sense that it's easier to really say 'I understand' when they tell me their story.

"This wasn't always true. Growing up in Reno, Nevada, as one of a very few Asian Americans, I wanted blond hair and blue eyes. When other children started the 'Ching chong Chinaman' routine, I was forced to realize that they did not accept me. My response only reinforced the stereotype. I continued to perpetuate the image of myself as quiet and passive, not one to get in trouble or do anything that would get me *noticed*. The only avenue was to excel academically.

"At the same time, I lived in a home where my parents never learned to speak English well. Our family was traditional in many ways, and I know that to this day I am still influenced by their values. For example, there are certain family issues that we just don't talk about. My older brother, for one. He's kind of the 'black sheep,' but we don't ever mention the trouble he has been in because, black sheep or not, he's still a *male*. As such, he has higher status and more value. My sister and I are basically taking care of my mother now, but she can't get past the fact that we are girls. She has a hard time acknowledging our contributions.

"Another way I knew I was Chinese was my certain knowledge that the only way to make something of myself was through education. Where did this drive, this instinct come from? I'm not sure, but I do remember my mother bragging about my brother who was in med school. And even though she herself never made it to high school, my mother would be sure to point out nieces and nephews who failed to get a college education: 'Oh yes, so-and-so may be making lots of money, but he's just a *plumber*.' I know that I still carry this prejudice. My current boyfriend is a building contractor. But I have to admit that I probably wouldn't have stuck with him if I didn't also know that he went to law school. He could have been a lawyer, he just chose not to be. I let the law degree compensate for his present choice of career.

"In terms of work, I can see that my parents' values and expectations had a lot to do with the choices I made. In college, I took classes in anthropology and loved them, but I always knew it 'was no real way to make a living.' Besides, how would I explain 'anthropology' to my mother? At the same time, I had a job doing bookkeeping. I didn't particularly enjoy it, but I was fairly good and so I just fell into accounting as a career. I worked as a CPA for eighteen years, and never really grew to like it. But my mother loved being able to say that her daughter was a CPA. That her daughter made a good salary and 'traveled internationally for her job.' Every time I got a raise, she'd ask how much, and I'd always tell her. I never considered not sharing that information with her. I knew she would be offended if I did not.

"Things at work deteriorated to the point where I realized I wasn't even doing a good job anymore. That was not acceptable to me. So I started to pursue the career I had dreamed of: working as a therapist who brings in the spiritual side. This is a concept that my mother and my siblings simply cannot understand. First, they think I'm crazy to give up a perfectly respectable job with its large salary and excellent benefits. To my mother's way of thinking, I have reached the height of my career and now I'm trying to throw it all away. Second, I don't think they comprehend the concept of altruism, of 'contributing to society.' I've noticed that Chinese families take care of their own, but they don't tend to do a lot of volunteer or community work. It is, however, important to me.

"I believe that the Chinese part of me has also brought with it real limits that I'm trying to overcome. Not being able to speak up, for example. Not feeling comfortable raising my hand in class or voicing my opinion in a meeting. In fact, I know for certain that when I worked as a CPA for the winery, they were disappointed that I failed to live up to the outgoing, assertive image I was somehow able to project in my interview. In general, the message I got in business was that I needed to be more assertive. But I'm not comfortable with people paying attention to me. I notice that when I'm asked how I am or what I'm up to, my answers tend to be very short. I don't like talking a lot about myself. After all, we were taught to 'Be good. Be quiet. Not stand out.' This is an issue I have been working on in therapy. Why is it so hard for me to speak up? What's really holding me back? Because I do see my behavior as a limitation.

"Making this career change has been difficult. Sometimes I

feel sad thinking about how much of my life I can no longer really share with my mother or my siblings. It's hard to go home and not say the things they want to hear, to have my sister point out jobs in the business section she thinks I should apply for. But I feel that I am doing what I truly love, what is truly important to me. And that's something I'm no longer willing to live without."

Karen is an attorney and currently the executive director of a group that works on legal issues important to the Asian American community. One of her concerns is the ease with which Asian American women are rendered invisible in the eyes of the dominant culture. Being invisible is not necessarily the same thing as being accepted: You don't stick out like a sore thumb but neither are you seen for the person you really are.

"We grew up with a dichotomy. From second grade on, we lived in the white suburbs of Seattle, where I experienced a strong drive to be American. Yet the subtle feedback from my parents was, 'Oh my goodness! You're not going to have the right friends, date the right (i.e., Japanese) people.' My thought was, 'Well then why did you move us to an area where it was very unlikely we'd be exposed to the proper candidates?' At the same time, my parents did involve us with the Nisei Vets, so we grew up believing that Santa Claus had Japanese features. Once, I invited a white friend to one of our Christmas parties, but I had no idea what she meant when she told me that 'something was wrong with Santa.'

"Although my father was agnostic, he sent us to the Asian Methodist Church when I was twelve, in hope that we would meet some nice Japanese boys. We also believed, as did many other Japanese Americans, that we had to outperform others. Still, I felt different and didn't particularly like that feeling. If we experienced prejudice from our peers, Dad's standard response was, 'But you should feel *sorry* for them because you are superior to them.' His words didn't take away the hurt: Certainly the rest of the world didn't seem to see us that way.

"My father was your typical stoic Asian man, so it was something for me to witness his expression of emotion when he finally received his redress check and the apology (for having been interned). Both my parents had been very close-mouthed about the internment, and my father's position had always been that restitution rightfully belonged to the Issei, who had been most affected by the experience. When he actually received his check, it had a very different impact on him than any of us anticipated. He was deeply moved, and witnessing it, so was I.

"My dad was also a Boeing engineer and believed I should go into the sciences. His reasoning was that science is very quantitative—either you're right or you're wrong. People can't make judgments about you or discriminate as easily. I was, however, interested in law, a profession with very little tradition in the Asian community. My parents weren't crazy about my becoming an attorney. I went to law school anyhow and then worked for a top Seattle firm for six years. This was a difficult time for me. I felt I had a lot to prove, and that old neurosis of working harder is very difficult to let go of. But I believe the pressure was more for being a woman than being Asian. In my second review I was told that I was doing great but appeared to be 'too intimidating.'

"Looking back, I don't think it is *possible* to do my job well and still preserve all the traditional Asian values such as modesty. This was especially irksome to relatives who would point out that I'm not married yet because I'm too tough. I scare the men away by my demeanor. On this point, my dad is very much old school, feels I'm not OK unless a man is taking care of me. Once I tried to point out to him that I'm making more money now as a single woman that he did when he had four kids to raise, so why worry about me? He didn't exactly see things that way.

"At the law firm, I was doing corporate work, which involves mostly phone contact. This was to my advantage because clients didn't usually see me until closing, at which point they'd remark, 'Oh, uh, you're not what I expected.' By then, they had already been judging me on the basis of my work, not on any potential stereotypes they might have held. As time went on, I got increasingly involved with Asian issues outside of work. This put me in two completely separate worlds, and although I felt comfortable in both, I'd have to suppress one trait or another depending on where I happened to be. The dissonance increased, and finally I left the firm to move to Washington, D.C., and work with Asian American legal issues.

"I'm very aware now that, as an Asian American woman, I'm in a very murky place. Either you're presumed to be white or you're invisible. Recently I was invited by Eleanor Smeal to speak at a press conference on affirmative action. I didn't expect press coverage, but *Newsweek* did come out to report on the event. They mentioned African Americans and Latinas, but completely overlooked my presence. It's as if I wasn't even there."

10 BLENDING IN OR STANDING OUT:

Stories of Racism and Discrimination

"Where are you from? No, where are you *really* from?"
"But you speak English so well!"
"You mean you eat turkey on Thanksgiving just like we do?"
"Oh, you Asians are all so successful."
"You must know kung fu."
"Ching, chong, Chinaman."
"Chink."
"Gook."
"Jap."

A memory. Disneyland, the Happiest Place on Earth. I was struggling with the burdens of a squirming toddler, a stroller, and various pieces of baby paraphernalia. The parade had just finished, and I was due to meet my husband in what unfortunately seemed to be in the opposite direction of prevailing traffic. I accidentally bumped into a man who took one look at me and said in disgust, "Oh, those *Asians,* always going the wrong direction." Another memory. Walking back to the parking lot after an exceptionally fine hike with my family, it was clear that a small group of young men and women wanted my attention. The leader made eye contact and then, when he was sure I could hear him, suggested loudly that I "go back where all you fucking Chinks belong!" It's not that I'd never heard this type of thing before, but on this particular day I really didn't want to

ignore him, passively accept the insult as I believe he probably
expected me to do. So, I flipped him off. A wide grin made its
way across the young man's face. "Well, no thanks," he said
with exaggerated politeness. "I already have someone here!"
And then they were off, leaving me sputtering with rage, help-
lessness, shame.

A very recent event, one not yet distant enough to be codified
into memory. My family and I had just spent a beautiful and
moving day touring the detention station at Angel Island (the
West Coast equivalent of Ellis Island, but one that symbolized
exclusion rather than a sense of welcoming the "huddled masses
yearning to breathe free"). On the way home, my daughter informed me that she needed to use the rest room, so we stopped
at an upscale bakery in Tiburon (site of the ferry crossing). Not
realizing that there were two separate lines, we headed straight
for the bathroom. A woman indicated that she was waiting, so
we got into place behind her. Then, a man I had not noticed
before wheeled around to face me. "I'm in line too," he explained. We moved back another place, but that did not satisfy
him. Summoning the full extent of his wrath, he shouted,
"Someone should teach *you immigrants* a lesson." He went on to
use the facility, but I could not move. I felt as if I had been physically assaulted, as if his words were weapons that could literally
knock the wind out of your gut. And then there was silence. No
one in that crowded bakery said a word. No one acknowledged
that anything whatsoever had happened. I was reminded again
that I am alone in this place.

What hurts about these specific memories is not just the remark itself, it is the unexpected and shattering suddenness that
wounds. As a child, growing up in Princeton, New Jersey, an
academically liberal town that kept the shadow side of its racism
under wraps, I had experienced enough of this to last a lifetime.
I was subjected to taunts on a daily basis. Children pulling up
the corners of their eyes as I passed by. Moving their hips in a
vaguely suggestive manner to the lyrics of Purina Dog Chow's
commercial, "Chow, Chow, *Chow!*" Spontaneous choruses of
"Ching, chong, walla walla bing bong!" My parents instructed

me to ignore the schoolyard talk and to concentrate on studying harder so that one day I could "show them."

What hurts is that I thought as an adult I would no longer be assailed by such attitudes, or at least that they would no longer have the same power to capture and humiliate. I had hoped I was beyond that. But what I learned is that the response to racism I developed as a child still lives within me. It will probably always be there. As a child, I believed that I *deserved* the treatment I received, that the kids in my school were right: Being Chinese *is* reason enough to feel ashamed. Something is wrong with me, not with them.

This is what psychologists call "internalized oppression." After a while, people no longer needed to call me names or demonstrate their contempt for me—I did that well enough by myself. However, most Asian American women do not grow up with this same longing to be someone other than who we are, this deep sense of shame about what we perceive to be our true selves. Many of us lived in white, ethnically diverse, or predominantly Asian neighborhoods and never felt the sting of singularity. And even those who do encounter racism in its myriad hurtful forms are more likely to externalize the experience, feeling angry about the mistreatment or a sense of resignation about the ignorance of others.

The response to racism also varies by generation. My mother is fairly typical of immigrants of her age. She believes the United States has been good to her, welcomed her with open arms, offered the opportunities to be successful, educated her children. A racist remark here, a taunt there is a small price to pay. "How do you think they treat foreigners in China?" she would ask. This difference in viewpoints can sometimes lead to intergenerational conflict. Advising their daughters to have patience, not to make waves, may feel like good judgment to the parents, but to the daughters this stance could be interpreted as a form of denial and lack of acknowledgment.

Among the Japanese, it is well documented that the Sansei, many of whom have never lived in camp themselves, articulate more rage and indignation about the internment than do their Nisei parents. The Nisei are known for their stoic attitudes, reinforced by the Japanese philosophy of *shikata ga nai* (it can't be helped). They do not talk about their life in camp, and their most common response to this massive trauma is to downplay its effects and dig in their heels, work harder at becoming "110 percent American" in the hope that their loyalty will never again be questioned. Perhaps women like myself have the luxury to explore the deeper ramification of events such as the internment— our parents were concerned more directly with survival.

In any event, the facts of racism are real and the imprints left on the soul and psyche undeniable.

Karen, a second-generation Chinese woman, tells her story of growing up in a small agricultural town in California's Central Valley.

"I grew up on a farm, which for children permitted a wonderful sense of freedom. There we were, with a hundred acres of our own to play in. But school was a different matter entirely. I came face-to-face with racism and discrimination every day of the academic year. To this day, I refuse to attend any high school reunions and I threw away my yearbook as soon as I graduated. Why would you want to remember classes where you raised your hand but were never acknowledged *once*? Where even the stupidest kids were given the opportunity to respond, but you were not? Who needs a record of school plays that you always, breathlessly, tried out for, but never got a single part in?

"My parents were poor and they always stressed to us the value of a good education: a way out for each of their seven sons and daughters. I focused on this as my personal goal, but it was difficult since I had no control whatsoever of my school environment. In my junior year, I had a teacher who was angry about my consistently high grades. One day, he gave us a history test. I got a 94 percent, but then I compared my answers to another kid who had received a perfect grade. Our answers were identical. When I tried to ask the teacher about this, all he said to me was 'Sit down. That's just the way it is.' And then, there was the time when I got the highest grade on a trig test. This boy, Joey, came up to me after school and spit at me. He was mad that I had ruined the curve.

"Perhaps one of the most upsetting things was a talk I had with my guidance counselor. I wanted to go to Cal, and I knew I had to submit an application. So I went into the office to see this man, whose name I've blocked from my memory, but whose face I can still see all too clearly. 'What do you need that for?' he asked. 'Why don't you just go to the JC [junior college]?' He insinuated that my parents wouldn't have the money to send me to Cal anyhow. And he absolutely refused to give me the form I needed.

"My parents were no help. They had no idea what to do or who to turn to. They did not speak English well and, true to tradition, did not believe in rocking the boat in any manner. So I had to do it on my own; I wrote to the university and got the form myself.

"I knew the teachers were wrong. I was angry and frustrated but I felt trapped. Nothing I could do when it was all those powerful white people on one side, me on the other. So I sat there graduation night and watched one student after another troop up to the stage to receive this award or that one. Melanie, a C student in history, got the history award. I did not receive a single distinction of any kind except the scholarships I earned on my own merit outside the school system.

"And I accepted the fact as if it were self-evident that I would have no dates, no chance to get on Student Council or be a cheerleader. I was always the last to be picked for whatever needed picking. And my friends would be those who were also shunned, like Mary, the girl who walked with a limp because of her polio. She was not accepted because of her disability, I because of my ethnicity, and so we had something in common, even though we were worlds apart academically."

For Frances, the images of Hollywood splayed, larger than life, across the movie screen formed a stark contrast to the daily routine she knew. Twenty-five cents could get you into the theater, but after the lights came on, you always had to leave again. Walk back into the heat and noise of the day, the poverty, the inescapable fact of being Chinese.

"We were very poor as children. My mother came here, through Angel Island, as a mail-order bride and found out that her intended husband was not the businessman she had been promised. Instead, he was a nobody who did seasonal work in the canneries, drifting from job to job. He wasn't around much and left my mother to raise five girls as a single parent with very limited resources. I remember a wealthy aunt occasionally giving us a quarter to 'buy a treat.' We'd spend that precious money to get a box of cornflakes, using little squares of toilet paper as napkins and dividing the food equally among us. I was often hungry.

"Growing up, we didn't have a real sense of all the struggles my mother went through. We just knew life was hard. At times, overcome by the frustration of her situation, aggravated by some misbehavior on our part, my mother would tell us that if she had had a son, she wouldn't have had any other children. I resented that. I also remember being punished by having to kneel at the foot of her bed for hours, not able to go to the bathroom, wondering if I should leave the room to start our chores and risk further wrath in so doing. I remember crying, but also telling myself, 'I'm alive. I'm breathing. Tomorrow will be different.' Today, you might consider my mother's form of discipline as abusive. But I don't really see it that way. My mother was in a very difficult position and yet managed to raise all of us, impress on us the value of a good education, and give us a sense of inner strength.

"Every weekend, we would be sent to the movies for the whole afternoon. As much as this cost, I imagine the peace and quiet were worth it for my mother. We mostly watched the big musicals—Fred Astaire and Ginger Rogers dancing from lavish set to lavish set. This is where I developed my fantasy of becoming a ballroom dancer, gliding down the marble steps. This is also where I started wondering whether my life would have been different if I had been born with blond hair and blue eyes. I'd scrutinize that Sunbeam girl on the bread wrapper with her ringlets of blond hair and think, 'Why not me? Why can't my life be like that?'

"The feelings were reinforced by the fact that each daughter, at the age of thirteen, was sent to work for a rich white family in Piedmont. We'd do housework and other chores in exchange for room and board. That was a common practice in those days—hiring black women as kitchen help and Orientals as 'mother's helpers.' I never felt resentful of my mother for the situation, but sometimes the contrast was just too stark: standing there with that hot iron starching the 'midis' worn by a girl who was almost my age but whose life in other respects was a world apart from mine. The lady of the house would say, 'Oh, we're going to mop the floor this Saturday,' and of course you knew she wasn't going to be on *her* hands and knees. Much of the work was physically demanding and I remember wondering if I'd have to do this forever. I'd see the black women cooking, and they were *adults*. Could I too be trapped like this for the rest of my life?

"I knew that education was probably my only way out, and I was accepted to Berkeley, but I had to work long hours in order to pay for school. The only jobs I could find were low-paying, menial jobs, and I believe that if I had been white, I would have done better. My mother always stressed the value of college and I was determined to get my degree, but in the back of my mind, I wasn't entirely confident that it would get me out of this life.

"When I graduated from Cal, the only job I could find was that of a clerk. I had majored in fashion design and originally looked for a position with the big department stores, but I never put my heart into it. I just knew I couldn't compete with all those pretty white girls. In fact, the only job I. Magnin's was willing to consider me and other Asians for was as an elevator operator. I took that job one summer, and we were required to wear little blue suits and white gloves, a clear signal from that high-class store that we were to be identified to their wealthy customers as 'help.' I used to feel some despair thinking, 'This is all we're good for. We'll never be better than the customers we are ferrying up and down all day.' At that time, my feelings about being Chinese were mixed. Maybe 25 percent felt proud of myself, who I am, but 75 percent continued to feel that I was the wrong race.

"Today, I look at my life and feel I've been successful. I worked very hard to get where I am. While I was still a clerk, a woman I knew said to me, 'What are you doing here? You have a degree from Berkeley and you're still *here*?' That made me feel terrible. But another man, an auditor, told me I could do better: get a degree in accounting and move up. I followed his advice and I ended up with five promotions in two years. Now I'm as high as I want to be. I'm content. I went back to school at the time affirmative action was just getting started. People would say, 'Oh, you're Asian. You're lucky to be in the right place at the right time.' Considering everything I've been through, I don't appreciate those comments. I don't think I've gotten anything because I'm Asian. I earned every bit of it.

"For my own children, I was mostly interested that they grow up believing they could be the best at whatever they wanted to be, without regard to color or race. Not to be white, exactly, but also not entirely Chinese. Once in a while, even today, I wish that my feelings about being Chinese didn't play such a large part in my identity; but mostly I'm content with the fact that I'm not one of those beautiful blondes I dreamed about as a child. It's OK not to be Ginger Rogers. Frances is just fine."

Keiko, a journalist in her early thirties, found that she could not really share the pain of being different with her parents. So she kept it in, which is a pretty common experience. In some cases, parents and children literally do not speak the same language, and there is no shared vocabulary by which to discuss such issues. The expression of feelings is not generally encouraged in Asian households anyhow. Parents also tend to honor more traditional values in terms of authority. Taking a stand against racism—especially in its institutional form—may be viewed as disrespectful. For Keiko, salvation at a very difficult time in her life came in the form of her ability to put feelings into the written word.

"I was born in Japan and literally came to the U.S. in a box resting on my mother's feet. I recently learned that there is a phrase to describe my generational status: 'shin Issei,' or first-generation immigrant. In the first few years of my life, I spoke only Japanese, and my family lived in an apartment complex with other Japanese colleagues of my physicist father. And then, when I was three, my parents sent me to this progressive nursery school filled with white children. I didn't speak a word of English. The teachers were most kind, but other kids, boys especially, teased me unmercifully. I came home every day not understanding what was happening to me, or why. And my parents' response was to get angry with me for returning home in this state. I remember the next summer, they wanted me to go to a summer camp that was just a short distance from home. As soon as they dropped me off, I'd start walking back home in tears. I *knew* I wasn't going through that experience again.

"I learned English. I had to. It was a matter of survival. I became extremely verbal and learned after a while that I could get attention by being the class clown.

"Second grade brought on the 'trauma of the school bus.' Around my home, in the neighborhood, things went pretty well for me. There weren't a lot of other Asians around, but the town in Connecticut where we lived was a multiethnic community. My best friend, Anna, was Brazilian, and her parents very old country. We'd find endless amusement in getting together to make fun of our parents, their accents, their lifestyle. But school was different. And getting to school on the bus was worse yet. Again, the boys would tease me. They called me Chink, Jap. They called me 'Flat Face' and asked if I enjoyed chasing parked cars. They would point out to me 'You lost the war!' I had no idea what that was about, so I asked my dad. He tried to instill pride in me, I'm sure, by responding that white people are barbarians. For the first time, I started to consciously understand that my race was an issue.

"One day, my father decided that he wanted to address the bus problem head-on. He waited with me at the bus stop, and when the bus arrived, he got on board to face and discuss the situation with the driver. I distinctly remember thinking, this short Japanese man—my father—was absolutely no match for this burly white bus driver. The odds were ridiculous; one man by himself simply could not turn the tide of racism and prejudice.

"In fifth grade, we moved to the suburbs of Chicago, ushering in some of the worst times of my life. I hated it there. I couldn't articulate what was wrong, but I knew I was miserable. So I turned into a bad kid. Until then, I had been obedient. But in Glen Ellyn, I found some bad girls to hang out with, the kind that came to school with their jeans full of holes. At first, we confined ourselves to mischief at school, throwing spitballs, peering into the stall of our fifth-grade teacher, who seemed to be able to spend endless amounts of time in the bathroom. In sixth grade, we graduated to stealing and smoking cigarettes. By seventh grade, we discovered the mall and its unlimited possibilities. My parents were in despair. Every night at dinner, I was the topic of conversation. I felt guilty about what I was doing, but I hated my parents, hated myself, and I could not stop.

"That was the point in my life when I turned to writing as an attempt to contain my misery. I'd open my journal with the same sentence every night, 'My parents are so screwed up.' But then I'd drop that line of thought and go on to discuss how everyone hated me, how my friends seemed to turn on me. Sometimes I'd blame my parents for all this: If they were more normal, if they celebrated Christmas the right way, didn't wear such shabby clothes, spoke better English, didn't eat all that funny-smelling food, were richer, etc. . . . If only I could be more like the people I was seeking acceptance from. I didn't consciously attribute this state of affairs to being Japanese, but it was certainly part of the picture. And once in a while I'd decide I needed to change. I'd resolve to be a better person.

"After school, I continued to cope with my pain by acting out, drinking too much, smoking, etc. I've recently worked through my problems with alcohol, but for a while, it was really a part of my life. Also with men: dating guys who were alcoholics, didn't have steady jobs, didn't have a real future.

"At some point, I just realized I had to get my life together. I had support from my friends, but I knew that my parents weren't going to be able to help me. For one thing, my mother has her own share of problems. She's very depressed and has been hospitalized for her depression. I knew I loved to write. It had been my saving grace at times in my life when I felt very much alone. I'm also very comfortable in foreign, even slightly sinister, places, so I believed I could be a journalist with my anthropological interest in different cultures. Finding a place for myself in the profession of journalism helped to put my life back in order.

"I also decided it was time to take a look at my attitudes toward finding a partner. For a long time, I only considered dating Caucasians. But I recently announced to my friends that 'I'm not dating any more white men.' I said that out loud because I want their backing. I've decided I have to adopt an affirmative action approach to dating, to seek out Asian men if I want to meet one. I want to confront the unconscious preference I've always had for white men and what they represent to me. So if I see a white guy now, I say to myself, 'No, this is not your next boyfriend.' I believe I can control who I am attracted to. For a while, I wasn't sure how to look for the right Asian man, but I recently attended an Asian American film festival and this videographer came up to me, started talking. So I think, 'This is what a guy that might work for me would look like, sound like, etc.' Before, Asian men were invisible to me; I need to work to make them visible.

"In coming to terms with who I am, I am also coming to terms with my parents. A few years ago, if they had opposed my dating someone black, it wouldn't have meant a thing to me. But family is taking on increasing importance in my life, and now I wouldn't want to marry someone they disapproved of. I would take their opinions into consideration, while reserving for myself the last word."

Growing up abroad can create a unique set of heartaches. The journey through racism to self-acceptance has been difficult for

Theresa, a literary agent in New York. It took a sojourn in California and exposure to an open and inviting Asian American community for her to start seeing herself in a different light. But the rewards are immense.

"Because my father worked for the UN, I have lived in several different parts of the world. We started in Wisconsin, where we were the first nonwhite family to attend the local elementary school. From there, we moved to Lebanon and then to Vienna. But it was not until I decided to go to college in California that I had any sense of belonging or affiliation. There was a large Asian population at UC Santa Cruz, and for the *first* time in my life, I allowed myself to acknowledge how incredibly painful it had been for me abroad, especially in Austria, where racism was a daily and unavoidable fact of life.

"In Vienna, it was like this. We were not Austrian and we were not wealthy. We didn't even fit into the group of other Americans or expatriates because we were not white. We were not anything. Being an adolescent is bad enough, experiencing all that angst in this very conservative and old-world city was doubly difficult. I remember one day riding in the back of the bus with a group of friends. We were loud in the way teenagers like to be loud, and this old man comes to tell us to be quiet. One of my friends says something to him about being 'an old fart,' and he wheels around to stare at us. 'The problem with all of you,' he says, 'is that *nigger* you've got with you.' He was pointing to the black girl in our group. I was absolutely stunned. I saw that she was silently crying and then I realized it could have been me. I could just as easily have been the target of his venom.

"I remember also the day this Canadian Korean girl at our school showed up with her hair curled in a tight perm. She was trying to look more Western, more like one of 'them.' I took one look at her and started teasing her unmercifully. I could not let go of it. Looking back, it's obvious that I was projecting my own desperate but unacknowledged desire to belong onto her. I could not deal with my own shame about being Asian, so I gave her hell for having the same feelings.

"Years later, I asked my father how he could have lived in

such a racist place. I knew he too had been subjected to racism, but he denied it now as he had denied it then, while it was happening. We would be eating in a restaurant where it was obvious that we were being treated like second-class citizens, and I would comment on it. 'Oh, you're just too sensitive!' Dad would say. 'But they're *staring* at us.' My mother would chime in at this point: 'That's just because you're such a pretty girl!' Right. I think my parents, as first-generation immigrants, found it easier to deny the discrimination and focus on the positive opportunities they found. But it was not so easy for me.

"At the time it was happening, I did not share my feelings with my parents. After all, how could I tell them that *they* were part of my embarrassment? How could I say, 'You don't speak English well enough to be American, and you don't speak German well enough to be accepted here?' I did know that my mother shared a profound sense of shame every time we encountered other Asians: Japanese tourists with their cameras and their bowing. To be identified as one of them was anathema. The feeling of racism was palpable. I have lived in other parts of the world, for example Uganda, and it's not like I haven't been stared at. But here it wasn't a friendly curiosity. It was hostility and contempt. As an adolescent already grappling with all those complex identity issues, this experience made it almost impossible for me to come to terms with who I was as an Asian.

"When I first got to school in California, I was shocked to see so many Asian faces, but I soon realized that these men and women were grounded in an identity, they had something I wanted. I became politicized and, for the first time in my life, discovered a positive connotation to my ethnicity. I even got my mother involved in this type of thinking, and she experienced a kind of cultural rebirth, reconnecting with the Japanese parts of her heritage she had shunned for so many years.

"One day, this white male friend of mine told me, 'You know, Theresa, you'll do well here. Asian women are at a premium!' This stunned me. I had never imagined that such a thing could be possible. In my opinion, all of us, with our flat faces and flat chests, were ugly. My desire had always been to find someone white and blond, but I didn't believe I really would.

"Today, I identify myself as Asian American. Of all the places in the world, including Japan and Korea, this country offers me the best chance to feel I belong. Not to say there aren't problems. But here, if I hear a racial slur, at least I can defend myself in my native tongue. I carry my sense of identity into my work as a literary agent. I'm interested in representing Asian American authors, in making our voices heard, especially on important issues such as race relations.

"I'm American because I live and work and feel at home here. But I'm also Asian. Coming to terms with my ethnic identity has also meant coming to terms with the inescapable fact that my father is and will always be a Korean male, with all the sense of privilege and narcissism accompanying that identification. As a child, I resented it. I saw my mother defer to him, trying to hide her sadness from me, sticking with the marriage for the sake of the children. But I'd fight back. There would be one piece of meat left on the table and I'd reach for it. My brother, six years older, wanted it too. 'I'm older,' he said. 'But you're done growing, you don't need to eat like that anymore,' I countered. Inevitably, my father would step in and tell me to give in, to be respectful to my brother. I could sulk all I wanted to but I wasn't going to get anything else to eat.

"My mother finally left my father when I was in high school. She went back to the States, and I was stuck with him for a full year. Things got so bad that we couldn't be in the same room together. I blamed him for driving her away. I had years of accumulated anger to draw from.

"But you know, that feeling has passed away. My father has mellowed and so have I. I am trying to salvage what I can from the relationship. He approves of me and of what I have done with my life, even leaving the law for my present career. And so I try to bear that in mind and just appreciate the support."

Tae, a clinical psychologist, believes that, as a young child, she learned to survive by filtering out the negative comments and rude remarks. She did not expect better treatment or feel much conscious anger about the racism; she simply found a way to remove it from her awareness. Recently, Tae found herself on the way to her car noticing a boy of about eight or nine walking with his mother in her direction. Suddenly, the thought broke through and became inescapably conscious: "This kid isn't staring or pointing at me! He's just walking over there, minding his own business, completely unfazed by the fact that there is this Asian lady a few feet away from him."

"Both of my parents were professionals who came to the U.S. seeking a better life. They came first on their own and then brought me at the age of seven. This was an enormous adjustment, and I still remember my mother dropping me off at the cafeteria (it was noon) on my first day of school, soon after arriving. School was a large, frightening place where children spoke a language I didn't understand. To this day, I can still remember being absolutely overpowered by the smell of all those peanut butter sandwiches being unwrapped around me. It wasn't until I started making this lunch for my own children that I could even tolerate the idea.

"My sister and I were the only Asians in the entire school. In a way, this worked to our advantage. For several years, school was primarily white, but then in a single year, there was a massive migration to the Philadelphia suburbs and overnight, it seemed, the student body became primarily black. As an Asian, I was treated like a novelty, a curiosity, and therefore not subjected to the harassment and even the beatings that the few remaining white kids suffered.

"But there was also this: I was learning all too well how to blend in, to acquiesce, to stay out of harm's way. This is a response to racism that is culturally sanctioned and it works. In addition, you have all these Asian parents pushing their children to achieve academically as a way to gain self-esteem. 'Just ignore what the kids are saying,' my mother advised. 'Make sure you are the top of your class, because actions speak louder than words.' I became good at filtering out the racist remarks. I developed a thick skin. In that sense, I believe it was good for me to grow up as I did. Today, I have a hard time when my kids complain about some small slight, real or imagined. 'Mom, he pushed me out of line when it was my turn to swing. And he hurt my feelings!' They don't look Korean (my husband is white) and I know this wasn't racially motivated. I listen to them, but I think to myself, 'How thin-skinned!'

"In high school, I was runner-up to the homecoming queen. I believed it was possible for me to be accepted by the dominant culture, but even getting this close did not mean that, inside, I stopped feeling different. My good friend had decided to nominate me for the title and I went along with her, but all the while I felt I was on exhibit. Several years later, I had an experience that confirmed those feelings.

"It was spring break and my boyfriend and I were on our way to Florida. We stopped in Columbia, South Carolina, for lunch. His parents had recently moved there. As soon as I walked into that restaurant, absolutely all conversation stopped. You could hear a pin drop. All eyes were on me as if I was the latest rare animal acquired by the zoo. It was very embarrassing, although at the time I covered it up with laughter, joked about it. But looking back, I know that what I really felt was that I had been invaded.

"I can't go back to Korea anymore and recapture that feeling of ease and comfort I experienced as a young child. I'm not really Korean, but then again, I'm also not white. I have to carve out my own identity and that's hard, because I have no role models, no guidance. I just have to invent it as I go along."

Racism takes many forms, wears many guises. At its most virulent, it assumes a murderous, genocidal rage. But even when it is innocent or unintentional, racism still has the power to hurt and to harm. My friend Linda told me the other day that she received a letter that was not intended to be insensitive. She was joined a group of therapists who put together a listing of various specialties they held. In order to save room, her ethnicity was designated by the simple three-letter abbreviation "JAP."

Looking back, I think one of the most hurtful parts of my

acquaintance with racism was the feeling of powerlessness, the sense of being totally unable to control others' judgments of or actions toward me. This is not an uncommon response.

Amanda's story is particularly instructive: She was raised by adoptive white parents and never knew her white mother or her Chinese father. Growing up, she really did not think of herself as Asian. And yet, the world sees what it wants to see, and children say what they want to say.

"I am in the middle of a course called 'Cross-Cultural Counseling.' One of the requirements was to write a paper on my culture of origin. For most of my life, I have had very little interest in or feeling of identification with my Asian background. In fact, the closest I generally get to Asian culture is when I sit in a Chinese restaurant and eat Chinese food. But because of this assignment, I have been thinking more consciously about the fact that, even though I was raised by white parents in a white environment, I am biologically half Chinese. And I made the decision to relate to the class an incident that took place when I was a child, one which I have never been able to share with anyone.

"I can remember the event like it happened yesterday. It was during the fourth grade that my peers and I began to notice that boys did not necessarily have cooties. On occasion, my friends and I would hang around with some of the more popular boys on the play yard. One day at recess, I was standing at the top of a small hill. For some reason, my girlfriends had already run off to join the soccer game in progress. I was alone with this one boy, who suddenly wheeled around, called me a 'Chink,' and spit in my face. To this day, I can feel the embarrassment and shame I experienced then.

"I remember standing there and wanting just to melt into the ground I was standing on. Instead, I quickly wiped the spit off my face and tried to act as if I was unharmed. I did not tell the yard duty or my teacher what had happened to me, nor did I tell any of my friends. All I wanted was to try to forget that it ever happened. The only redeeming piece was that none of my friends had been close enough to witness the incident. From that day on, I knew I *was* different. I learned never to go near that boy again. Throughout my school years, there were times I have wished for fine blond hair and blue eyes or even brunette hair. I would have loved to have been able to get rid of my thick black hair and almond-shaped eyes.

"Although I do not believe that this incident continues to affect how I see myself today, I know that for some time afterward, I was unable to accept a compliment with respect to the way I looked. I would downplay and basically dismiss any compliments about my physical appearance because I did not think that my physical characteristics were worthy of praise. I believed that the shape of my eyes and other Asian-like characteristics could not be good attributes. Fortunately, after learning more about who I am as a person from the inside out, I have been able to learn to lovingly accept the way I look.

"Today, I feel I am both white and a person of color. White not only because the woman who brought me into this world is white, but also because my adoptive parents are both white and have raised me as their own daughter. At the same time, I cannot deny that part of me would be considered a person of color. In addition to the knowledge that my biological father is Chinese, I am reminded on a daily basis, every time I look into the mirror, that I have Asian characteristics. So it is sometimes a struggle to try to honor both parts of who I am and be OK with each. I keep working on it."

Sometimes, we get pushed too far and we push back. We may not feel proud of our actions, may cringe in the retelling, but the fact is that it happens. Being a victim of racism, unfortunately, does not prevent us from passing it on. Among Asians, there is certainly intergroup conflict and prejudice. Even within a single country, there is intolerance of others who look like me but do not speak the same dialect. Terry, a thirty-two-year-old writer, speaks about her own experience of being on both the receiving and perpetrating side of racism. Either way, it hurts.

"In Alexandria, Virginia, I experienced the only intense period of racism I have known in my life. It was fourth grade, and the city had just started to enforce busing. Blacks were brought to our school; my younger brother was bused to the inner city. I was not particularly aware of my racial identity, but we knew there was a lot of racial tension. At that time, my best friend was Belinda, a light-skinned African American. We were very much the target of other black children, and I would come home daily with visible bruises, bloody noses.

"One day, in the cafeteria, I learned the difficult lesson that not only could I be the victim of racism, I could also be its perpetrator. Belinda and I were both crying, sick and tired of being bullied by the kids who called us 'Chink' and 'Chink lover.' The lunch monitors did nothing to intervene; they were probably scared of being accused of racism themselves. Finally, I had had it. I did something horrible; I screamed out, "Leave us alone, you niggers!" I didn't really understand what that word meant, but I knew it was something bad. Complete silence. Then Belinda and I were both sent to the principal's office to be disciplined, because we should 'have known better.' Shortly afterwards, my parents put me in an all-white parochial school. I never heard from Belinda again."

I would like a second chance with the man from Disneyland, the young men and women in the Great Falls parking lot, the patron in the Tiburon bakery. Depending on my mood, I would either like to come back with a really fine retort that leaves no room for further discussion, or if I'm feeling ornery, forget the wit and go for the jugular. I still think from time to time what I could say that would get through. But I guess what I'd like most of all, and fear will never be, is to live in a world where this doesn't happen. A place where we realize that causing pain and humiliation to others may provoke a few laughs or a moment of false bravado but that it ultimately diminishes the self, thus diminishing us all in the process.

11 ETHNICITY AND IDENTITY:
What It Means to Be Asian American

One fine autumn day when I was in seventh grade, my civics teacher called me to the front of the classroom. I assumed he wanted me to say something about the day's lesson, which I was more than prepared to do. Instead, he pulled out a yellow piece of construction paper and asked me to lay my arm against it. "See, class," he explained, "her skin isn't really yellow at all, it's more like an ivory color." He made his point and then dismissed me to my seat. Walking back to the fifth desk, first row nearest to the door, I could not have been more stunned. I was not angry with him. I knew this was his way of trying to confront racial stereotypes. Instead, I experienced a wave of self-loathing and shame that still crashes at the edge of my consciousness some thirty years later. The teacher was not at fault—it was *me*, with my ivory skin, my slanted eyes, my high cheekbones and foreign last name that was responsible for this situation. I have no idea how my classmates actually related to the civics lesson they were witnessing, but in my heart and in my memory, I still hear the giggles, the snickers, the jokes. They cannot be erased.

My sister and I used to fantasize about how our lives would be different if we could wake up one morning with blond hair and blue eyes. We would be popular. Boys would pay attention to us. Girls would not giggle and whisper when we walked into the room. In other words, we would be just like everyone else.

But for me, the desire to be white went a step further. What I did not fully understand at the time, what I kept to myself, was that I hated being Chinese. I was embarrassed about how I looked. I believed Chinese were rightfully second-class citizens, less worthy or valuable than whites. I did not want any Chinese friends because looking at their faces provided an unsettling and undesired reflection of my own countenance. I dated only white men and vowed to marry one. And when I did, I found myself feeling grateful to this man—who could trace his ancestors to the *Mayflower*—for marrying me despite my ethnicity. It is not just that I wanted to be white, or that I hated being different, it is that I hated *myself* because I was Chinese.

And yet, at the same time, I had very little real understanding of what being Chinese meant. As far as I was concerned, my language, my values, my dreams were no different from those of my white classmates and peers. I thought it was only my physical appearance that made me Chinese, and so I lived with a sense of despair that things would never change. I could be sixty years old, living in California or Texas or Lithuania, and would still be identified as Asian. Whatever was inside me would always be tempered by the fact of my facial features. The best I could hope for was to act as white as possible, and perhaps those around me would forget my ethnicity.

Today I am at a point in my life where I no longer wish I were someone other than who I am. Now I know that, for better or worse, I have more Chinese in me than just the genes for black hair or short stature. My mother may have baked brownies for us to take to school, but *her* grandmother struggled to walk from room to room with bound feet. I am *both* Chinese and American, a product of history and present circumstance, and if I choose to devalue or reject either side, I will never be able to experience myself as a whole person. Now, because I have had a taste of wholeness, because I feel like a woman who has taken secrets out of their ancient hiding places and exposed them to the clear pure light of day, I recognize that there is no turning back.

The quest to integrate ethnicity and identity is not an easy one, or a singular event, but a process. I will probably always have questions and doubts. I may never be able to fully eradicate the shame I felt as a child, but each new bit of information or shared connection is one more piece of the puzzle in place.

Part of the journey for me has involved discovering what it is about me that I can attribute to being Chinese. This is probably a question with no definitive answer, but there are certain things I know to be true about myself that feel more Asian than Western. This intuition has been confirmed in my conversations with women of similar backgrounds. For example: my relationship with my mother. My elitist attitudes about education and occupation. My work ethic. My discomfort with promoting myself or my work. My deference to authority. My need to excel. My reserve. My ability to save money and defer gratification. My self-control and my discomfort with others who do not censor strong displays of emotion in public. Some of these traits have been helpful, others have probably held me back; but they are still part of who I am, where I come from. And in the act of making this discovery I have experienced the joy of recognition: "Oh, you mean you also have a hard time expressing affection? It isn't just me? Maybe it's one of those Asian things." I feel less alone, less strange, and in me a deep human longing for connection and twinship is satiated.

I have also had to come to terms with being different. Several years ago, a Caucasian friend told me that he didn't think of me as Asian, simply as Claire. That statement was something I had been longing to hear all my life. What surprised me, however, was that it didn't have the kind of magic I thought it would. In a way, I no longer want this. I felt like saying to him, "Well, the fact is, I *am* Chinese. I'm not exactly like you and I wish you could see that. Otherwise, I feel denied and unacknowledged." In fact, I realize that I have lived with differentness for so long that it has become part of who I am. Some of my self-esteem derives from being set apart from the crowd; I'm starting to feel a little threatened when I see all these other Asian American women wanting to become therapists. You mean I'm not the only one anymore?

How do other Asian American women identify themselves? Not an easy question to answer, but I believe it is the core around which life choices, perceptions, and values revolve. The extent to which one identifies more with one's Asian heritage or more with American current circumstances influences the whole of a woman's life. Subtly or not, that identification colors her choice of career, marriage partner, friends, child-rearing philosophy, and allegiance to family of origin. When she stands at the crossroads and needs to make a choice, it is from this reservoir of ethnicity and identity that she will draw inspiration. In other words, whether or not she was born here, a woman with strong ties to her Asian background is not as likely to marry an unsuitable husband or embark on a career that her parents find unacceptable.

Very broadly speaking, women seem to find a place of identity in one of several venues. Many women would describe themselves as essentially American. They do not necessarily reject their Asian heritage, but neither do they give it much thought. It simply does not play a critical role in their self-image. They may be able to speak a few words of Japanese or Korean and celebrate the occasional New Year's with their family, but otherwise, they would be hard-pressed to say what it is about themselves that makes them Asian. These women believe they fit into American society as it is constructed; they tend to emphasize what it is about being human that transcends skin color or national origin.

For others, the attempt to locate ethnicity in the overall scheme of identity is more of an ongoing struggle. Women like myself tend to use the term "Asian American" (or, more specifically, Chinese American) to describe ourselves. I think we do this for several reasons. First is the recognition that our identity really lies somewhere in between, in a place that is hard to pin down. But also to recognize that both the Asian and the American influences are important, twin magnetic poles that hold in suspended animation the globe of our lives. I use this admittedly nebulous term because I don't feel fully American or fully Chinese. I am some kind of strange new hybrid and I have to make my own way. I have to decide what "being Asian American" means to *me*. And this is both the challenge and the obstacle: possibilities are limitless, but I am walking in uncharted territory without benefit of a map or a guide.

"Asian American" also has political overtones. Some women choose this designation because "American" too often means "white," and they do not feel that Asians or other women of color have a place of value in the dominant culture. For these women, the legacy of the internment, the history of repressive legislation against Asians of all origins, cannot be disregarded. The stories of our parents and grandparents trying to make a life in this new land become a part of us. We enjoy comforts born of their sweat and their tears.

Finally, there are women like my mother's friend Carol who have lived here many years but still see themselves as "100 percent Chinese." She says, "I eat Chinese food, have Chinese friends, think Chinese. When I have some money, I send it to my parents because I was taught from an early age that I should obey them whether they love me or not." Carol is in her seventies and this is her view: "I am deep rooted in the Chinese way. I believe that the exact same flower—a chrysanthemum or a rose—grows differently in America than it does in China. Maybe it is the same for people. If I was born here, even to the same parents, I would be a different person. But since I was born in China, I am Chinese." For these women, the core of their identity was fixed in China, or Japan, or Korea. External Western layers can be added, a woman can grow to feel comfortable among her American peers, but at the deepest place of identity, she still feels Asian.

For Cathy, ethnicity is very much a part of her identity. The dilemma she faces is how to keep her cultural legacy alive through the generations, how to pass it on.

"I feel I have a very strong Korean American identity. I grew up primarily with Caucasians in a rural community in northwest Washington state, but my first language was Korean and I spoke it until I went to kindergarten. I am concerned that, in a few generations, the Korean part of our family will just fade away, that my grandchildren won't even know how to use chopsticks—or that's the *only* Asian thing they'll be familiar with. To me, being Korean American means that I could never go back there to live, but I'm not entirely American either. I'm somewhere in between. And that is a place of identity for me.

"My dad came to the U.S. to get his Ph.D. Because there were so few other Koreans at the time they arrived in Pullman, my parents felt it was important for us to assimilate as quickly as possible. They knew no English when they came, but by the time my brother, two years younger, was ready for school, he already spoke the language quite well. I learned English easily, but I never had the sense of not wanting to speak Korean. In fact, we still speak a mix of the two languages at home. Some concepts are just better expressed in one language or in the other, and I feel lucky to have access to both.

"As an adolescent, sometimes I felt my life would have been easier if I were white. I think all Asians go through that to some degree. Things would have been less complicated if my parents were more like the parents of my friends. For example, if their English was perfect. Or if they weren't always making people take off their shoes every time they came into the house. Stuff like that. But it wasn't a major issue. I never disliked myself or felt others disliked me for being Korean American.

"I was aware that some things about our family set us apart from many of my peers. Definitely grades and school. Even though many of my classmates were also the children of professors, they seemed to have much more leeway. Getting A's wasn't the big celebratory thing it was in our house. But then again, they didn't think a B+ was a bad grade. My two best friends were very social. To them, it was a good semester if they didn't get too many C's. Part of what kept our friendship intact was that we never compared report cards. I do remember occasionally getting less than an A in math (my father has a Ph.D. in that subject) and wishing my parents wouldn't make such a big deal about it, but mostly, I wanted the good grades for myself. Now, in grad school, where everyone else also works really hard, I feel right at home.

"I also know that my parents have a pretty traditional Korean marriage and that they put up with a lot in each other. Dissolving the marriage is never an issue. My mother is a feminist in some ways and she has confided in me that she doesn't feel she has fulfilled her potential because her culture relegated her to the role of wife and mother. I want something different for myself. That's why, at this point, I'm not sure I want children. I don't want to face that conflict. Of course, my mother tells me I'll change my mind, as she did.

"I am dating a Caucasian man right now. He's interested in Asian issues, does environmental work in Vietnam. No one in my family has yet married Korean. But in a reversal of how I felt as a teenager, I believe it would be simpler if *I* married a Korean American man. Sometimes I think to myself, 'Oh, my God. If I marry this Caucasian man, my family is no longer going to be Korean from *here on out.*' I know I am putting this pressure on myself, but it is a real conflict."

Meg is a Japanese American woman who has given a lot of thought to her own struggles around the issue of identity.

"For me, the question of ethnicity and identity is very important, but also very complicated. So much of me is American, but at the core, I am really Asian. This makes for a lot of confusion in my life and brings up questions I can't answer. For example, I observe a number of Japanese customs, such as tea ceremony. I value these traditions, they enrich my life. Yet, at the same time, knowing that Japanese have the highest rate of out-marriages of all the Asians, I foresee that in a few generations, our culture will be lost, indiscernible. On the one hand, this is a loss, but on the other, I have a Zen orientation and believe that, fundamentally, we are all one. Part of me also believes that when people attach to their differentness it is part of the process of gaining self-esteem, but that it may not ultimately be what we should be seeking. I feel torn.

"My parents were both interned, and I was born in camp. However, I didn't really find out anything about my parents' experience until I was seventeen. They just did not talk about it. Same with Hiroshima. My grandmother was killed in the bombing, but for months afterwards, my mother couldn't get any word on whether her mother had survived or not. Finally, she did get some sort of communication saying that my grandmother had died. She didn't talk about that either. My parents and others like them were experiencing a kind of amnesia about the facts of war, life in the camps.

"I think that for them, and for myself, one of the primary effects of these experiences has been the abiding need to prove myself, to overcompensate. So if my brother goes into Boy Scouts, he's got to be an Eagle Scout. Good is never good enough. That's partly why I dropped out of grad school almost thirty years ago and am just now able to return to work on my doctorate. The Japanese part of me was very uncomfortable speaking up in class, raising my hand, being recognized. I had a very hard time being successful in that environment.

"I also feel that some of my Japanese attitudes or beliefs are not helpful in the work I do (social work). I grew up believing in the value of stoicism, 'pulling yourself up by your own bootstraps,' etc., but I don't think I should impose those values on people who come from a different culture than I do. So I try to be aware of them, to rein them in.

"This has been such a thorny issue for me. In the sixties, I went to see a therapist. The question I was trying to ask was 'Who am I, really?' I don't think the therapist, who was white, could help me. I wasn't able to articulate how I felt as a marginal person, a 'hyphenated' person. What it means to live day after day, twenty-four hours a day, as an identifiable minority."

As a psychotherapist, Marion is particularly interested in the ways that culture interacts with personality. She speaks to a dilemma shared by other Asian American women: What do you do with Asian values learned as a child that hinder your progress in the world today? For example, if a supervisor challenges you to be more assertive, if a professor marks you down for not actively participating in class discussion, do you seek to *overcome* those traits of modesty and reserve that may be deeply ingrained? Or, is it possible to retain some of these values and work instead to educate peers and colleagues as to a different way of looking at the world? If you find yourself consistently opting for Western behavioral traits, what does that do to your sense of identity?

*   *   *

"I am more assertive now. I just can't let things go the way I used to. If something is wrong, I will call the manager. Maybe I'm becoming more Western, maybe it's just that I'm too old for this. But I still hope I've retained some of my Japanese values, that I haven't lost all my modesty.

"I grew up in central California on the family farm. My parents met at camp. In fact, three siblings in one family married three in the other, so that we formed a very tight-knit community that was also traditionally Japanese. I grew up with Japanese language school and memories of my grandmother, a Shinto Buddhist, saying her prayers every morning as the sun rose. I don't remember not liking who I was although I know I had some desire to look more white. One time, a Mexican kid named Peter called me a Jap, so I chased him around the playground. I didn't understand what he was talking about, but I knew it wasn't good.

"I went from high school to Reedly Junior College, which was only a half mile away, but a world apart. Sophomore year, I suffered a major depression, slept all the time, gained twenty pounds. My mother never said a peep. Now I realize she simply didn't believe it was real. I thought the problem was that I had a crush on this guy who never even noticed me. But I think the larger issue, which I couldn't really see at the time, was that moving from high school to college was a step closer to the real world. I realized for the first time that racism really did exist, we weren't all equal, and that my being Japanese might not be viewed positively by others. Things were so segregated—whites sat at one table, Asians at another, blacks at yet another. It was very discouraging and shattered my worldview.

"I decided that I needed to find some answers for myself and applied to San Francisco State. I was accepted, but I had to apply for financial aid because my parents only had enough money to send my older sister to school. This provoked a big fight. Applying for a loan required a W2, which would show how little money they made. What would other people think? The whole thing was shameful to them, but I had to get away. The atmosphere in Reedly was suffociating. People knew everything that happened to you as soon as it occurred.

"Then the strike at SF State took place and I became involved with the Asian American student movement. Cesar Chavez was trying to organize and I got very rhetorical, talking about the oppression of workers, etc. I even tried to politicize my parents, who at least tolerated me. From college I went to Japan, where I realized I was really an American. Then I went to Berkeley, where I studied mental health and got involved with dance, founding a repertory group called 'Unbound Spirit.' As our group started to receive favorable press, my uncles would point out to my parents that 'Marion is in the newspapers again.' So my work was legitimized and my parents could accept it.

"After leaving the dance company, I married a Chinese man from whom I am now separated. My friends all tried to warn me, 'You're going to marry the *only son* of a Chinese family?' They were right; the generational differences proved to be unbreachable. He has not separated from his mother yet. I understand the Asian notion of interdependence, but in this case, it was excessive. That kind of connection may be healthy in China, but not here.

"I am interested in what the concept Japanese American really means. I realize that I carry a lot of values that the Japanese who live over there might have, but here they are distorted; there isn't the cultural consistency. For example, if someone compliments me, I would say, 'Oh no, this isn't really a nice dress. It's just something my sister handed down to me.' But here you are supposed to acknowledge the giver of the compliment by accepting it. Now I'm just trying to bite my tongue and simply say thank you.

"When I'm with other Japanese, I tend to be more humble, which Westerners would call self-effacing. For a while, I tried to figure out whether this meant I lacked self-confidence. But now, I see it this way—it's only a problem if we believe what we do *is* self-effacing.

"At the Psychotherapy Institute, I was the only Asian among white and Jewish students. I felt like a fish out of water. One day, I was supposed to make an oral presentation to my class on dreams. I stood up and prefaced my remarks by saying, 'I've done my best to record these dreams, but I'm not sure how accurate they are. . . .' The professor interrupted and said, 'Don't apologize, Marion, just go ahead with it.' I was mortified. Being Japanese, I wanted the group to accept me, I didn't want to appear boastful in front of them. A white client told me, 'You know, Marion, sometimes you say things I just don't understand. You're so circumspect.' What I realized then is that I still 'talk Japanese' although in English.

"Now, with my kids, I take the position that they need to know they are Japanese because I am Japanese. In fact, I chose to give them Japanese first names because their last names already provide the identification with their Chinese side. A friend of mine, a Sansei even, once asked me what I had named my children. When I told him 'Kenji and Yuki,' his response was, 'Why would you do a thing like that?' He tried to suggest something more Anglo sounding and I got so mad thinking, 'Why should we try to hide who we are?'

"I'm aware that I still have that self-consciousness, that Japanese paranoia about what others will think. So when my kids start screaming at me to buy Doritos in the grocery store, I tell them flat out, 'If you keep that up, Mom will be embarrassed.' I don't think there is anything wrong with teaching them about family honor, family ties, but I know that ultimately they will learn more from my behavior than my words. So they may learn some modesty, but they'll also see me upholding Western ways of being. I'd like my kids to go to the Buddhist church, but I'm also a psychotherapist. I'm weird that way."

The first time I interviewed a woman from Hawaii, it was a real shock. I couldn't imagine being American but growing up in a part of the country where Asians are part of the dominant culture and where ethnicity is really not an issue. Annette shared her views on growing up Japanese in Hawaii. Like others in her situation, it was not until she traveled to the mainland that she got a taste of what life as a minority might feel like. But because she was grounded already in a solid sense of self and culture, this experience did not fundamentally alter her view of herself.

* * *

"I was born and raised in Hawaii and I think that really colors my perception of how I see myself as Asian or, more specifically, as Japanese. There is such a large Asian population there—Asians in political office, as the superintendent of schools, etc.—that in a sense, there was almost a form of reverse discrimination against whites. They call Hawaii the 'melting pot' and I think it's true; the races really do get along. So I grew up feeling comfortable about who I was. I never felt excluded in any way.

"My mother was raised in Japan and my dad was a Kibbei (born in the U.S. but educated in Japan). In some ways, he was a traditional Japanese man, stoic and quiet. For example, my sister and I recently discovered some clippings, papers in an old scrap album that indicated my father had had to go through the courts in order to get his citizenship back because he was studying at Meiji University (in Japan) at the time of the war. He never said a thing about this before, and he still doesn't talk about whether he was angry that it happened. But my mom is different—she speaks her mind, is very outgoing, and sort of 'wears the pants' in the family. In my marriage now, I also have a lot of say in how things are run. That's part of the reason I have no real burning interest to go back to visit Japan anytime soon; I think it would be hard to be in an environment where women are expected to be so deferential to men.

"My sister is much more into Japanese cultural issues and traditions. I'm kind of spending my time working on my business and professional connections. Sometimes I feel bad that I don't share her drive to reestablish our cultural roots.

"Last year, we went on a pilgrimage to Tule Lake, one of the internment camps. I remember a certain building, kind of a prison for the more unruly detainees, bare cement floors, two or three levels of beds. Much of the rest you just had to imagine. It was interesting, but I have to say I probably wouldn't have made the time to go there if my sister wasn't so interested. We're very close, so I felt I'd like to accompany her. I think that because I didn't actually know anyone who went to camp, not even relatives, it doesn't have a real or personal significance for me. Simply the fact that Japanese men and women were detained there is not enough to make that connection.

"At the same time, I do notice I feel more comfortable around Asians. If I'm at a sales function, I guess I naturally gravitate toward the other Asians in the room, even if they only make up 1 percent of the people there. I've dated Caucasian guys, but I knew I'd prefer an Asian man; there would be a comfort level there that would just make life easier. For example, when I was invited to a boyfriend's home, I liked to observe the traditional Japanese custom of bringing a gift. The white men I dated were always like 'Why do you bother?' Or, 'You don't need to do that, don't get so stressed out about it.' They didn't understand that it made *me* feel more comfortable. I also think we are in fact more repressed, don't share as much of ourselves. Because of this, whites see us as uncommunicative. You don't run into this issue as much with an Asian partner.

"I have not experienced much racism. Growing up as I did, I expect equitable treatment—both in business and interpersonal relationships. Even coming to the mainland, *I* didn't feel like a minority. But I experience, while traveling for my job, being on the receiving end of racism. My husband and I were leaving New York, standing in a long line waiting to get our bags checked. We were tired, eager to be on our way, when this lady pushes ahead of us. I said, 'Excuse me, but there is a line here.' She took one look at me and suggested I 'go back where I came from.' I was shocked. I hate to admit this, but I turned right around and told her she should shut up. I'm sure she expected me just to be quiet, mousy, not say anything. She didn't say another word. Walked off to another line.

"When we have children, I hope they will feel as comfortable with their identity as I am with mine. If they experience some type of discrimination because they are Asian, I would tell them they are worthwhile, special people, and they should be proud of themselves. I want to pass my self-confidence and belief about fairness on to them. But of course, I realize it's easy to say this when it hasn't actually happened yet. I just hope it works out that way."

Gloria also grew up in Hawaii and felt no sense of discomfort with her Japanese heritage. However, in moving to the main-land, she started to take a closer look at what about her is Japanese: both the positive things and the traits that might make her life more difficult.

"I was raised in Hawaii, running around barefoot among the coffee and sugarcane plants on my parents' farm. I was always surrounded by extended family: aunts and uncles and even a great-grandfather. My grandmother has a very special place in my heart—she took care of me while my mother worked. She always knew exactly how to console me when my parents might have harsh words for me. And when we stayed at her house, I was the one who would sleep with her.

"Japanese are the majority where I grew up and I have always felt very proud of my heritage. Almost all my teachers were Asian, with the exception of Miss Williams, the imposing white-haired battle-ax of a kindergarten teacher. One day they served macaroni and cheese at school. We never had cheese at home and I told her I could not eat this. 'Yes, you can!' she replied, then proceeded to shove a forkful into my mouth. Which I promptly threw up. She made me clean up the mess. Somehow, my father got wind of this incident and he let her have it.

"I remember a white friend in fourth grade. She was the daughter of one of the two doctors in town and the granddaughter of a very wealthy landowner. But one day at recess, she told me that she had always wished she was Japanese.

"Moving from Hawaii to the mainland, even if northern California, involved real culture shock. At that time, Stanford had only two hundred Asians out of a student body of more than four thousand. I used to sit in class and count how many of them there were, how many of us. I still do that. I also got my first real exposure to the fact that Japanese were not always liked. This was very depressing.

"As the oldest child, I was always expected to set an example. I knew that if anything ever happened to my parents, I would be the one responsible for my younger sisters. Perhaps that is why I see myself as the most Japanese of my siblings. After my father died, my mother wanted to honor the traditional Buddhist rituals, with ceremonies at forty-nine days, at a year, and so on. The next anniversary is coming up this summer and there's no question that I'll go. My youngest sister and her husband, however, thinking they hadn't had a 'real vacation' for a while, preferred to use their time off to better advantage than spending it with family. That's not how I see things. But recently, I've been starting to let go of my need to always be responsible for my sisters. If June says she can cook the dinner, I now tell her that would be nice.

"In my present position as the director of a college counseling center, I am finding that I have to learn how to stand up for myself, be confrontational if confrontation is called for. I'm probably most comfortable with the softer, nonassertive approach, that 'Asian woman's stuff,' but I can fight my battles if I need to. And I have finally done something about a stereotype that is definitely projected onto me as a woman, as an Asian. I am expected to do the nurturing of the staff. I used to plan birthday parties, open my house for staff retreats, etc. My contributions were expected but never acknowledged. So I recently made the decision: I stopped offering to arrange everything. You know what? We don't have parties here anymore."

The question of identity becomes very complicated when additional influences are added to the mix. May grew up in a Chinese family headed by a traditionally matriarchal grandmother, went to school in a predominantly black neighborhood, wrestled with conflicts between the words of her Catholic priest and the practices of her parents, and ended up in corporate white America.

"As a little girl, I played mostly with black children and, until the age of seven, thought I, too, was black. One day at school, a friend informed me otherwise. I didn't believe her. I ran in to ask my teacher. She looks at me and says, 'Sweetheart, you are not black.' 'Oh,' I asked, 'you mean because my hair is different?' 'Well, actually, it's more than just that . . .' Her words were quite a revelation, but they did not fundamentally alter my view of myself. Later in life, I would pass this information on to my friend Albert, a Chinese man who also grew up in a black neighborhood, wore dreadlocks, and thought of himself as African American. 'Albert, honey,' I told him, 'I've been through that already and believe me, you *are not* black!'

"For me, the real identity conflict of childhood came about because the Catholic Church was telling me one thing, but my grandmother was telling me another. Po Po, who is really the one who raised me while my mother worked in a sweatshop to try to supplement Father's income, expected her family to participate in ancestor worship. We would burn paper money and other items to honor the spirits of dead relatives. My priest, however, forbade me to carry out such practices, saying it was against the religion. So there I was, participating in Chinese traditions by day, feeling horribly guilty, and praying at night for forgiveness for my sins.

"To make things even more complicated, my father was this very flamboyant man. Once, working as a bus boy on his way up to Canada, he stopped in South Dakota to practice his archery, a skill he had learned as a young boy in China (where, incidentally, he had been treated like a little emperor—never having to walk anywhere, always carried on people's backs). This Indian chief watched him and was so impressed that he asked my dad to teach his son archery. They became friends. Dad helped Chief White Cloud secure water rights for his tribe. And then, after we were born, he put together this cowboys and Indians show, complete with us onstage, holding balloons on our heads as targets for his arrows. A modern-day William Tell.

"I went to UC Berkeley. But after a year of college, the academic and financial pressures got to me. Plus, as the oldest daughter, I was still expected to run out to Po Po's every Friday night to do her bidding. So I married this African American man I was dating as a way out, but several months into the marriage realized I had made a mistake. We split up, but I was too ashamed to tell anyone. After a few years, we got back together, had a baby, split up again. By and large, my family supported me, but what really hurt was that my brother, whom I idolized, turned his back on me. He hated blacks. Po Po was OK with the relationship as long as it didn't interfere with my taking care of her.

"Now I'm working in a largely white corporate environment. I try to maintain a good relationship with my co-workers, but don't reveal much of my personal life to them. The thing that gets to me is that I'm treated as if I am ethnically invisible, so I'm privy to all the racial slurs, the ethnic jokes tossed around the office. 'Niggers' are called 'losers' in my presence. I don't want to be confrontational, but I will ask people to change the subject. I know they don't realize that I am in a relationship with another African American man I have known for twelve years. I just don't talk about that. Even people who know us still look at Ben and me like some kind of 'mystery couple.'

"I see myself now as 'multilayered.' I can call on different parts of myself in order to feel comfortable in a given situation. A white friend once confessed to me that she had never been exposed to Hispanics or blacks and therefore wasn't at ease with them. I appreciate her honesty and have learned to value other attributes. And while I pride myself in being able to cross color and class lines with no difficulty whatsoever, I don't necessarily expect my friends to be able to do the same."

Susan, who has spent half her life in Taiwan and half her life here, is in a unique position to comment on what ethnicity means to her. She was raised in a traditional Asian household, but was also exposed to Western ideas as a young adult. As Asian American women, we all have to make choices about how much to pursue the lead of the dominant culture, how much to retain values and ways of being from our culture of origin. For many women, this is a seemingly effortless and largely unconscious process that leads to acculturation. But for others, it takes a deliberate effort to sort out the various strands of influence and to retain certain Asian cultural values, incorporate these into one's self-concept.

"Two years ago, I thought to myself, 'I've lived here just as many years as I lived in Taiwan.' Twenty-five years in each country, to be exact. At this point, I couldn't go back there to live. The standard of living, the relative lack of freedom would make life difficult. I have a theory that, after three years of living anywhere, it becomes home. So this is home for me now and I am trying to make it work. Still, I know there are Chinese parts of me that will never change, just as there are American parts. For example, I can swear in English, but even though I know the words, it is impossible to say them out loud in Chinese. Same with sex. Can't even mention the concept in my native tongue.

"This is what it was like for me growing up. China has been an imperial country for five thousand years. Everyone wants to be the emperor or the empress. The bus driver is the emperor of his domain, yells at his passengers. At home, it's mother or father, depending on who has the power. In our family, my father was the emperor when he was home from military duties. As soon as he stepped in the door, all noise would cease, and he would give his orders. The rest of the time, my mother tried to be the empress, but she had a number of problems and couldn't carry out that role. So it fell to my oldest sister.

"After three daughters, my mother finally had a son. But he died before I was born and somehow I took on the expectations she had for him. When I look at old photos, I see myself always dressed in pants, wearing a short haircut. As the 'boy,' I felt I could do whatever I wanted and consequently grew up with greater self-esteem than my sisters. My older sister would deny this, but I know that she dated only men with our last name so that when she married, she could carry on the family name. She believed she had to do this.

"But as the 'boy' I also suffered. When I was seven years old, the fuses blew one day. If we couldn't fix it, we'd have to wait a week for Dad to come home and live without electricity in the meantime. So, without any hesitation, I offered to change the fuses. It was a dangerous, scary thing to do. I told myself, 'You can do this because you are a boy.' Then they were all praising me, telling me how brave I was. But inside I didn't feel brave, I felt I had no choice.

"I married almost exactly the man my parents would have chosen for me, had it been up to them. The perfect résumé: Harvard, good temperament, even the right height. When they heard the news, my mother said, 'Everything about him is fine. Except that he is Cantonese.' Cantonese or not, I already knew what they were most interested in. My oldest sister had announced her engagement and been greeted with the automatic first question: Where did he go to school? And the automatic follow-up: What did he study? So, when my brother-in-law introduced me to Mitchell, I was overwhelmed. I told myself, 'This is too good to be true! It must be fate!' We got married three months after we met.

"As I get older, I am becoming more and more Chinese. Earlier on, I was more Western, but now I am trying to hold on to the positive parts of my culture and to live them. One way I know I am Chinese is the value I place on extended family. In my thirties, I dated this white high-priced lawyer, we had a lot of good times together. He owned a Cessna and we'd fly halfway across the state just to eat dinner at some restaurant. But I knew by the way he treated his eighty-year-old mother that a serious relationship between us would never work out. He was very wealthy, and while his mother was not exactly living in poverty, she had only her Social Security check to depend on. Once I asked him how much money he gave to her, and he said, 'Why should I give her any money? She'd probably just smoke it away anyhow.' He seemed so heartless to me.

"And then I asked him if he'd like to meet my family. He got all excited, all dressed up. We went to have dinner with my aunt, and Ted was flabbergasted. He absolutely could not fathom how I conceived of her as family, and felt that I was doing things for *her* that he wouldn't even consider doing for his own mother. After we left, he asked 'Why did you lie to me?' To me, 'extended family' and 'nuclear family' are pretty much the same thing. I don't make those kinds of distinctions and this incident just proved to me how different we were.

"Sometimes I get discouraged about trying to reclaim my heritage. But then I am reminded of an old Chinese proverb, 'Water will prevail.' The hardest ax may not be able to split the rock, but water, one drop at a time, falling persistently, will eventually erode it. If you do the right thing, eventually things will work out."

Finally, a story of a woman who has lived in the United States for nine years. Xiao-Yen is a filmmaker whose feature film, *Monkey Kid,* garnered honors as an official selection of the Cannes Festival International du Film. Her perspective on identity is drawn from the wellspring of varied sources: her experience as a little girl growing up in the Cultural Revolution, the influence of her parents—her mother particularly—her exposure, at the age of twenty-seven, to life in the United States, and most certainly, to her own indomitable spirit.

"When I first came to the U.S. from China nine years ago, a fellow employee at the restaurant where I was working said, 'You need an American name. Something people can relate to. How about Shirley? That sounds like Xiao Yen.' So I said OK, and I was Shirley for a while. But now I don't care if they have problems with the *X* in my name. My name is my name and that's the way I'm keeping it. It's the same with my identity. I may live and work in the U.S. with my Caucasian husband and our four-year-old daughter, but I *know* I am Chinese. I don't even think of myself as Chinese American. To me, that means people who were born in this country and don't speak Chinese.

"I am very proud of my Chinese heritage. I love the stories, the history, the folktales. I love to tell the story of the Monkey King! And yet, as soon as I stepped foot in the U.S., I felt happy. In fact, I even wrote home to my mother that I had learned, for the first time in my life, how to really smile. It didn't bother me that I now looked different from everyone around me, because in China, I had always *felt* different inside. My mother was not typical for her generation. She was very encouraging and supported me in becoming my own person. My father wanted me to be a doctor because he is ill and hoped that I could take care of him, but my mother gave me art lessons when she noticed how much I loved to draw. Back in the dark, gray days of the Cultural Revolution, she would dress me in bright cheerful colors, which always set me apart from my classmates. And when it was allowed, she even encouraged me to try using rollers to curl my hair!

"Some things I definitely like better about the U.S. For example, how they raise children here. In China, everything is very rigid, you must behave just a certain way. But it takes constant supervision and fierce looks from parents and teachers to maintain that discipline. As soon as the teacher's back is turned, the kids go crazy. Here, kids may look less well behaved, but if they follow the right path, it's because they want to, not because they feel they *have* to. In China, although children are loved, they have no rights. It is the parents' place to put children down, to tell them that they don't know what they're talking about because they're too young. I don't want that for my daughter. In fact, as much as I'd like her to continue to speak Chinese, I hesitate to send her to one of those Chinese schools where much attention will be paid to children lining up in straight lines.

"It's difficult to say exactly what may have changed in me as a result of living here. Those are really very subtle shifts. But I guess the way I see it is that, even though the core of my identity is fixed, I am flexible enough to take on ideas or values if they work for me. I *am* Chinese, but I can talk to my daughter and really listen to what she has to say!"

I believe that, for Asian American women, ethnicity is part of identity. No matter how Western or "white" we may feel or act, there is a way in which we view the world through the lens of our ethnicity, there is a way in which the Asian values that were passed on to us—even if diluted—resonate in our lives today. For some women, this process may occur at a subtle or even an imperceptible level, but it happens whether we realize it or not. My friend Joanne shares this example.

"My parents were visiting recently. One evening, my mother helped me to cook dinner, when she burned an expensive new pot I had just received as a present. I spent a lot of time scrubbing and trying to restore it. My mother hovered and hovered. It was clear she felt bad, but she just could not bring herself to say those simple words, 'I'm sorry.' I became angrier and angrier, but I didn't say anything. Finally, I was able to get the pot clean. My mother turned to me and said, 'I'm glad it's OK now.'

"And in that instant, I understood that this was the closest she could come; it hit me with the force of lightning that my parents had never *once* apologized for anything they had done. Somehow, this time I was able to see the behavior in its cultural context: Parents simply do not apologize to children. I saw my mother's words to me in a new light and I found, as she was speaking, that there were tears in my eyes. And I realized that *I* do this too: I have a very hard time saying I'm sorry to people I care about."

Ethnicity influences identity not only because of internal processes (ingrained expectations, values retained or rejected), but also because of interactions with the world outside. No matter how we personally feel about being Asian American, others will continue to see us from their vantage point, and that can run the gamut from idealization to cold, hard hatred. Thus, a Chinese baby adopted and raised by white parents in a white community still has to live with the fact that others will see her black hair and make certain assumptions about her.

For myself, after the painful years of childhood, I entered a long period of my life when I really didn't think much about being "Chinese." I concentrated on being the "Claire" my friend had spoken of, worrying about jobs or making money, or finding a mate. Once in a while, a racist slur would break my composure like a slap across the face, but on the whole, I gave my ethnicity very little conscious thought.

All of that has changed. Understanding and accepting the Chinese part of me provides a new perspective on myself, on the world. Even if I wanted to, I would not return to the vision I once held. A vision notable for what it lacked as much as for what it contained.

12 ETHNICITY AND IDENTITY: *Creating a Sense of Self*

Who can say how ethnic identity is formed? Is it nurtured like the seed in the soil by parents who cultivate ways of thinking, values, preferences? Does it develop in response to the external world, a reaction to the stereotypes and perceptions promulgated "out there"? Is the simple fact of distinctive physical appearance enough to form the core of an identity, around which other influences solidify, the grain of sand that eventually becomes the pearl?

This is not a question that can be answered with certainty. But I believe there are a number of factors that influence the extent to which a person identifies with one or both cultures. First are the demographic characteristics: age, generational status, date of personal or family immigration. Also significant is the availability of extended family and ethnic community (especially as a child), peer influences, relationships with parents, sociopolitical events such as the internment, and exposure to political ideology, for example, the movement to ensure civil rights for Asian Americans. But perhaps the single most important factor is simply individual preference, which itself is based on life experience and temperament. Thus, two children growing up in the same house could come to maturity with different ideas about their ethnicity.

I believe that by the time an Asian American woman reaches

adulthood, she chooses how to identify herself. That choice may be largely unconscious, but it is still a manifestation of individual will. After all, isn't this the grand and glorious thing about the American experience: the opportunity to define yourself, to forge your own image? Living here, the notion of the frontier, with its promise of transformation, beckons to us all.

In this chapter are stories of women who have worked, sometimes against tremendous odds, to resolve this question of ethnicity and identity.

Doreen, who lives in a small town in North Carolina, talks about her struggle to hold on to the Asian half of her heritage.

"Today began as all others with a quick shower and a look in the mirror asking myself, 'Who am I?' Then, off to work I went. It is early fall and my skin is beginning to fade back to a natural yellow-ivory color. This is one of those minor features of mine that always provokes a question in the minds of curious people. In the course of this day, a co-worker placed his arm next to mine and asked, 'Are you one of *those*?' 'Yes,' I answered quietly. 'My father was Chinese.'

"Ever since I can remember, I have felt different, I have had this sense inside that I was not like the people who surrounded me. Everyone in my family is tall, red-haired, green-eyed. I'm short and on the stocky side. Doing good at five five and a half. No legs. Eyes slanted just a little too much. Face just a little too round. In the fourth grade, the teacher had us project our profiles on an overhead. My nose was so flat, the kids all started laughing. And when my beautiful, tall white mother, who is of Welsh-Scottish descent, got mad at me, which she did frequently, she'd scream, 'You have such a *fat, flat, ugly* nose.'

"My mother put her maiden name on my birth certificate. No father. Virgin birth, of course. When I was twelve, she admitted that the man she was married to was not my father. But she refused to tell me who my real father was. One Christmas she asked what I wanted. 'The name of my father,' I said, not missing a beat. No answer. So I continued to feel different, to look at myself in the mirror and try to figure it out. I used to cut that long blond hair off my Barbies; it made me mad that I was never given a doll who looked like me. For a long time, I was bitter about the Miss America pageant, never a dark-skinned or dark-haired beauty queen.

"Two years ago, I got my hair cut very short, almost a bob. I had a picture taken of myself and gave a copy to my mother. She was furious. She hated that photograph. Finally, my husband said to me, 'You've got to pursue this. You need to confront her.' So I did. And in her anger, my mother told me the one true thing, one of the very few things I could ever believe. She told me that my father was Chinese. That statement helped put things in place, gave me an explanation that made sense. But at a deeper level, I didn't really need to hear her say those words out loud, because I *knew* it was true. I have always known, it has just never been articulated before.

"Learning about my parentage explains a lot. Like why, as a small child, I always treasured Oriental things. Like why I feel more comfortable around Chinese people than whites. Not even Japanese so much, but Chinese. Like why, at eighteen years of age, I left the South, took a bus to New York City determined to live in Chinatown. I remember arriving at Port Authority, sitting in a coffee shop for a few hours and then telling myself, 'OK, this is why you came here, to live among Chinese people. Now go do it!' I had a wonderful experience. The Chinese would confirm stuff about me. Look behind my glasses at my eyes. They knew. I learned to speak Cantonese, a little Mandarin. They didn't treat me like a whole Chinese, but that's OK because I didn't expect them to. But at least they didn't treat me like I was white. I've never really felt white.

"Perhaps if my mother hadn't treated me the way she did, my need to know my father wouldn't be so great. Perhaps if I didn't have this feeling that I made my mother uncomfortable, that she doesn't like to look at me, doesn't want to be reminded of my Chinese father, I might not have quite this drive to pursue my heritage. But that's not what has happened.

"My husband and I now live in North Carolina. I'd love to be somewhere where there are more Chinese people. For example, Hong Kong. I'd love to have been there in '97, watching the clock tick off the minutes until the country reverted back to China. But we're here now because of my husband's job. When we bought our house a few years ago, one of the neighbors stopped in to say hello. She also asked, 'What is your nationality?' When I told her, she said, 'I knew you weren't pure white.' Now I want to ask you, what the heck is 'pure white'? *Who* is 'pure white'? All these white people came here from somewhere else. So I call myself a mutt.

"I would like to know more about my father. But I'm afraid that I may never be able to trace him. The only thing I have to go on is what a relative once told me, that a Chinese doctor from Manchuria brought over a group of his friends to live here when the Japanese were invading. Perhaps my father is one of those men. But my mom will not give me his name or his identity. In the meantime, it just helps to be able to look in the mirror and have a better sense of who that person really is. What I want is this: More than anything else, I want my Chinese heritage."

The adoption of an Asian child by white parents adds another level of complexity to the question of developing an ethnic identity. Renée is thirty-two years old, lives in Oregon, and works with battered women.

"A few years ago, I hired a good attorney, got a restraining order, and after eight years of marriage, left my abusive husband. Now, maybe for the first time in my life, I feel free to find out who I really am: as a woman, as a Korean American, as a person worthy of dignity and respect.

"My Korean mother abandoned me as an infant. I was adopted by white parents through an agency when I was twenty-four months old and moved to Salem, Oregon. I'm not too keen on the agency these days. Their philosophy, at least back then, was that the little Korean children should be grateful to be raised by white Christian families. I still have a letter from the woman who ran the agency saying that 'since an orphan has no place in Korean society, you were a nobody and now you are a person.'

"My mother is religious in a Bible-beating sort of way, and she also bought these notions of gratitude and Christian service, which she has tried to impose on me. She wanted me to go to a Bible college, but when I went to an academic school instead and majored in social science, she was convinced I would be doomed. Now I have this nice purple candle in my living room. It has a sun, star, and a moon on it, sits in a simple brass holder. She asks me what I need that for. I tell my mom that it's my way to honor witches and lesbians. My ex-husband also thought I should be grateful. He loved to introduce me as his Korean wife who should be 'serving him,' and frequently pointed out that if I had stayed back in Korea, I would be 'eating dogs and worms.'

"I grew up thinking I was white. After all, I was raised in an all-American family, with all-white relatives, on hamburgers. In fact, sometimes I blame all those cow hormones for my overdeveloped bust, which was a source of constant discomfort for me as a teenager. I used to think, 'If these things keep growing, one of these days I'm just going to fall over and die.' My uncle and aunt, whom I call the 'King and Queen of the Right Wing,' also would treat me as if I was white. In their eyes, I *was* white. So the fact that I'm a woman of color, that I do oppression training in my work, completely eludes them. They love to talk about how the Mexicans in our town are always the ones getting picked up for DUIs, etc., right in front of me. Usually, I just let it go, but once in a while if I do decide to speak up, I feel like one of my relatives is thinking, 'We better cool it, the race police is here.'

"I was never pushed to excel academically, but I became an overachiever all on my own. I worked hard for good grades, joined all kinds of clubs, etc. I even got elected to be on the homecoming court. But even so, I always felt unattractive. In high school, I got into this big thing about eye surgery. My mother had a cousin who was a plastic surgeon and I went to see him when I was fifteen. He refused to do the surgery and tried to convince me that my eyes were in fact pretty. That didn't stop me from trying to curl my lashes with one of those curler things, which always caught my eyelid instead of my lashes anyhow. And my nose was too flat. So flat, in fact, that at the time of the *Roots* thing, kids were calling me Kunta Kinte. And my breasts were too large, especially for an Asian, who should be petite. And my hair was wrong too. It was black, not blond. My hair stylist had to break the news to me that my hair just would not feather like Farrah Fawcett's.

"After high school, I suddenly started getting asked out a lot. There was this whole 'all Asian women are beautiful and sexy' thing going on. White guys would come up to me and start gibbering, then tell me, 'In Cantonese, that means you're beautiful.' I bought it. I was only attracted to white men and there were plenty available, so that was a period of my life marked by a lot of oversexualized behavior. I also used to go to the library and check out books in the Asian section and look up the chapters on women's roles. I read about geishas, I learned that we should be compliant and passive along with being sexually enticing. In fact, I have to admit that I used my 'Asianness' to attract my ex-husband. The stereotypes allowed me to project an image of myself that was exciting to me, one that made me stand out a little from the crowd. Besides, at that period of my life, I was screwed up in so many ways that this gave me at least *some* kind of an identity.

"The main reason I was screwed up is that I hadn't resolved the sexual abuse I suffered as a child. When I was nine years old, a Chinese pastor came to live with us. He was married to this nutso woman whom my mother had fostered. One day, when I was eleven, I was asked to pour him some tea at dinner. I was so mad that I deliberately spilled hot tea on his leg. My mother asked my why, and I started screaming, told her that he had been touching me for two years and I wanted him *out* of the house. What really got to me was that no one said anything after that. They just wanted to get on with dinner. Later, I repeated my message to my mother. She tried to tell me that he was a pastor, sometimes men do something they're sorry about, etc. etc. But finally, she did kick him out. After that, I never wanted anything to do with Asian men again. I was afraid they'd all be like this guy, who preyed on me because of my ethnicity. Who was also, I realize now, the perfect pedophile in the most insidious way.

"Marrying a white guy unfortunately did not spare me further abuse. During those terrible years of marriage—the name-calling, threats, the jokes about taking nude pictures of me to send to Asian porno magazines, and the rape (my ex claimed there was no such thing since he 'owned me')—my mother's only response was to 'pray about it.' Well, I don't know about prayer, but I do know that divorce has made a fundamental difference in my life. At my divorce party (where I gave away wedding presents from his family, who hated me anyhow for being Korean, as door prizes), I realized I had all these friends who really supported me. They clapped and cheered for me and I knew that this was my real family, the place where I could really be myself. A Korean American woman and proud of it!"

Sarah, like Renée, was adopted by white parents. Unlike Renee, however, Sarah was encouraged by her family to pursue her cultural roots. But even with this support, she describes a lifetime of grappling with the question, "What makes me Asian?"

"When I was twenty-five, I went to Hawaii to meet my birth mother for the first time in my life. The day before I was due to leave was very hard. I cried a lot and she held me. As I curled up in her arms, I could hear her heart beat and I said to myself, I *know* this. I can't describe the feeling any better. It was amazing to see her, to touch her, to know it was her. I look a lot like my birth mother and I realized that for the first time in my life, I had a *match*.

"All my life, I have been searching for my Asian heritage. I was adopted by white parents who tried hard to give my sister (also adopted, and Filipina) and me a connection to our culture. My mother took lessons in Chinese cooking, brought us along to her Asian studies classes, bought us books about Asian women. But still, somehow, it wasn't enough. I'm not sure I could say what exactly I needed, all I know is that something was missing.

"In third grade I decided to try to copy my Asian friends' behavior. They were quiet, reserved, polite. They knew how to make themselves invisible. I learned to imitate them, but it never felt right. Rubbed against the grain. Still, to this day, I sometimes fall back on that behavior. I'm quieter in groups, more polite than a lot of people I know. I'm sure what I felt was that if I could be more Asian, I could find my identity. And if I could be more Asian, I could be more like my birth mother.

"At the same time that I was trying to figure out what it meant to be Asian, my teachers would take one look at me and know what it meant to *them*. It was naturally assumed that I should be in the gifted and talented program even though my test scores didn't quite justify it. Also, I could do no wrong. I looked so innocent. Who would suspect that I was the one responsible for those paper airplanes sailing across the classroom? I loved it! I played it for all it was worth. And yet, I always had the sense that 'I'm Asian, but I'm not.' I had a lot of Asian friends, but my home life wasn't nearly as restrictive as theirs. Unlike them, I had the freedom to follow my heart's desires. And I'm grateful for that.

"My grandmother also treated me on the basis of how I looked. I used to get so mad because she could never tell me and my sister apart. We don't look that much alike aside from both being Asian. She'd ask, 'Now, which one are you?' and every year would give us identical presents. Two red sweaters. Two white bears. As a result of all this, I felt that I didn't really fit in anywhere. I had a bunch of friends, but I floated from group to group. A true chameleon.

"I had another chance to experiment with my ethnic identity in college. I went to Humboldt State, where I was one of a very few Asians. I cultivated the 'long-haired exotic Polynesian' look and dated anyone I set my sights on. I got what I wanted. In this guise, I could get away with things my friends wouldn't dare to try. For example, I was able to date three different men and one woman at the same time, be perfectly open about it, and not have to justify my behavior to anyone. That's 'just Sarah,' my friends would say. A package deal.

Then, I cut my hair very short. My whole life changed. I was no longer the enticing Asian. No one asked me out. I was now the 'dyke,' even if I was dating men. I knew when I cut my hair this might happen, but it was still disappointing. Two and a half feet of hair does not a person make. I wished they could see beyond that. The whole question of my identity was up for grabs again.

"I also had the experience, at Humboldt, of feeling for the first time in my life that I wished I was not Asian. One evening, my friends and I went out to a bar. Somewhere along the line, I noticed this scruffy-looking guy in the corner just staring at me. He gave me the creeps. But it was more than just being a woman and feeling vulnerable to the power of a man. I had this sense that he was one of those white supremacist types who wanted to hurt me because I was Asian, and I was reminded of nightmares where men in white hoods would hunt me down, of hanging from a tree. I realized that, in this town, I had *nowhere to hide.* I could not blend in, I would always be identifiable.

"Today, I call myself an Asian woman. I don't like the term 'American,' because to me, American means 'white male.' I still may not know exactly who I am, but at least I know who I'm *not.*"

13 NAMING NAMES

I have always had a love-hate relationship with my last name. For many years, I considered it to be one of the most obvious—and therefore detested—indications of my ethnicity. CHOW: a momentary grunt of a syllable that, to me, screamed Chinese! Foreign! Out of place! Once, I learned from my mother that our family name actually sounded more like "Drow" but was anglicized to Chow by immigration officials who did that sort of thing. My instantaneous reaction was, well then we should call ourselves the "Drews." A nice respectable name that people could hear, pronounce, and identify with. A nice respectable name to hide behind. It also didn't hurt that it just happened to be the name of my favorite female sleuth.

Every year, the beginning of school brought a new agony, because, in the calling of the roll, the name Chow would be declared for all to hear. Even if my classmates didn't giggle and twitter, I always assumed they would. One year, my seventh-grade math teacher mistakenly read my name as "Charlie Chow." Everyone laughed, of course, but that was one time I could laugh with them. Seventh grade was probably the time I started dreaming in that very math class about the day when I could call myself Mrs. Claire Johnson, or Mrs. Claire Smith, or something else in that vein. I remember covering sheet after sheet of notepaper with elaborate calligraphy, practicing the spelling of my new married surname (although I had no candidates in mind at the time). Certainly, part of my fantasy was about marriage and adulthood, but it was also about having a legitimate reason to discard my last name, to divest myself of that part of my identity.

When it actually came time to make the switch, however, I was at a very different place in my life. I married a man with a perfectly suitable Anglo name, but I decided *not* to change mine to his. Primarily, my thinking was based on feminist principles; none of my friends at the time believed that marriage should require women to forsake an important part of themselves, to make the symbolic gesture of acquiescence to ownership. But the other reason to retain a name I had never liked was that I was no longer ashamed of being Chinese. Changing my name would mean losing a part of my identity, albeit one I have reviled and struggled against for much of my life. I knew that if I became Mrs. Beattie, people who did not know me would look at that name and expect me to be something that I am not. I did not want to live with that discrepancy anymore.

Today, in my everyday life as a mother, I am called Mrs. Beattie more often than not. It is no longer politically imperative for me to correct folks who assume my last name should be the same as my children's. Sometimes, I am mistaken for the parent of one of the purely Asian kids in my son's class. I know they have a hard time associating the name Beattie with this woman and her black hair and high cheekbones. But I don't really care anymore. I guess I have gained at least this much maturity: Their assumptions about my ethnicity do not have to interfere with my own.

Work is a somewhat different story. At the risk of sounding paranoid, I can't help but wonder if my last name, glimpsed on a business card or mentioned by a colleague (among the obligatory three alternatives) poses problems for clients considering therapy. I imagine that some clients may have doubts about my ability to speak the language or to connect with their experience. I would probably keep these questions entirely to myself except that a friend and colleague with a very Asian Indian–sounding name recently shared with me similar concerns. And, my cousin's husband, a successful psychiatrist, told me that patients at first do express concern about whether he will be able to speak English fluently. (He was born in this country.)

The issue of names takes on a new life in succeeding generations. When my husband and I had children, we settled on the expedient measure of giving them his last name. This is the solution most of my feminist friends have adopted. For me, however, it felt important to acknowledge in some way that my children are half Chinese. So I modified a centuries-old custom to give them Chinese middle names. By tradition, the Chinese have three parts to their names. The first and most important is the family name. Second comes a syllable to denote one's generational status. This part of the name is obtained from a piece of writing produced by the family patriarch, which prescribes names for many generations. By this method, cousins can easily be identified because they carry the same second syllable. (At least the children of sons—another relic of sexism inherent in the culture is that the children of daughters don't matter. When they get married, they take on their husbands' full names anyhow.) The third syllable is equivalent to the Western concept of a "given name" (Mary, Mark) and trails the family and generational name in significance.

Theoretically, the generational name would have come from my husband's family, but since we had to make do, we settled on generational names foretold by my grandfather. For my children, this was Hua, meaning "glorious." If you ask Rebecca Hua Beattie or Julian Hua Beattie (ages twelve and ten) how they feel about their middle name, they will tell you they wish it was one that people could easily pronounce and spell correctly. (Rebecca claims that her friends say "Hoo-wa" and no amount of coaching can convince them it is otherwise.) They do not reject the name, but at this point in their lives, neither do they embrace it. I am hoping that one day it will be a treasured part of their identity. In the meantime I guess they are stuck with it.

What's in a name? For an Asian American woman, this is not a trivial question. The name she carries, and in some cases *chooses* to carry, makes a statement to the larger world about her ethnicity and perhaps its relationship to her identity. Asian names are distinctive and easily identifiable. People may not, for example, be able to recognize that she is Korean, but there is no doubt that someone called "Seung Sook Myung" is most likely one of those "foreigners." Many immigrants gave their children unmistakably American first names, in part out of a sense of patriotism to their new homeland, and in part to help their kids blend in more easily. Still others voluntarily gave up their own Asian names in order to accelerate the assimilation process, or they accepted without question the anglicized version of their name given by a teacher, immigration authority, or other white contact.

The opposite is also true. Especially for women of my generation, the desire to reclaim heritage may motivate women to take back an Asian name or at least to give their children such a name. Perhaps the most poignant example I know is that of a friend, Korean but adopted as a little girl by white parents, who wrote to tell me that she was now calling herself Jin Ah Renée Kim (instead of Renée Swan).

Issues related to names vary somewhat from culture to culture. Japanese Americans, for example, tend to follow a pattern where the Issei retain their full Japanese names, along with the language and as much of the original culture as possible. Things for the Nissei are mixed, some having Anglo first names, although many were given a Japanese one. A common practice for this generation was to shorten a name (first or last) to one syllable and henceforth be known by that designation. Thus, Yoshi became Yo, Takasu became Tak, and so on. The shortened name has the flavor of an affectionate nickname. And for their white peers and their own children (many of whom speak little or no Japanese), one short syllable is clearly less daunting than the multisyllabic original. The Sansei almost all have Anglo first names. Some have Japanese middle names, but many do not. These are generally the sons and daughters of Japanese Americans who spent time in internment camps, and clearly one of the motives in choosing names such as Judy or David was the desire to help their children appear to be as American as possible. Sansei sometimes also call each other by a shortened version of their last name. This tends to be a practice that they reserve for use among Japanese Americans or other Asian Americans. They may not feel as comfortable with non-Asians using this shortened form.

Jan's family story is not unusual.

"There were ten kids in my father's family. He's the middle son, and he's the only one with an English name. Henry, to be precise. I guess I always took that for granted, never really questioned why that would be. But recently I asked my mother where the name came from. Her answer: 'The doctor gave it to him when he was born.' Then I started thinking about my mother and my uncle John on her side of the family. How did they become Mary and John? It turns out that when they first went to school, the teacher decided that their Japanese names were too hard to pronounce, so she gave them English ones. The new ones just kind of stuck; my mother became so used to being called Mary that she made it her legal name. Her two siblings, however, had Japanese names that were easier to deal with, so they didn't lose them.

"My brothers and sisters all have very ordinary American names. Janice Gay. Keith Henry. Judith Ann. I did ask my mother if it had even occurred to Dad to give us Japanese names. She couldn't really answer that one. But I wonder if it was because he was in the same place that I am about our Japanese identity. For me it just wasn't really an issue. I know who I am. So when I married Dave, a Caucasian, it didn't make any difference to me if I changed my last name from Sakaguchi to Sechrist. Changing my name doesn't change who I am.

"I think I feel the way I do because I grew up with so much extended family around me from which to draw my Japanese identity. I also think it's because I didn't experience much prejudice. I never was conscious of feeling different. Perhaps that's because we lived in Colorado, the only state with a governor who refused to sign Executive Order 9066. But maybe it's also because I overlooked or denied the prejudice. As far as I could tell, the only thing really different about me was that I was so tiny compared with my friends. Yes, teachers sometimes mispronounced my last name. One even tried to spell it as if it were Italian. But we just corrected them. We never felt hurt."

For Tae Hyun Moon, a Korean American, the question of names has certain similarities but also some variations that may reflect culture-of-origin differences.

"My name is Tae Hyun, my second sister is Tae Kyung, and my oldest sister is Tae Im. Our last name is Moon, which in Korea (as in China) would come first. When we moved to the U.S., however, we reversed the order so that we could conform to American practices. In second grade, the teacher called me 'Toe' for the whole year. At first, I didn't speak English well enough to correct her, and by the time I did, she was so used to calling me Toe that I just let it be. I would have been too shy to say anything anyhow. Another thing about my name. Tae is easy to say, but not Tae Hyun or Tae Kyung. So my sister and I were both called Tae. We didn't care. We knew we were our own unique selves, so sharing a name didn't make any difference. If someone called on the phone asking for Tae, we'd simply respond, 'Do you mean the Tae in fourth grade or the Tae in sixth grade?' My oldest sister, on the other hand, had a name that was easy to say, so she remained Tae Im (which people pronounced as a slightly elongated version of the word *tame*, 'Tae-Im').

"I was proud of my name. I never desired an Anglo name and never wished for anything other than Tae. Ironically enough, Tae is not even a girl's name. My grandfather so desired a grandson that he gave us all a boy's name. My mother finally did bear a son, but by that time, she had divorced my Korean father, married an American, and named her boy John.

"Why was it so easy to feel comfortable with these Korean names? I think it's because my mother is a very proud woman and she passed on a sense of family pride to us. She loved to regale us with stories of how we came from such a good family.

A *superior* family if you really want to know. My great-grand-mother was a large landowner at a time when that was virtually unheard of for a woman. We scoffed at other Asian kids who anglicized their names because we felt no need to do so. To this day, I can hear my mother telling us about how 'white people were still running around in skins, while Koreans wore the finest silks.'

"For my children, however, it's a somewhat different story. Their middle name is Kim. They were named after my mother's family, the family I most associate with. I asked Stephanie (eleven) and Caroline (nine) how they would feel if their middle name was something like 'Pak' instead of Kim, which is identical to the English name. Stephanie said she would not like it. Why? Because Kim is a 'more unusual name.' Caroline feels that Kim 'sounds better, like a real name.' I guess it's because my children are so acculturated that they don't have the same sense I grew up with, that being different in our case means being better."

Linda's story is an example of a woman who is seeking to re-claim heritage. This process is complicated because Linda's mother was Mexican, her father Filipino. She grew up in poverty but the support of the Filipino farm community in which she lived gave her a real appreciation for this half of her heritage. In a sense, you could say she had a choice: whether to identify most closely with her Latin or her Asian roots. Linda is now at a point in her life where she wants to hold on to her Filipino culture and to take back her family's original name.

"You know how Loretta Lynn talks about being a coal miner's daughter? Well, I'm a migrant farm worker's daughter and proud of it. I'm half Filipino and half Mexican.

"My father left the Philippines when he was sixteen, stowed away aboard a ship to come to Hawaii and work the sugar plan-tations. My mother, who was from a relatively well off and edu-cated family, fled Mexico during Zapata's revolution. They met in Southern California. I have pictures of my dad from that time, showing a very dapper, handsome fellow who used to ride a motorcycle, act as an extra in Tom Mix movies, even had a life as a prizefighter for a while. But after they married, my parents ended up having twelve children, sometimes as many as three cribs at a time, and my father had to work tremendously hard just to keep us fed and sheltered. My mother would wake up at three in the morning to start cooking for the field workers and then tend to the business of raising her kids, whom she always referred to as her 'precious, precious children.'

"We lived in shacks provided by the white landowners. I used to go by their large houses, and I would always think 'It must be *warm* in there.' When it came time for us to go to school, the town wanted to send us to the 'minority school.' My mother felt this was absolutely wrong, took on the principal, and single-handedly paved the way for all of us to attend the white school. Soon other Filipino families followed suit. At school, I mostly played with Asian kids. I never thought much about racism, I just accepted that this was how it had to be. But I would get a chill every time I would go by the elaborate Victorian home of one of the rich ranch owners. Their son was in my class and he gave the impression that he was better than me, that you didn't even have the right to talk to him. I still got a chill when, just recently, I came across a picture that had been painted of that old house.

"At the same time, we did have these Filipino youth clubs where we'd play basketball and volleyball with kids from other towns. We'd get to know Filipino kids our own age and we became really close. In fact, we still meet for reunions some thirty years later. That helped to provide a sense of community.

My mother suffered tremendous hardships. Being the traditional Asian male, my dad didn't take on any of the responsibility in raising the kids. So she had to try to keep up with all twelve of us. We always had clean clothes to wear, even in that environment. She also had to put up with our father's jealousy. Once, she went to a funeral of a family member. She came back a day later than she had planned. He got so mad that he burned all her clothes. My sister and I still find that hard to accept. But as far as we knew, he never crossed the line of violence towards her. And they loved each other—they married for love against the wishes of her parents, against even the laws of the state. They had to go to Arizona to get the union legalized. My mother was also very much accepted by the Filipino farm community in which we lived. She learned to speak three dialects, and cooked mostly Filipino food. Once in a while, she'd make some Mexican dish, and we considered that a treat.

"I think that is why, as much as I love my mother and my Hispanic culture, I identify more with being Filipino. I love history, and I'm now involved with a group trying to preserve the history of Filipino Americans. I'm also the unofficial family historian; one of these days, I *am* going to get all these pictures into an album! I think it is an important record to preserve and cherish.

"After high school, I got a job as a flight attendant. I was one of the few minorities hired. At that point, you no longer needed to be a nurse to qualify, but I noticed that all the other minorities, except me, were RNs. As a flight attendant, your whole life revolved around the airlines. You lived with your co-workers and socialized with them on layovers. There were times, however, when I felt excluded from these activities. They would forget to invite me to meals with them. And once, I was in the limo riding back from the airport. The pilot and other flight attendants were in the front seats; I ended up in the back. I think they just forgot I was there. So they started talking very freely. One blond stewardess said how much she hated Filipinos. I didn't say a thing. I just wanted to hear what they would say next. So the pilot chimed in with something about Filipinos and monkeys. I was absolutely crushed, but I just sat there in silence.

"Another time, a friend of one of my roommates started talking about how bad Mexicans were. They were dirty, uneducated, etc. 'But,' she continued, 'the *worst* are the Filipinos.' At this point, my roommates did step in and told her to be quiet. I just left the room. Later they asked me why I didn't want to invite her to my wedding. 'I'm afraid she won't be comfortable,' I replied. 'There will be a lot of those *Filipinos* there.'

"The passengers also reminded me that I was 'something different.' I'd walk up and down those aisles and they'd always have that look of puzzlement on their faces. Invariably, they'd come out and ask, 'What *are* you?' It was always like that, and I did feel insulted. But I'd say, 'I'm half Filipino, half Mexican.' Or they'd look at my nametag and say, 'You don't look like a Miss Mahoney.' Actually, that isn't our family's real name. When my dad was fighting, all the other well-known fighters were Irishmen, so they got him to change his name from Maghanoy to a more recognizable name. So I'd either explain, or sometimes I'd say something flip like, 'It was my Massa's name.' But once they opened that up, they were going to hear my story, like it or not.

"Let me say it again. I am *proud* of whom I am. Lately, I've been thinking of changing my name back to the original, Maghanoy. I identify with that more than Mahoney. Some of my siblings are very much against the idea, but it feels like something I need to do for myself. I need to acknowledge where I really come from. It's a big part of who I am."

To conclude this chapter, a story by Thanh Tran, a sixteen-year-old Vietnamese teenager whose essay won Honorable Mention in the 1996 contest "Growing Up Asian in America."[1]

"When I was younger and people used to ask me what language I spoke at home, I would always answer 'English. I used to speak Chinese really well, but I lost it all when I went to kindergarten.' I was so proud whenever I said this because I wanted to be as 'American' as possible. I also told people to call me 'Jessica.' It sounded so pretty and American. I couldn't stand the sound of my name. I wanted to be like everybody else. I didn't want to associate myself with my heritage because I was in America, not Vietnam. Why should I know my parents' language? I would never use it. I brought this attitude with me to Vietnamese school on Saturdays. I thought that attending the

[1]"Growing Up Asian in America" is a program of the Asian Pacific American Community Fund, a tax-exempt organization based in San Francisco, which invests in communities and provides for the diverse and emerging needs of Asian Pacific Americans through programs of grants and services to community agencies.

volunteer-run school was a form of punishment inflicted onto me by my mother. I was determined not to learn anything. This attitude was shared by my sisters. We were better than the other students because we spoke perfect English, so we didn't really want to associate with them.

"The belief that I was better than other Asians because I was more 'American' stayed with me for a very long time. My attitude changed one day when I was in Chinatown with my mother. I had always hated Chinatown because it was so dirty and crowded with people I couldn't relate to. I never went into the supermarkets, and always stayed outside in the street with my arms crossed. I only went to Chinatown because I felt an obligation to keep my mother company. She always complained that she could never buy enough groceries because all of the bags would be too heavy to carry herself. The guilt was so strong that I made myself go with her. I was standing outside one Sunday when I noticed some teenagers also standing outside. They looked like me. They had these haughty superior facial expressions that made it obvious that they didn't want to be there either. Looking at them, I suddenly realized what a snob I'd been.

"I was just like the other teenagers; ashamed of their parents and of their heritage. This realization hit me very hard. I didn't want to be snobby like the others. What right did I have to feel superior to people who had been through so many more hardships than I would ever have to face? I finally saw these people of Chinatown not as a mass, but rather as individuals who had tried very hard their whole lives to guarantee their children a better future. I was very ashamed of myself.

"I've learned now that I was wrong to be embarrassed of my background. There are some aspects of my culture that I have had a hard time accepting, but after examining them from my parents' point of view, I realize that the intentions behind the actions are good. I had always resented my parents for being so strict. I could never go out and have fun like my friends, which I thought was unfair. I realize now that my parents have been looking out for my best interests. They don't want me to impose on other people. For the longest time, my parents would not let me sleep over at a friend's house. I had always thought that this was due to a lack of trust, but I've learned that my parents just don't want me bothering my friends and their families. They also worry about me. It's natural for parents to worry about their kids. I had always wanted my parents to let me do anything I wanted, but I know that they are so strict because they care about me and being strict is their way of showing their love. I realize that where they grew up, 'family' didn't mean its 'looser' American equivalent. It meant fierce pride, responsibility, and unspoken love. Their expectations and limits are the ways they know how to care for me and my sisters.

"I always took for granted one of the most important aspects of being Asian, which is that the Asian family supports and loves one another. There is an interdependent tie with the family. Nobody is ever alone; there is always someone to support and encourage you, and there is never any hesitation to help a relative in need. When my sister went to college, all of my relatives chipped in money to help with her tuition. They give her money whenever she comes home so that she doesn't have to get through college alone. My mother explains to me that parents will do anything for their children; they are the first priority. My father never buys anything for himself. He hasn't had new clothes in a very long time. I had thought that his lack of clothes was due to his stinginess. This explanation, however, contradicts his actions. If he took us out shopping, he would never hesitate to buy us something. My mother told me that my father doesn't care about himself and only wants to use his money on us.

"The love and care they give us will be returned. When my parents become older and can no longer take care of themselves, we will bring them into our homes and return the care we have received. The meaningful ties that we obtain from our family enable us to have a foundation to accomplish many things. We can do so much because we know that our parents will always support us. In America, success is valued by the amount one has accomplished independently. This is different from Asian culture because we value working together and helping one another. These values enable us to get through life a lot easier because we are always aware of the support given to us.

"Another benefit of being Asian is that my parents make me

strive for the best. They want me to accomplish their dream of a better future in America. This drive for perfection used to make me angry at my parents. I never understood why they could never be happy about my grades, and always told me to try hard, as if I hadn't been doing that before. I always tried harder to please them, but nothing seemed to be enough. I now realize that my parents are very proud of me, and that they just don't know how to express their pride to me. I would hear my mother tell her friends about the latest accomplishments that we, her daughters, had just achieved. I used to think she did this just to brag to her friends and I was always embarrassed at my mother's obviousness. I understand now that she didn't know how to tell us how proud she was, so she was expressing her pride to her friends. Her hopes for us to grow up successful are being achieved.

"I never fully understood the sacrifice my parents made when they came to America. They left their homeland in order for me and my sisters to have a chance of success in America. They brought their culture with them and tried to pass it on to us. It has taken me a very long time to accept and value this culture. As much as I denied the Asian influence on me when I was younger, it is the one thing that has continually shaped me into who I am.

"My parents recently became United States citizens. I, being under the age of eighteen, immediately became a citizen too. I had a chance to change my name. I pored through books, trying to find the perfect name. I thought I found it. I was going to be Adena Tran. At the last moment, when I had a chance to have an American name like my sisters, I signed, on the line that said 'Name of Citizen,' Thanh Tran."

14 A SENSE OF BELONGING:
A Place to Call Home

I think all of us, being human, experience the need to belong. I am no different. I want to feel that I am a natural part of the landscape, not an aberration to be tolerated. I want to be comfortable in the presence of others and know they are comfortable in mine. But this is not the message I received as a child, and I believe it has affected me to the core. For I have long believed that I am here—whether in this class or with this Girl Scout troop—through the grace of others who allow me to be present, but who could just as easily close the door. In a sense, I'm not ever sure I have a right to be where I am. I don't belong here. Even the well-meaning comments of others who reassured me that my "English is so good" only reinforced the sense of being the stranger, the one who does not fit in.

When I was fourteen, I was invited to my best friend Mary Hedberg's summerhouse for a week. Her family owned a beautiful ramshackle house on Martha's Vineyard overlooking the ocean. The clan would gather there every summer, trading stories, sharing meals, and creating memories. Mary's father was a professor at Princeton University, and she is the girlfriend who shared with me her passion for horses and things equestrian. The Hedbergs had certain time-honored rituals, including reading out loud, every evening, from books that family members might be interested in.

One night, after the places had been cleared, Mary's mother called for suggestions of a new book to tackle. I had a wonderful idea in mind, and immediately leapt out of my seat to retrieve the book from the bookshelf. I had made it about two feet when a voice as cold as ice hit me. "You do *not* leave the table until you have been excused." This happened midweek of my visit, and after that, I never felt comfortable in the home again. My dreams of being accepted and fitting into a group such as this, reminiscent almost of the Kennedys, were once again destroyed. I remember that we had read *The Scarlet Letter* in English class that year, and felt I should start walking around with a huge *A* pinned to my chest. I knew, without having to be told, that growing up in a Chinese household had not equipped me to move in other social circles, especially those I most desired to be a part of.

Looking back, I can see that I have used several different strategies to cope with my feelings of not belonging. At first, aided by the developmental pressures of adolescence, I simply tried to conform. Be as much like them as possible. Hide or cut off everything that indicated a difference. I am aware, even as I write this, that most adolescents, Asian or not, have similar memories of this difficult time in their lives. But for me, it was not so much a different struggle as it was a different order of magnitude. I had no role models; there were no Connie Chungs or Amy Tans at the time to give me even a glimmer of hope that life could be different. And the fact is, as far as we have come, I am aware that in the waning years of the twentieth century, there are still Americans who believe that people like me are to blame for this country's problems and would just as soon we left or made ourselves scarce.

At the same time that I was striving to conform, a small part of me was moving in the opposite direction. My mother had told me—and I wanted to believe her—that Chinese were better people. Those girls with their blond ponytails and pom-poms were not headed for a "good college." They were not as diligent or really as bright as I was. They would not end up with a doctorate or a faculty position. This was small consolation, but sometimes it worked. Sometimes it kept me going.

A third and more recent attempt to settle the question of belonging: I am trying to create the community where I feel accepted. I instigated our family's move from the East Coast to the West Coast when my daughter was two years old because I got tired of fellow stroller pushers assuming I was Rebecca's "nanny." I wanted my children to grow up in a place where Asians and biracial faces were common, where black hair or "mixed" features merited no special attention, where ethnic diversity was a fact of life. I have also actively pursued friendships with other Asian American women. And here is a place where I feel a level of comfort unlike anything I have ever known. Not that these are more important connections, but I am grateful to simply have time with women who understand my experience firsthand. I have also made opportunities for us, as a family, to visit with cousins and other relatives. Now we get together at least once a year for Chinese New Year's. I have to call my mother to get recipes for traditional dishes because we did not honor these customs as a child. I have to make it happen.

Yet even if I am now living in a place where I generally feel accepted, old habits die hard. I am aware that, whenever I am in a group, I always have my antennae out to detect subtleties of behavior that might indicate rejection or exclusion. I can't seem to help it, whether I'm sitting on the side of a Little League game or eating lunch with colleagues, I can never entirely let go of the question, "Do I really belong here? Do they *really* want me here?" Viewed from a Western model of mental health, this attitude borders on paranoia. But I only have to remember the time that Wayne, in front of the entire tenth-grade mathematics class, asked me if I wanted to come to a party with him—and how my heart leapt with joy at the thought—only to realize it was a joke, told for their benefit, at my expense.

And as much as I would like to get rid of *this* habit, I still find myself falling back on the superiority defense. If I start to pick up the vibrations that, for whatever reason, I'm not being included in any particular group, I say to myself, "Well, these are just Little League parents. You're a psychotherapist." Or I say, "Well, these are just psychotherapists. You're an involved parent."

I know that my particular experience of inclusion/exclusion is partly a product of personal insecurity and vulnerability that would have manifested even if I had been born white. But this personal trait does not diminish the reality of racism and intolerance. I believe that all of us, as Asian American women, have to answer for ourselves the question of belonging. Some may feel that this is no longer an issue, but my response is this: The experience of internment still exists within the living memory of many thousands of Japanese Americans. Who among us can guarantee that it will never happen again?

Where do we belong? In which neighborhoods, communities, or geographic locations? What helps us feel comfortable and what keeps us separate? Another way to look at this question is to ask, "Where is *home* for me?" Because whether or not life is entirely comfortable here, it is almost certain that we can't go back to the land of our parents. Even though many of us have had the experience of being admonished to "Go back where you came from! Go home where you *belong!*" this may not be possible, let alone desirable. Women who were born abroad usually feel they have become "too American" to return. Those who were born here and have an opportunity to visit Asia say, "In America I might not have felt fully American, but after traveling to Japan, I realized that I am definitely not Japanese." So here we are, and somehow we have to find a place for ourselves.

Lori is a Methodist minister who found a way to satisfy the need for belonging: She found a Japanese church to serve.

"My father was a Methodist minister, meaning that he served a denomination with a policy of itinerating pastorship, so we moved around a lot. For much of my childhood, I lived in different small towns in the Deep South. Every time we moved to a new place, there was always that first awful trip to the grocery store. We knew people would stop their carts mid-aisle and stare. Or point. Or pretend not to notice, but notice all the same. Something like the way a Martian would be greeted. My parents always warned us in advance. 'OK, we're going to the store now.' But they took the attitude that this was simply something we would have to gut out. An icky reality, but also a passing one. Still, I had my moments of wishing I was white, of standing in front of the mirror practicing making my eyes bigger.

"Going to a new school had some of the same flavor. Kids would crowd around, touch my hair, my skin. I never felt inferior in any way, but I definitely knew I was different. I also knew there would be a waiting period, a season of advent if you will, before I met friends and gained entrance into the community. But sooner or later, it always came. Plus, I have kind of a nasty or a mean streak. Not too long ago, I was one of several judges at a contest. Another judge looked across the room at me and said quite loudly, 'Does she even *speak* English?' implying something about my fitness to be in that room. 'Yes,' I answered equally loudly. 'Yes, she certainly does speak English.'

"From the South, I moved to the Midwest and bit by bit found myself called to ministry. I ended up serving rural churches in Kansas, living at the end of a dirt road in a town of nine hundred. At first, I was kind of oblivious to the fact of my ethnicity. I had a lovely naïveté about whether I would be accepted by the congregation. Part of that has to do with my personal style. On the Myer-Briggs, I'm an 'E' (extrovert), off the end of the scale. My father is this way too, and he used to encourage me to be the very best but also to seize leadership opportunities, to be comfortable being 'out there.' My mother was proud of me and also awed by my ability. I used to wonder why she herself was so reticent, so nervous about accepting the invitation to join some women's club. Now I understand that she was worried about not measuring up to those white women. And I realize too that my extroversion is, at the core, an essential survival skill. It keeps me afloat.

"Somewhere along the line in Kansas, I realized that I could not do this anymore. This subconscious but constant taking into consideration, 'Well, they really haven't been around Japanese people before, they haven't been exposed to diversity.' There was no one around that I could even begin to talk to about subjects such as the internment, about the impact it had on my mother's life and therefore on mine. I knew I felt shame about that experience, as did she. But with no context in which to explore these issues, I really couldn't look at how they affected me. What I felt instead was almost visceral, a feeling of churning inside. Being turned upside down and having my identity called into question. And then I started to become aware of feeling angry and experiencing flashbacks of memories that had to do with being different, that didn't feel good.

"Just at that time, I got a call to serve a Japanese American church in California. My father, who generally supported me in whatever I wanted to do, had some reservations about my leaving Kansas, 'which has been so good to you.' But I was ready. I arrived at my new church a few days before Obon and went to a community celebration, where blocks and blocks were closed off and absolutely brimming over with Japanese faces. At first I was freaked out, stunned. But soon I discovered what an incredible high this was. At worship, I'd look out over the congregation and think, 'This is *me*! I belong here!' Such a wonderful feeling.

"Being in this place has allowed me to explore much more fully my identity as a Japanese American. I've even joined a group called Sansei Legacy, and it feels great to be able to talk about all this stuff with others who have been there too. Because I am a Methodist pastor, I know that my time with this church is limited. I take the position that it's not good or healthy to become too attached to the idea of 'where to go next.' But I do believe it's important for ethnic churches to have ethnic leadership, and there just aren't enough of us to go around. Yet. That's something I'm working on now. I guess you could call me a role model, and it makes me feel good to be that."

How do we, as Asian American women, find a "home place"? A place where we feel comfortable, a place we can return to after an absence? For Miyo, it was a conversation with her Caucasian husband that helped her understand that home is not really a geographic location, it is a place in the heart. Melinda's story, which comes after Miyo's, has a similar flavor.

"Recently, my husband was discussing the concept of home-
town with a good friend. Both men have long histories in the
town they grew up in. Bruce's family goes back at least ten or
eleven generations in Hanover, where we live. Bruce made a remark that caught me off guard. 'I don't really feel comfortable,
I'm not really myself unless I'm in Hanover.' For me, it's my
family and extended family that define home. I feel very connected to this community, I enjoy my life here and feel accepted,
but I know that if something were to happen to Bruce, if the kids
had moved away, I wouldn't necessarily stay here. Home to me
is not a physical location, it's the people in my family that I love.

"I grew up in New Jersey, where my father had a fruit or-
chard. The Quakers had been very kind to him after he left camp,
so Tak decided to raise us in that community, even scraping the
money together to send us to the Friends School. I would say
that being a Quaker was the strongest influence on my childhood. Although we went to a few social activities with my parents' JACL. [Japanese Americans Citizens League] friends, we
basically grew up with white kids and school friends.

"However, I realize that, in some ways, my parents did have
traditional Japanese values and attitudes. At times, this caught
me off guard. In my junior year, I was trying to decide between
Occidental College (Southern California) and Middlebury (New
Hampshire). Both were similar in many ways. One day, I came
downstairs and found my mother ironing. She kept moving that
iron back and forth, back and forth, while managing to get this
message across to me: 'You know, there are more Japanese boys
in California.' (I went to Occidental although I did not end up
with a Japanese boy.) And when I was leaving for a trip to
Ghana, my father found the leader of our sponsoring organization and personally thanked him for the care he would take of
me. That was very Japanese. We also stopped off at the cemetery
to pay our respects to my grandparents and give them an accounting of our actions.

"After college, I decided to go spend some time in Japan.
Mostly, I just enjoyed the opportunity to travel, but I also wanted
to make a connection with my roots. While I was there, I realized

that I could never be Japanese like them. The only way would have been to fall in love with a Japanese man and learn to accept the restrictions of that society. Restrictions primarily against women: Even the language women use is different from that of men. I couldn't handle that, and inwardly rebelled against learning those differences.

"From Japan, I came to Hanover where Bruce had already reestablished himself. (We met in college.) Neither his parents nor mine were keen on the idea of our living together. Dad especially was concerned about 'what the other people will think.' Interracial dating was not the issue. At first, it was difficult for me to make friends here, I was lonely. I didn't feel that other people were excluding me, but I also didn't know how to get plugged into the community. But once I became Bruce's wife, everyone breathed a sigh of relief and life got easier.

"Today, if you asked me who I am, I would say I'm Jessie and Trudy and Cal's (the golden retriever) mom. I'm involved with our local chapter of Planned Parenthood and with the YWCA. I'm fascinated with Japanese culture and aesthetics, but I know I'm American. I think the culture you grew up in *is* your culture. My eleven-year-old, Trudy, says she feels mostly American. 'What's Japanese about you?' Her answer, 'My hair, my face, my skin shade.' Jessie, age fifteen, feels that our primary link to being Japanese is the food we eat, the fact that we know how to use chopsticks.

"For pictures, I have dressed the children in kimonos. We spend Christmas with Bruce's family and then go to New Jersey for Japanese New Year's, where I notice the decibel level of gatherings is significantly higher. But perhaps most telling is my daughter's comment at about age five. We were giving a guest a tour of the town. Trudy proudly pointed to the cemetery and said, 'That's where my great-grandparents are buried, and that's where *I'm* going to be buried!' "

Melinda, a professor at a large East Coast university, tells her story.

"Where is the place I can identify as my 'heartfelt home'? This is a concept that evolves over the years, but I'm not sure it can ever be answered with certainty. My family and I now live on the East Coast. For a while, I felt this could only be a temporary situation, I had to get back to California where I 'belonged.' But as our life progresses, the kids make friends, and we feel connected to the community, any urgency to return to the state where I was born becomes more and more remote. Maybe this is one of the legacies of the [internment] camps, but I really don't know where 'home' would be; in one sense, I feel displaced all the time.

"Growing up, we moved around a lot, so that I found myself living both in white and in largely Japanese American communities. In some ways, that was to my advantage, but it also made me feel that I didn't really fit in anywhere. Once, I came into a new school where there were a lot of Japanese in the middle of the year. At first it was hard to make friends because my Japanese American classmates felt I was trying to act 'better than them' although really it was just that I was shy. Eventually, I did find a place with this group, but inside, I never stopped feeling somewhat different. Curiously enough, it was here that I got into the Scotch tape and eyelids thing. Like everyone else, my friends and I were experimenting with makeup but found ourselves continuously frustrated that eye shadow and eyeliner didn't work the way it was supposed to. So someone got the idea of sticking little pieces of Scotch tape on your eyelids, which would make them double and thus easier to apply makeup to. Thing is, we were doing this in a group of Japanese American girls, in order to be attractive to other Sansei boys, *not* to the white guys.

"My parents didn't communicate about a lot of things, particularly their own history. I used to think the internment camps were something like what the Boy Scouts did. But over time, it became clear that *something* had happened but it wasn't anything we were supposed to discuss. I had to piece together bits of the puzzle though my own efforts. Now, I feel a sense of social obligation. I believe that this is a story that needs to be told. I can articulate for my parents and for others like them what they experienced but have not been able to give words to. I can *feel* it for them.

"They also didn't push me into a certain field, although they certainly wanted me to study something 'practical.' But my parents did manage to convey important beliefs about how to behave, how to conduct yourself in the world, that I retain to this day. For example, I don't talk a lot in meetings. I'm not what you would call very assertive. So I struggle with a lifelong issue: Do I speak up enough? As a child, I learned certain rules. Don't talk back. Don't do anything that would reflect badly on the family. Don't offend anyone. Something as simple as, if someone offers you some food, don't take it all. These are inhibitory codes that make me feel I need to monitor my own behavior. I don't necessarily see my white colleagues or peers living with the same inhibitions, so they seem at times rude or brazen, and that puts a distance between us. I can also remember as a child hearing my parents talking about Americans in connection with the word *yakamashi*, talking too much and too loud.

"Where can I feel at home? Here on the East Coast we have access to wonderful historic sites, generations upon generations of history. But I'm always aware of the fact that even as I enjoy a place like Williamsburg, this isn't *my* history, it's not about me. The other day I was at my daughter's soccer game. I tend to stand apart from the other parents, have a hard time entering into their conversation. I wonder what they see when they see me. And then, the thought occurs to me, they probably never have to do this, never have to go through this type of questioning. I was reminded of my differentness even by my own daughter, who takes a real interest in the Japanese half of her heritage. Once, when she was small, she listened to 'Rudolph the Red-Nosed Reindeer,' and then said to me, 'That wasn't very nice what they did to Rudolph, was it?' I was gratified that she had picked up this message of tolerance and said something to her like, 'No, it wasn't. We shouldn't judge others by the way they look.' To which she promptly replied, 'Yes, and I don't even notice that you are dark-skinned!' Dark-skinned? I had never thought of myself that way before. I asked her what her skin color was. 'Peach.' And Daddy, and sister? 'Peach too.' What I realized at that moment was that in her child's eye, that differentness was attributed to *me*, not to my husband."

Jean was born in Korea, but even that does not give her the type of connection to the country of her birth that she thought it would. Like many other Asian Americans, regardless of origin, her psychological and ideological allegiance is to the United States, not to Asia.

"I was born in Korea. My parents immigrated to the U.S. when I was six for the standard reasons: better opportunities, better economic potential. But when they came, they also brought their traditions and culture with them, making a concerted effort to ensure that we would continue to speak the language. We returned to Korea every several years to visit relatives, and these trips for me felt like coming home. As a child, I identified myself very strongly as Korean.

"It wasn't until after I graduated from college and spent a year working in Korea that I realized I was much more American than I had thought. In a sense, this was an unsettling revelation because the Korean part of my identity had always been a fallback position. I used to believe that I could go live in Korea at any time if things didn't work out for me here. But during that year of working in a law firm, it dawned on me that I did not fit into this society. The lawyers where I worked were 100 percent male, the secretaries 100 percent female. Since I was going to law school in the fall, I didn't exactly fit into either category, and received special treatment from the men. As a result, the women all resented me, never asked me to join them for lunch.

"Also, I dressed differently, and the women subtly pointed this out to me. I never tried to present myself as pro-American, but the anti-American sentiment in the country was evident. My views clashed with theirs. Until now, my visits to Korea had been restricted to family gatherings; now I was being exposed to the larger society, and I saw some things I didn't like: the gap between rich and poor, the display of wealth put on by the nouveau riche.

"Growing up in a traditional household, I felt it was my place to be obedient. I knew my parents wanted me to go to medical school and then marry a Korean man. So I went to school with no doubt in my mind that I would be a doctor. But one summer, I did some volunteer work at a hospital and discovered, to my utter dismay, that I didn't like medicine. This caused me great anxiety. How could I think of switching careers when it was clear what my parents wanted of me? I had never acted against their wishes in my entire life. Clearly, this would be the Big Disobedience.

"Then came the issue of marriage. I met my husband during my first year of law school, and by Christmas, we were engaged. I had never expected to fall in love with a Caucasian man; I'd always assumed I would marry Korean. During Christmas break, I announced my intentions to my parents. 'What?' my dad asked, then, 'Who is he?' 'He's not Korean,' I answered. 'Well, then, is he Chinese?' 'No, he's white.' Complete silence, shock registering on both their faces. My parents accepted my decision in the sense that they would not try to stop us. But even now, they're not fully comfortable around him, which has something to do with what is considered proper in Korean society. Korea is very homogeneous and marrying out is not well accepted.

"I can't say I don't feel guilty about my decision. I want my parents' approval but I also want to make my own choices. And some part of the guilt I feel is not just for disappointing my parents, it's that this was never my *own* plan for my life. I just never imagined not marrying someone Korean."

A sense of "where I belong" may also have its shadow side, a feeling that I may be Asian American, but I'm not purely Asian. A desire not to be associated with Asians who are "FOB" (fresh off the boat). Those of us who are aware of being between two cultures can find a sense of belonging by stressing one connection, sometimes at the expense of the other. I remember visiting

Hawaii five years ago and being struck by the island's ethnic diversity. But I was also very much aware of not wanting to be identified with those "hordes" of Japanese newlyweds dressed in their designer jeans and sporting expensive cameras. If given the opportunity, I would have clearly pointed out that I am American, not Asian. I don't belong with them.

Stephanie grew up in Hawaii but now lives in California with her Chinese husband. She has experienced the issue of belonging from several different points of view.

"I got married in college. Ran away from home to marry this haole [Hawaiian slang for white] guy. My mother hated his guts. Only once had she ever told me to 'find a nice Japanese boy,' but I knew I didn't want to get stuck in a bossy marriage like hers. My father was eighteen years older than my mother and we all had to cater to him. If we made any noise, he'd yell, 'Is this indoors or outdoors?' Around 5:00 every evening we'd start checking the clock, trying to get dinner ready so it could be served precisely when he wanted it. And we'd have to surrender the newspaper to him even if we were in the middle of reading something, because it was 'his paper.' So I said to myself, no way I'm putting up with that.

"My mother likes to complain about the fact that nothing ever turns out the way it is supposed to. For a while, the only thing that made her happy was that her three kids at least graduated from college. But we all married people she didn't like, so she would say, 'The best thing that could happen to me is if all my kids got a divorce.' I have been fighting with her all my life, it's only the last five years or so we could start to have a relationship. I kept saying, 'Mom, I'm thirty-three (or thirty-four, or thirty-five), it's time to let go of the past. I know I made a bad marriage, but now I'm with someone you like, OK? He's Chinese, but at least he's Asian.' Every year I'd add another year to my age and finally, I said, 'Look, I'm *middle aged* now. We don't have to fight anymore.' I think it finally sunk in.

"I tell my husband John, 'Being married to you is like culture shock all the time.' I grew up in Hawaii, he grew up in Hong Kong. His parents can speak English, but mostly they converse in Chinese. I associate that with my grandparents' generation. Once, I told his father, 'I hope you're not talking about me when you say things I can't understand.' John has a hard time speaking up for himself. He'll say things to me like 'I can't believe you got so upset at that ticket agent, yelling and all.' I have to say, 'Well, thirty dollars is thirty dollars.' I think his family also expects me to act like him. So I had to make it clear. 'John, you better get this straight with your mother. I may look Asian, but I'm not what they think I am. I do things my own way.'

"Coming to California from Hawaii was another source of culture shock. When we first came to this area, we saw very few Asian faces. My sister and I would find one at the mall, point her out, and say, 'Can you *believe* there's another one?' Now my husband and I live in the East Bay [California]. It's strange. We fit in because we're not black, but there aren't many Asians here. I also notice a difference between Japanese Americans in Hawaii and here. Here, they seem to do more Japanese stuff, stick together, etc. I think it's kind of sad that they feel they need to do that. And then I realize how lucky I was to be raised in Hawaii.

"When we leave the area, it gets worse. Once I was stranded overnight by an airline in St. Louis. I had my two kids with me and a voucher to get dinner at this restaurant. We stood around waiting and waiting. Finally, this white guy came up to me and said, 'You know, they are not going to serve you.' That pissed me off, so I went to clear a table by myself. I told the waiter, 'I'm sick and tired of being ignored, start taking my order.' He did, but brought my kids these burned hot dogs. That city with the big old arch? I'm never going *there* again. But it was even worse for my brother when he went to visit my sister in Georgia. He had long hair at the time, a good suntan. He looked Mexican, and the Klan actually burned a cross because of him.

"I'm fine with being Japanese American, but one thing I don't like is being associated in any way with those recent Asian immigrants who are pushy, loud, rude. They don't have any concept of personal space. If they want something, they just smash you out of line. I told John, 'Hey, this could be a great business! Teach them some manners. Teach them how to act in an acceptable way in this society.' I also don't like the rich Chinese in L.A.

who just spent tons of money at the mall. Talk about conspicuous consumption!

"I would rather be Japanese American any day than white. I think I'm better off. My daughter's first name is Mariko and she used to go around all the time saying, 'I'm Mariko, I'm Japanese American.' But my husband's daughter (from his first marriage), on the other hand, says she is white. She tells me, 'I don't have black hair like you. I told my teacher to put down that my hair is *dark brown*.' I feel sad for her. But it's partly her mom too. In Hong Kong they have this thing about white skin, they wear gloves when they go out in the sun. I got her this brunette Barbie once and she said to me she wanted the blond one. I'm afraid someday someone's going to point out her squinty little eyes and call her a banana. I'm afraid that will hurt."

And then there are Asian American women who feel very much at home in the dominant culture, who do not particularly seek out other Asians, who do not have a sense that they, in any way, have been excluded from the life of the mainstream, illustrating again that our experiences in this country run the gamut from complete acceptance to exclusion and rejection.

Anne works in a high-level position with the federal government.

"I recently attended a diversity training workshop and the question was asked, 'Have you ever felt discriminated against?' I have to say honestly, no. I can't think of a single situation in my life where that has happened. I grew up in Southern California in a very normal family, led a sheltered existence. My parents were briefly interned in camp, but even that was not a terrible experience for them; my mother was too young to remember it as anything other than a change of routine.

"Like many other Japanese Americans of their generation, my parents wanted us to assimilate. Most of my peers were white, although I realize that my best friends tended to be Japanese. I never felt that I didn't fit in. I knew something about my heritage because we celebrated Japanese holidays, especially New Year's, but we were never pushed to learn the language. My sister now resents that; she wishes we had had more of a Japanese American community as we grew up and that we had learned to speak. But it doesn't affect me the same way. If you ask me if I was raised with traditional Japanese values, I'd have to say I really don't know. I do notice that the Japanese Americans I interact with tend to be more polite, more considerate than the general public, but for myself, I have to ask, 'Is that a Japanese trait or is that just the way my family raised me?'

"I've only been in my present position a short time. Already, I'm realizing that I'm going to need to be a lot more aggressive. I don't see this as something bad, however; I believe that being tougher will make me a stronger person. I don't generally talk just for the sake of being heard. That's what I consider a 'whiteboy' trait. But if I need to make my point, I'm confident I can do it. Being Asian has *not* been a handicap. Nor has it been a problem to be a woman. If anything works against me, it's probably my age—I'm younger than almost all the people I work with.

"One thing I do resent is when people say, 'Oh, you should meet so-and-so. She's also Asian and you should get to know her.' Why should I get to know her? People who make these remarks don't know anything about our backgrounds. We may have absolutely nothing in common. Like the time I attended some inaugural function. I saw this Asian American woman sitting at a table near me and I noticed her glancing in my direction. I'm thinking she probably feels we're going to 'bond' because we have the same color hair, the same features. This thought disturbs me, and I'm like, 'no way!' "

15 BECOMING MY OWN PERSON:
A Woman in Her Own Right

When Terry's aunt had her first child, a girl, her uncle brought a box of chocolates to the hospital. The next child was a son. Two dozen exquisite long-stemmed red roses. The third and final child was another girl. Back to the chocolates.

In traditional Asian societies, boys were more valuable than girls. They carried the family name, an important honor to bear. They were also expected to take primary responsibility for the care and financial well-being of their elderly parents. The hopes and dreams of the clan were thus concentrated in the promise that sons represented. When a daughter married, her name was removed from the family records; the thread of her identity was interwoven into the fabric of her husband's lineage. It was expected that she would serve her mother-in-law dutifully and with respect, and then bear sons. Becoming a woman in her own right was not a goal to be pursued. If undertaken, this process often led to suicide or other disastrous consequences, as in the case of daughters who had a specific mate in mind rather than the arranged marriage presented by her parents.

My mother recently shared with me what it was like for her to grow up in a society and a family where girls were viewed as intrinsically less worthy than boys. She remembers her father coming home on a cold winter's day, his pockets stuffed full of hot roasted chestnuts. Their tantalizing fragrance would permeate the house; the very thought of such a treat made your mouth water! But Grandfather was only interested in sharing this delicacy with his sons. If my mother happened to be in the right place at the right time, he might grudgingly toss a few her way, then it was "Shoo—down to the basement to eat those." Another memory. As a young girl, my mother was terrified of slave traders who roamed the land. But more than once, she found herself left at school to walk home alone, afraid every step of the way that they were after her. Servants had been sent to pick up the boys, but she was left to fend for herself.

Mei also knows the pain of disregard. Her husband has suffered from episodes of mental illness and was once driven to travel more than forty miles at a time looking for a McDonald's where his food might not be poisoned. Mei's husband lives every day with the unrelenting guilt of feeling responsible for his mother's death. His mother had five girls in a row, and was so ashamed of herself that she located a concubine for her husband. Took the woman into her home, treated her with extreme courtesy. Finally, her sixth pregnancy produced a son. But by that time, she was so feeble, so broken down from years of shame, that she managed to live for only seven days after the birth of her long-awaited son.

Today, I listen to my mother's stories of the lives lived by girls in China and I am fascinated, saddened, but I don't really take them in. They don't belong to me. This is probably one aspect of Asian culture that I relate to least. There were only two girls in my family, and we never got the sense that my parents wanted a boy. In fact, to this day, I can hear my mother telling me the story of my sister's birth. Her obstetrician delivered Barbara, and then turned regretfully to my mother, saying, "I'm sorry it's not a bouncing baby boy." But what the doctor did not realize was that she actually preferred a second daughter to a son. Having experienced all that oppression, she found it easier to relate to little girls.

For many other women, however, there is a definite sense of having grown up in a family where boys were preferred. Which is not to say that women in the dominant culture here do not also bear the scars of sexism. But I believe that the experience of a woman from a traditional Asian family is quantitatively and qualitatively different. It is not just that women are expected to play different roles, possess different skills, like different things, but that they are considered less valuable as *human beings*. American girls may still be getting lower test scores in math and science because of cultural biases in the education system, they may still be steered toward traditional occupations and roles. But at least they are not left out on the streets to starve to death so that Mom and Dad can try for a boy.

How then does an Asian American become a woman in her own right? How does she take advantage of the relatively freer climate in the United States to come into her own? Obviously the answer is different for different people, and some women may choose not to break the mold in which their lives were cast. But others, through tenacity, determination, and maybe sheer chutzpah, achieve their goals. Here are their stories.

At the age of seventy, Rosalyn, a community activist, reflects on her life.

"At my age, I think I have learned some very important lessons. Number one: I can be a wife, a mother, a daughter, but I also have to be my own person, I have to make my own choices. Number two: The world is full of people not like me. And that is perfectly OK. Number three: We seniors need to fight our own battles, we can't depend on our children or younger generations to do it for us.

"I was born and raised in Shanghai. Both of my parents came from families with exposure to Western ideas. But my father, Harvard trained as he was, had little regard for women and told my mother that he would educate the boys but not the girls. My mother had to acquiesce to the traditional right of the paternal grandparents to have the oldest grandson come live with them. He did, and died as a young child. The next son was also sent to the grandparents, but after they in effect killed him off too, my mother said, 'No more.' She was required to tolerate my father's 'right' to girlfriends outside the marriage. All this was a very bitter pill for her to swallow, having been raised as the daughter of one of the first Presbyterian ministers in China, a man who believed in treating his daughters as well as he did his sons.

"As a child, I keenly sensed my mother's unhappiness and had an awareness of the injustice toward women inherent in Chinese culture. In fact, I got that from her. I was sent to McTeer, a girls' boarding school in Shanghai, where I learned English, social graces, and how to please people. I also learned the notion of social service. So after graduating, I decided to go to Yenching Province, help the poor. I was so righteous. I wanted to reject the decadent society of my parents. But my mother put her foot down. 'Absolutely not. You're such a radical, you'll surely become a Communist.' As a compromise, they decided to ship me off to Mills College in the U.S. The fact is, if I had stayed, I probably would have gotten into trouble, landed in jail.

"I didn't fit in well at Mills. There were a few other Asian women there at the time, but the policy was to integrate us, not have more than two or three in a single dorm. They were afraid we would just stick together. I was not happy, and I spent a lot of time trying to figure out what was going on with me. I was very clear about what I didn't want. I rejected out of hand the life my parents led in China, the opulence, the wealth. But, for the life of me, I couldn't figure out what I stood *for*.

"So, after two years of this, I dropped out of college and enrolled in a business school where I was able to show up for classes only occasionally. Where I had quantities of time to read, to take walks, and to figure out how to be the first generation here, how to make it work. Because clearly, I wasn't going back to China.

"That's when I met my husband, who was from a very traditional family: one father with three wives all living under the same roof, who collectively produced only one male heir (my husband). He saw me walking down a crowded city street dressed in Chinese clothing and tracked me down. I asked him, 'What do you think woman's role in society should be?' Frankly, he hadn't even given the question much thought. He was just looking for a date. But I observed by the way he treated animals and babies that he was a very gentle man, a good person. So we got married. I told my husband, 'We're starting this marriage with new rules. The old ones don't work anymore. For example, I don't know much about cooking. In fact, I hate to cook! You're better in the kitchen, you can do that.' And then I told him I wanted to work. That provoked one humdinger of a fight. He said, 'People will think I can't provide for you.' I told him, 'Well, that's true! You can't provide what I want, which is the ability to be my own person. Not just someone's daughter. Not just your wife.'

"Sometime after we had this conversation, his mother got sick and my husband left the country to be with her. While he was gone, I went out looking for a job. The only thing I could find was as a secretary with the public relations department of the United Way. I didn't even know how to answer the phone, but someone took pity on me. However, as soon as I arrived in the office, my colleagues took one look at me and said, 'You're going to die here.' So they took it upon themselves to educate me in the ways of the world. We went to a bar. After one glass of orange juice (which happened to be a screwdriver), I found I could no longer stand up on my own power. So I had to call my husband and ask him to drive me home.

"After a while, my husband got used to me. Nothing surprises him anymore and we've now been married forty-two years. Following the United Way job, I ended up at the Mental Health Clinic at Berkeley. Right smack in the middle of the Free Speech movement. They had all these tests lying around—personality, IQ—plus answer keys. I took them on my own and one day discovered that I was neurotic. A professor happened to be walking by, so I asked him about my results. 'Oh, don't worry,' he said. 'Everyone is neurotic.' For the first time in my life, I became friends with other professional women who validated my feelings and experiences. And for the first time ever, I stopped thinking of myself as an abnormal Chinese woman. Regardless of the fact that my husband thought I should be content staying home to raise children. Regardless of the fact that my friends thought I was weird to hold on to this relentless drive to be my own person. I told myself, 'I am OK.'

"From Berkeley, I went to the financial district, hoping finally to make some money. I got a job at an architectural firm and became the first nonarchitect principal in the profession. I lost all my self-consciousness associated with being Chinese. And then, thirty years after launching my way into the work world, I quit in order to have time to give back to the community, to fulfill the dream I had as a young girl in China responding to the terrible poverty I knew lay around me. Now I am involved with a group to provide elderly Chinese in our community an option besides depending on their children. Which really doesn't work here anyhow.

"At this point in my life, I would have to say I'm not very Chinese. For one thing, I have long ago rejected the sexism inbred in Chinese tradition. But certain values are still there. My sense of ethics, my commitment to deliver on my promises. And my relationship to my mother, who was a very demanding Chinese mother. I brought her here to live with us and she stayed for sixteen years before asking to return to Taiwan to be cared for by her son. I felt I owed it to her. I'd heard many times the story of how she stayed in that terrible marriage because of her children. So I felt guilty. Until one day it dawned on me that no matter what I did, I would never be able to satisfy her. Even if I got run over by a truck, my obligation would not end. And I do not want my children to grow up as screwed up as I was. So I forgave my mother and I forgave myself. And I deal with any traces of lingering guilt by throwing myself into my volunteer work, my service to the elderly. It has been a kind of redemption for me, and I can now face the rest of my years without anxiety, without fear."

We all find different ways of coming to terms with ourselves. For Edith, it was a return to the Buddhist way of thinking that helped her to "get through the garbage."

"From my earliest memories, I have wanted to be a boy. My father always claimed to treat us equally, but I could never forget the story my mother told me time and time again. 'When your younger sister was born,' she said, 'your father was so sure she would be a boy that he made a bet with your uncle. He lost.' I saw that my younger brother, the only boy, got a lot more freedom. My parents bought him a car. They gave him spending money. I wanted to do something with my life. I had great dreams: to be an opera singer, or a UN translator. But all my father saw in me was the potential to get married and have children. And when I brought home straight A's, he would only take the time to shrug his shoulders.

"In high school, I found a boyfriend who seemed to be the kind of man I was looking for: supportive and agreeable to whatever I wanted to do. So we got married a few years after graduation and had two children right away. Married or not, I was still determined to pursue my dream of an education, to satisfy my hunger for knowledge. But every time I asked my husband if I could go back to school, he only said, 'No money.' Case closed, no discussion. I had two small children to take care of, but I knew I wanted more. So I would also tell him I needed my own life. He had an answer for that one too. 'My mother didn't need her own life, so why do you?'

"I wanted a family, but the truth is, I wasn't mature enough to be a good mother. I had all this fear in me: fear of not being adequate and the fear my mother passed on to me. She was the oldest daughter and she had always felt responsible for setting the standard. So, when I, her firstborn, ran around noisily as two-year-olds will do, I got treated very harshly. Plus we were living in internment camp at the time and the thin walls just did not permit families to disturb each other's peace.

"When I was first pregnant, people would say, 'Oh, you'll just love being a mother!' But when my daughter was born, I did not have those feelings and it scared me. There was a coldness inside me that I could not get rid of. Part of it was postpartum depression. But it was also that while I seemed happy on the outside, inside I had learned to wall off all my feelings. I got teased a lot by my family for being so dark-skinned and fat and I coped with that by developing a shield of armor. The shield certainly came in handy in the fifth grade when a group of the 'popular girls' decided that their activity for the day would be to make me and Billy, a lonely, awkward, and unpopular boy, walk around school with our shoelaces tied together. I determined not to let them get the satisfaction of seeing me humiliated, so I pretended that this was an enjoyable activity.

"My daughter looks back on her early years and says, 'Mom, you really were a witch!' I freely admit it. I yelled, I spanked my kids a lot. I *knew* something was wrong, but I didn't know what to do about it. Finally, one day, after a study session at my Buddhist church, I found myself alone in the room, in a place I felt very comfortable. I started singing out loud. All those sad songs like 'Song Sung Blue,' 'Downtown,' etc. I must have sat there singing for an hour, until I finally realized that my feet and hands were getting cold. But incredibly, inside, I felt a tremendous amount of warmth rising from the center of my body. Even my palms started to sweat. I felt completely warm for the first time in my life and that's when I started to grow as a person and as a woman. Now I call that my 'garbage time,' and realize there were years of accumulated pain I needed to clean out.

"After this day, I no longer asked my husband about school. I told him I had made my decision to go back to finish my degree. I got pregnant again and I was absolutely ready to be a mother this time; even the childbirth was wonderful, breech baby and all.

"I have been asked—and asked myself—why I stayed with a marriage that in many ways was unsatisfactory. Perhaps it's partly that Asian thing, not giving up, putting family as my first priority. But there were other reasons. I did not want to be a single parent. And I hold on to the Buddhist idea about impermanence. Everything changes. Even my own father, who mellowed over the years and reached out with delight to cuddle his grandchildren when he never touched us with affection. I also hold on to the notion of the 'middle path,' not middle of the road, but choosing the appropriate way for the particular situation. In my case, it makes sense to blend the best of Asian tradition, Buddhist teachings, and Western feminism to find my own direction.

"When I was a little girl growing up in rural central California, I remember at Obon every year this Chinese man who always came dressed in his elaborate silks, wearing a traditional headpiece. He could not speak our language, nor we his, but he joined in the celebration, bringing his fan dance and his gentle presence. I think he was a lonely man looking for community, but he never seemed disheartened in any way. I would always look for him. Now, I realize he is my bodhisattva. He showed me that you can be different and still be OK. That our humanness transcends race, culture, age, gender. My children are also my bodhisattvas. They have been my mirror; showing me what a devil I used to be so that I could change and be the person I was meant to be, the person I am today."

Is it possible to be a feminist and still identify with a culture that promotes the subordination of women? Marissa acknowledges and values certain aspects of her Japanese heritage, but she is quick to point out that she is not what she would call "typical Japanese."

"I see myself as a feminist, have been for a long time, even before it was really acceptable. I kept my last name when I got married, established my own credit at a time when that was almost illegal. But that's me. I don't seem to have adopted this Japanese thing of obligation, duty, always doing the things you are supposed to do. You know how Japanese bring gifts to your house and say, 'This low, dishonorable person is bringing this worthless gift to you, etc. etc.?' Well, I don't fit that pattern. I'm independent and quick mouthed; I know how to do things to 'fit in,' but generally I like to see myself as kind of a rebel, one who prefers to run on the opposite edge of things.

"At the same time, I associate very positive things with being Japanese. I like the culture (although I definitely don't agree with their traditional view of women as subservient). I like Japanese things, the sense of style. I was born at Amache (a camp in Arizona), and when I read that the Japanese got their gardens to grow in those bone-dry deserts and even sold vegetables to townspeople, I thought, we're a very resourceful people. I like that!

"It has also worked to my advantage that teachers always looked at me in a very positive light. And in my job now—interviewing people for cancer studies or other research projects—I think one reason I'm accepted by so many different people (white, blacks, poor, etc.) is that, as a Japanese American woman, I'm nonthreatening. I figure I'm kind of this neutral thing, it's OK to let me into your house.

"My dad was a Methodist minister and after we left camp, we settled in Omaha, Nebraska. My sister and I were the only Japanese in the school, but I don't think I realized I was Japanese or something different from everyone else. As I recall, I was quite popular. Maybe they saw me as this cute little Japanese doll. I even had a boyfriend, Eddie, very blond-haired and blue-eyed. In second grade, his dad drove him to my house to give me a Valentine's present, so they couldn't have thought too badly of me. In third grade, we moved to Berkeley. There were obviously a lot more Asians there, but I don't remember being particularly struck by that. But by junior high, I was hanging around with all Japanese kids. We put ourselves on the same teams, in a sense voluntarily segregated ourselves.

"Sometimes I wonder why I feel so positive about myself, when others in my situation might not. One thing is that my parents were always very encouraging, never said I couldn't do this or do that. And I've had a clear sense of my own path from a very early age. I remember at twelve my mother saying she was going to spank me for some reason. I told her, well you'll have to catch me first! Later, I told her she better not try to tell me what to do because I'd turn around and do just the opposite.

"After graduating from college, I spent a few months in a social welfare job for the county. Just before my six months' probation was up, a friend convinced me to move to New York. My boss, a single parent, was appalled that I would just pick up and leave. You mean you won't just stay *half a month* more and then have a guaranteed job with the county? She could not fathom it. In New York, I met and married a white man who was quite wealthy. We got divorced three years later. My uncle thought it was because of cultural differences, but really, I just didn't care for the country-club life. It just wasn't me. Here—on the tennis court and at cocktail parties—is where I got the most negative reaction because I was Japanese. Little kids would stare. Their parents would say things like, 'Where are you from?' 'Oh, California.' (Puzzled looks.) 'No, I mean where are you really from?' Well, being the snotty person I am, one day I said to this guy, 'What I've always wanted to ask is where are *you* from?' 'Wisconsin,' he answered. 'No,' I persisted, 'I mean where are you *really* from?'

"I felt no embarrassment about the divorce, no sense of failure whatsoever. My mother also said nothing to me, either because she was scared to, or because she didn't need to put anything on me. From New York, I went to Tahoe, where I skied for eleven years. I was a guide, I raced, it was great! I love to do things we women are not supposed to be good at, i.e., sports. I love people to know I can work on my own car. I met my second husband in Tahoe. He was from Finland and had always been interested in Japanese culture. But if he had been on the prowl for an Asian woman specifically, I would have run the other direction. I'd be afraid he was looking for something I'm not. Looking for a woman to be subordinate to him; and if there's one thing I refuse to be, that's it."

Rosa grew up in China and was introduced to the traditional notions about the role of men and women. But through the sheer force of her personality she rejected those that did not suit her ways.

"I'm part Western, part Chinese, and part Latin. And when all those three act in combination, you better watch out! I speak my mind and I don't let the vice president or head honcho so-and-so rattle me. Once, at the bank, I fought with the deputy chairman. In doing so, I put my job on the line, but I don't tolerate being treated poorly. 'How dare you yell at me?' he asked. 'If

I didn't raise my voice, you would never listen to me!' was my reply. We never had a problem after that.

"My grandmother was very broad-minded for a Chinese woman of her generation. Her marriage, to a cripple, was arranged when she was three years old. When she turned sixteen, the families decided it was time. But being a good swimmer, she just plunged into the lake and swam off to the home of a relative. Eventually, she had to submit and the two newlyweds fought for a time like cats and dogs. They produced no offspring until the mother-in-law bolted the bedroom door. Unfortunately, her husband died when my grandmother was seven months pregnant with my mother.

"Because of this experience, she refused to arrange a marriage for her own daughter. But she also found that she had a very hard time controlling my mother, who sought equality from an early age. When she was told she could not sit in the same area as the boys, my mother demanded to know, 'Do the boys weigh more than I?' She was sent to school and decided she did not want to be a girl anymore, started dressing herself in boys' clothing. Grandmother asked her why. 'Then I'll be treated fairly!'

"When the Japanese invaded China and were raping women in the countryside, my grandmother thought it would be safer for my mother in Shanghai, and sent her to live with an uncle, who owned a small convenience store. This is where my father, who is Portuguese, met and fell in love with my mother. Mixed marriages in that time and place were fairly common. My mother had a very good life with her husband, but sadly enough he died from drinking wood alcohol only five years into their marriage. She was left with four young children and desperately wanted to jump into the grave after my father. I learned the hard way it was not my place to bring up that loss. Once when I wanted something she did not want to give me, my mother threatened, 'I wish your father could see you like this. He'd straighten you out.' Without missing a beat, I told her, 'I wish so too. He'd have a thing or two to say about how you're treating *me*.' She burst into tears and my brothers all scolded me for upsetting her.

"When I was ten, we left Shanghai for Macao. My mother worked five days a week caring for a Russian woman and her invalid son. My brothers were all sent to boarding school, but I refused to go. 'Try to make me and I'll run away from school every single day.' I was sent instead to the local Catholic school were I was 'half-half.' That was OK because there were lots of other half-halfs. At least we thought of ourselves as one step above the locals. Some kids called me names, but it didn't bother me too much. I decided to just accept and live with it.

"By the age of thirteen, I was financially independent. I had a job as a tutor, but I always gave half the money I earned to my mother, because there is one thing I just can't tolerate, and that is to see my mother unhappy. It brings up overwhelming sadness for me. I fought with my brothers. 'You should be sharing your money with Mom too. Not just Christmas and birthdays. Do you ever see her spend a cent on herself? Now, I demand you go out there and buy her something she really wants!' My mother never scolded her sons. She'd say, 'OK Rosa, OK, that's enough.' '*NOT OK*,' I'd tell her. I was the middle child, I was smaller than my brothers in size, so I had to be bigger in temperament.

"My mother did try to correct me. She'd try to get me to say I was sorry, but I refused because I didn't *feel* sorry. She warned that, the way I was going, I'd never marry a nice Asian man. I told her I didn't like that tradition anyhow, the double standard. 'I won't bow to anyone,' I told her. 'Only to God.'

"I immigrated to the U.S. via Canada in 1973. For one thing, I was concerned about what would happen to Hong Kong (where we lived after Macao) when the Communists took over. For another, life there was just too easy. Want a cup of tea? Just ask and someone will bring you one. It wasn't real living. I needed to prove to myself that I could survive on my own, away from my family. Another problem: all those rich Chinese boys pursuing me. Rich Chinese boy equals spoiled Chinese boy. I wasn't about to get myself into that situation, kowtow to some mother-in-law. My mother would warn me, 'Rosa, you're going to die a spinster.' 'Mom,' I'd say, 'I'd rather die a frustrated spinster than be an unhappy wife.' After I made my decision to leave the country, my mother cried for months. My brothers tried to persuade me to change my mind. But my mind was made up.

"Two years after I arrived in the U.S., I married my husband, Bill. But I got a few things straight first. One, if my mother can't control me, don't think you can. Two, you can look at this face and think I'll say, 'Yes, dear,' but you're sadly mistaken. I want a partnership—you run your life and I'll run mine. In the beginning, my husband wanted us to do everything together. I was so glad when our son was born, because then there would be someone else to do things with him. 'Look, Bill,' I said at last. 'If something happens to me or Mark, you'd be totally lost. You need to develop some connections of your own.'

"We get into good fights once in a while. Mark worries, but I tell him, no, it's healthy. One day, Bill failed to pick me up from work as he had agreed to and I was forced to ride the bus home. He made no attempt to contact me, simply forgot to do what he had promised. I walked in the front door, told Mark to clear out of the kitchen, go into the family room with Grandma and turn on the TV 'real loud because now I'm gonna let your father have it!' I confronted Bill, gave him a piece of my mind, got it out of my system, and then we all went out for ice cream. Best of friends!

"As I get older, I believe I should command more respect. I will not tolerate rudeness, not from the teenage clerk in the store, not from the bank VP. My Latin blood starts to boil. When a bank VP came in the office and brushed by me as if I was a nobody, I gave him back the identical treatment. 'But he's *so-and-so*,' warned a colleague. 'Well, does he shit any differently than me?' I asked. 'Rosa, you're terrible!' 'Yes,' I said, smiling. 'Yes, I *am* terrible!' "

16 GRIEF AND ITS AFTERMATH

The morning four years ago that I discovered my father had died sometime during the night, I started crying and felt that I would never stop. But we managed to make it through the day, to drive to the mortuary and pick out an urn, to notify friends and relatives. And in the stillness of the evening, I realized that what I was grieving for was the father who no longer lived as well as the father I never knew. Over the days and months to come, I would often feel the sharpest pain when I happened to notice a father and daughter intensely engaged in conversation one table over, or a father simply walking quietly with his daughter, an arm casually draped around her shoulders. The legacy of losing my father has been an increased awareness of what has always been missing from my life, and the plague of questions that ensues: What if it had been otherwise? What if my father had been able to make evident and tangible his love for his firstborn?

Grief is a universal human reaction to loss. But it is also true that culture plays a role in shaping the form in which grief is borne. The meaning we attribute to a particular loss has a profound effect on how we take it in, how it *feels* to us. Consider the Oklahoma City bombing. In this country, the death of the young children was seen as the highest tragedy. But in Japan, media coverage of the event expressed a concern for the older people—

who also died in that fiery explosion. We see the loss of all that potential; others mourn the loss of all that accumulated life experience. In China today, baby girls are abandoned to the streets and to starvation, a devastating consequence of the one-child policy. But while their mothers may feel personal pain at the loss, their grief is tempered by the belief that this is a cruel but necessary way to have a son.

In my case, I believe that cultural factors did play a role in the expression of my grief. That role was a subtle one, and it was not until recently that I could discern its presence. Now I realize that what I was grieving most of all was the fact that my father never measured up to the fantasies I harbored for him. Fantasies nurtured by spending time with my white friends' families, watching TV, reading books. After all, Nancy Drew's father was *very* attentive to her. The truth is, my dad was a good father in many ways: responsible, stable, devoted to my mother, an excellent provider. By traditional Asian standards, he fulfilled his role admirably. But all I knew is that he never opened his arms to embrace me. He never played a board game or read a book or threw a ball to me. He did not adjust the training wheels on my bike and he did not once call me his "little princess." Or tell me I was pretty. Or tell me that he loved me.

When a young girl loses a parent, that loss can become a central element in the organization of her life, with repercussions that resonate throughout a lifetime.

In Joanna's case, one eventual consequence of her mother's death was that she also lost the country of her origin, a fact of life for many Asian American women. While the emotional aftermath of immigration is not always immediately evident or even consciously understood, the grief of culture loss can sometimes persist for several generations.

"My dream is someday to own my own business. I love to bake. I can see myself with a place that sells pastries, different types of coffees. But sometimes, I also think I'd like to stop working altogether. I've been working all my life; in fact, I feel like I was born in my parents' grocery store. My whole childhood was spent there, and I'm still in a grocery store as a checker for a large supermarket.

"I wonder what would have happened to me if we had stayed in Peru, the country my family fled to after escaping the Communist takeover of China. I'm not sure why Peru was chosen, I think it's just where the boat stopped. And of course, I can't stop wondering how my life would have turned out if my mother had not died when I was seven. I remember that period of time vividly. My mother had some female problems, was hemorrhaging badly. Probably for some time, but my dad did not believe in Western medicine and wouldn't take her to the hospital. Finally, one of her friends said she'd better go. She died after the surgery. I can still see my dad, literally being carried home by a few of his friends, hysterical, crying uncontrollably. I wasn't in any way prepared to face the news he brought with him. No one had told me a thing.

"We had a traditional funeral for my mother. I refused to go up to see her in the casket, but they dragged me up there anyhow. I think that's cruel. In my mind, I was trying to tell myself, 'This is all a bad dream. You'll wake up from it soon.' After my mother's death, my father threw himself into his work, opened the store earlier and earlier, moved back the closing time. The five of us brothers and sisters tried to hang on the best we could. I was the youngest, so I didn't really understand what was happening, but I remember hearing them talk about how angry they were at my father. Blaming him for my mother's death.

"When I was eleven years old, my oldest sister convinced my father that the children should all come to the U.S. She had been here for a year as an exchange student and was concerned about Peru's political instability. He let us go, but he stayed behind. My thought was, 'Hey, this is great! A brand-new life.' My sister, nineteen at the time, was essentially in charge of us. By the time I got to high school, it was just me and my older brother, a coin dealer, living in the apartment. I was going to school and working to help support us. I didn't have much time to study. Kids would come up to me and say, 'I thought you Chinese were all so smart. How come you don't get straight A's?' The only thing I could think of to say was, 'Well, I must not be 100 percent Chinese then.' Living in L.A. was awkward in several ways: I was the only Asian in my class, I didn't speak English that well, and I had no parents. I had to sign my own permission slips.

"Thinking back, I can't visualize my house in Peru anymore. I guess I want to forget about the fact that I never really had a childhood there. In terms of identity, I remember kids calling me 'Chinita' in a way that showed how they felt about us. But I never thought I wanted to be Spanish the way I wanted to be white when we came to the States.

"Without a mother, I had no one to tell me about men or relationships. What information I did get came piecemeal and sometimes inaccurately. Once, my oldest sister happened to be in the apartment when I was taking a shower. She looked at me and asked, 'Have you had sex?' I was probably fourteen or fifteen at the time, and her question stunned me. 'What are you *talking* about? I have no idea what you're getting at.' She pointed to the stretch marks on my belly and explained to me that that proved her point. And at about that same age, a guy at work asked me out. I agreed, but when I found out he was twenty-three and divorced, I knew enough to say this isn't right. This isn't for me.

"I have dated white men almost exclusively. In part because that's mostly who is available. But also, the Chinese guys I knew weren't physically attractive and I was concerned they would find me too Americanized, not submissive enough. One thing, however, that I really hate is when a man—and this has happened to me both with white and black guys—expresses interest because 'I've never *had* an Asian woman before.' I tell them, 'Well, you're not about to have one now.' I find it insulting and degrading. I don't feel I'm sexually different than any other woman, Chinese or not.

"I got married at eighteen. I moved to a conservative small town in northern California to be with my husband, and used my college money to buy a house. One day, out of the clear blue, I get this call from my father. He's living in Hawaii now. He's been out of touch for many years, but somehow he heard that I was planning to marry a white man. 'How could you do such a thing? How could you marry someone white?' he scolded me. 'And you haven't even finished college yet.' I ignored both my father and his advice.

"That was in 1977 and I found a job with a grocery store

because they had just been told they needed to hire some minorities. I was hired but not accepted. My manager never said a thing to my face, but you know he didn't want us around. We had been forced on him so he gave us—blacks, Mexicans, Asians—the worst shifts. I was written up for things no one else would have been. Like the weekend I wouldn't work because I was getting married. The manager said I refused to come in. Today, I probably would have said something. In fact, when an auditor recently came to the store and was giving us a hard time, I surprised myself by taking him on. 'I think you have an attitude against me,' I told him. Then we talked and I learned where he was coming from. But back then, I just kept my mouth shut.

"My first marriage didn't work. We were too immature. So we split up, sold the house, and I used my proceeds to buy a condo. I went through kind of an irresponsible period after that, but when I realized this one boyfriend I had was using drugs, I knew I had to get back on track. That's when I met the man I'm now married to. He's *very* responsible.

"We hit it off well, but it was a different story with his parents. The first time I went over to meet his grandmother, she asked me to write my name and phone number down, 'just in case.' She picks up the piece of paper I had written on, looks at it, and says, 'Oh, your name tag says you spell your name with an E.' 'My name tag?' 'Oh, yes, well we, uh, happened to be at the store the other day, we were out of coffee.' I knew his family wasn't driving twenty-five miles just to buy some groceries. They wanted to check me out without my being aware of it because they weren't at all crazy about their son marrying Chinese.

"Later in our marriage, their attitudes were responsible for a big fight between my husband and me, one that led to us separating for a while. There was an older woman in my life who has been very good to me, a kind of mother figure or a mother substitute. One of her sons is gay and I think of him like a brother. We were having Christmas at my house and I decided to invite Dave and his partner. When my father-in-law found out that they were coming, he asked, 'How dare you do such a thing?' I got really upset. I even said to him, 'I thought you considered yourself a Christian.' His parents refused to come over to the house until my sister-in-law phoned them to say the coast was clear. But I think what hurt most was that my husband did not back me up. That crushed me.

"Right now things are tense in my life because my fellow employees are out on strike. I'm not sure how long we can get by without my income. Sometimes I wish I had a professional career. I think if my mother had lived, I would surely have a college degree by now. But that's in the past. Now I'm just trying to be me. I'm looking at my situation optimistically and saying, 'Hey, this is a golden opportunity to find something else to do.'

"And for the first time, I think, Mother's Day was OK this year. I didn't dread it and I didn't feel sorry for myself for not having a mom. I guess you'd have to say I'm doing pretty well."

Clara's initial reaction to the death of her mother was to shut off the pain it evoked. But over the years, she has learned to come to terms with her loss, and part of that involved adopting a philosophy of life that has its roots in Chinese traditional thinking.

"The night my mother died, I made the decision not to react in an emotional way, and that choice has had a profound effect on who I am and how I have chosen to live my life. I was eight years old, living in Hong Kong at the time, and I still remember one of our servants picking up the phone, getting the news from the hospital, and then slamming down the receiver. In a very angry voice, she informed me that my mother had just died. For me, it was as simple a matter as turning off the light; I vowed at that moment to stay calm regardless of what happened. I would not cry at her funeral; nor really allow myself to cry about much of anything else.

"My mother suffered from a brain tumor for two years before she died, but in that time, none of us made any preparation for what was to come. After she died, my father completely clammed up and I was not close to either of my younger siblings. The death was traumatic to everyone, including my mother's family. Grandmother, in fact, was heartbroken, and in order to spare her the pain she experienced every time she saw us, my mother's family simply cut themselves off. At the time, I was angry, it was hard to understand why they weren't stepping forth to help out, but now I can look back and say, these weren't cruel or malicious people, they just didn't know how to handle us. Is this a cultural reaction to bereavement? A Chinese thing or just a people thing? I don't know.

"My response to her death was to become very independent and stubborn. No one could stop me from doing what I wanted to do. In high school, we had this picnic every year. It really was a fraudulent event; we were supposed to act like we loved school, loved our teachers, when I felt the opposite was closer to the truth. So I organized my own picnic, and when one of the students voiced her concern about the lack of adult supervision, I just invited some of our substitute teachers to chaperone. We were more comfortable with them anyhow.

"At the age of nineteen, I came to the U.S. to complete my education. According to Hong Kong standards, my grades, especially in math, weren't good enough to get into a top university, so the alternative was to go abroad. I was much more interested in music anyhow, and my father, who was a self-made musician, supported me. Besides, I always had a convenient excuse for my lack of academic success—I was born with a heart problem and had surgery at the age of thirteen. Recuperating took two months away from school and I was never able to catch up after I returned. I had an uncle in Princeton, New Jersey, so I went there. Pennington H.S. was a wonderful experience. I had no self-consciousness about being Asian, in fact it was great—no competition! The teachers took a real interest in me and I even learned some of the math I had struggled with for so long. It was the first time in many years I felt cared for and nurtured.

"Having been independent for so long, it was hard to contemplate marriage, although I knew it was something I wanted for myself. That kind of commitment both attracted and scared me off. But in considering a partner, I was never concerned with issues of ethnicity or race. I dated a few Caucasian men and then met my husband through a mutual Chinese friend. Marriage was a big step for me. I cried a lot those first few years and wondered why I put myself through this. I'm sure part of it was not wanting to lose my independence and the protection it gave me in shielding myself from additional loss. But over the years, my husband and I have worked out a very good marriage, aided by a recent midlife crisis which provoked us to communicate at a very deep level.

"The way I look at things now is this: We're all going to have to face trauma in our life. It's inescapable. You can either let the bad times overwhelm you or you can learn from it, you can grow. You can make something good come out of a tragedy. Recently, we got a little kitten and became very attached to her. Unfortunately, we found out not long afterwards that she was very ill and would have to be put to sleep. I cried and cried, I was a real mess, but we got through it. We talked to the kids about death, we even discussed what we could do with her before we took her to the vet that last time. Love her unconditionally. Love her knowing she's going to die. One thing I learned from my mother's death is that I can't let my fear of loss keep me from loving again.

"In that sense, I have found the little I know of Buddhism or Eastern philosophy to be more useful than Christianity, which has provided no real comfort. I am reminded of an ancient Chinese tale. A man loses his horse. All the people of the village gather around, tell him how sorry they are. He responds, 'How do you know it's a bad thing?' Three days later, the horse returns. The villagers rejoice. But he asks them, 'How do you know this is a good thing?' And three days later, the horse dies. If you are too attached to the happiness of having your horse return, the grief of losing him later will be all the greater. And another way of looking at it is that we never really know how a given event will play out over the course of our lives. What looks horrible today may turn out to be the seed of something wonderful for tomorrow.

"I could still be upset about how my aunts, my grandmother weren't there for me when my mother died. But who knows how my life would have turned out if I had received what I wanted as a child? Maybe I would have been adequately comforted, adequately nurtured, and never left Hong Kong. The life I have now might never have happened."

Viewed through the lens of culture, the loss of a family member can reveal difficult truths about the way a family functions. For Janet, a clinical psychologist, the death of her father brought this issue into sharper focus.

"I believe that when a parent dies in a Chinese American family, the surviving spouse is likely to cling all the more tightly to traditional values, traditional ways of being. The cross-cultural dilemmas are intensified. My father died a few years ago, and since that time, my mother has become increasingly difficult to cope with. As the oldest daughter in a family of seven, I was already familiar with the role of parentified child. So I went out looking for a two-bedroom, two-bath condo, and then invited my mother to come live with me. I was the logical choice: unattached at the time and making good money. But she turned me down. In her mind, it would be number one son or it would be no one.

"Early in her life, my mother, through an arranged marriage, had fallen into the role of traditional daughter-in-law. In China, that meant enduring physical and emotional abuse from her husband's mother. In this case, her husband wasn't even around, he was off in the U.S. trying to make a living. Eventually, my father did send for her, but not quickly enough to prevent the development of deep emotional scars. My mother believed that she was being whisked off to Gold Mountain, where life would be easier. Instead, she ended up working day and night at a laundry on the East Coast, cut off from her family, her culture, and from contact with other Chinese.

"My mother's primary goal for me was to get higher education and to marry a Chinese man. I was sent to college in California, since the town we lived in held no promise of such a union. When my mother and the rest of the family followed me to the West Coast, as had been the plan, I introduced her to all the Chinese boys I knew—five or six at least. She rejected every one. Their skin was too dark and their feet were too big.

"I believe that if it had not been for my father's openness, his ability to encourage me, his hunger for knowledge and the arts, which he passed on to me, I would not be the person I am today. My mother is a very different story. On the one hand, she was more traditionally Chinese than my father. But she is not above adopting Western attitudes when it is to her benefit. She infantalizes us. When I come home from working all day in my private practice, there is dinner sitting on the table, the steam still rising from the chow fun. No matter how many times I tell her I need some time to unwind first, to have a Scotch, to chill out, she never changes the routine. And if I don't drop everything and pick up the chopsticks, she feels rejected. Withdraws and goes into the dying swan routine.

"For a while after Dad died, my mother tried to make my oldest brother fit the fantasy of what a number one son should act like. But within months, she had disowned him because he did not live up to her traditional expectations. She felt so rejected, so insulted. And this was the only one of her children who got it right: married Chinese! Then commenced a period of nomadic homelessness, where she would move from the home of one of us to another, never feeling that things were right. Eventually, number three son got into trouble. She was pissed at him because he had decided it wasn't a viable option to build a separate wing to his house for her.

"Now, sadly, my mother is showing early signs of Alzheimer's. We had a family conference recently to talk about what to do. But there isn't really a lot we can do. I am watching her become more obsessed with tradition, holding on to the past as a defense against the erosion of her faculties, her known world. I don't take it personally. And if it gets bad enough, there is always number one son's solution: He times his use of Valium to coincide with her visits. He calls it 'the best antidote to mother stress in the world.' Clearly a modern technological solution to an age-old problem."

Even if the loss is not of a family member or close friend, grief can still have a profound impact on a person's life. Sachi is a real-estate agent who has developed a successful business by blending her Japanese origins with Western attitudes. Recently, the death of a client's only child threw her into a prolonged period of grief and reexamination.

"About a year ago, I sold a beautiful, half-million-dollar house to a client. I became friends with them, as I do with all my clients. One night I was out and got paged. Their little boy, Derrick, had drowned in the swimming pool in the backyard. I was devastated. I cried all day long, and I felt so responsible. I shouldn't have sold that house to them. When I was showing it, I noticed the little boy running at the edge of the pool. I said to them, 'You're going to have to keep a close eye on him,' but I should have done more. The other agents all told me, 'It's not your fault. You don't need to feel guilty.' I did not want to hear that. It didn't help because I felt very guilty.

"I was born and raised in Japan, but I've lived abroad or in the U.S. for many years. I go home to visit often, but I don't think I could live in Japan anymore. I'm too American! In Japan, a child's life is already set by the time he goes to kindergarten. I myself did not go to college because at that time, women weren't supposed to worry about higher education. Just get married. I loved my parents and grandparents, but I also had curiosity and I wanted to get away from home.

"I had always assumed I would marry a Japanese man and be a good wife, and of course, so had my parents. They weren't too happy when I stated dating a white man I met at the naval station where I was working. I had a hard time too because I didn't want to disappoint my parents or my grandparents, who had lost their first son in the war. But it worked out fine and my husband and I have been happily married for twenty-five years.

"Being so far away from Japan is hard in the sense that I can't be closer to my mother. I tried to get her to move here, but she didn't want to be so far from home. She doesn't try to make me feel bad, but I feel bad anyhow. I was raised to respect my elders, even ancestors I never knew. My grandparents and I were very close, they taught me a lot. That kind of connection is missing here, it's not valued the same way. So to make things up a little, I am trying to help elderly Asians here. They have suffered a lot, paved the way for people like me to be successful. I deal with my guilt that way.

"Something else about me that is more Japanese than American. This piece of fruit on my desk. In Japan, you'd never eat it by yourself. You'd always share it—you eat half, I eat half. That's not how things are done here. Here people are self-centered. It's OK because they were raised that way. But to my way of thinking, the fruit *tastes* better when it's shared! Sometimes too I feel I do so much for other people and it's not that I look for something in return, but . . . I get hurt.

"Eight years ago, I realized I wanted to be in a business again. My parents were very successful store owners, but they weren't home often, and I decided that wasn't the life for me. I married a man who is very easygoing, a paycheck kind of guy. But I started feeling like I wanted my own business. First I thought a Japanese restaurant. But when the banks said they wouldn't loan me money unless I was married to a chef, I gave up that idea. Then my daughter says, 'Mom, why don't you try real estate?' She had a great idea. People thought I couldn't do it because of the language barrier. But I fooled them.

"I know the language problem is still an obstacle. One thing, I don't do cold calling. I'm aware that I've lost business because of being a foreigner. But that doesn't hurt my feelings. If I was in Japan and some foreigner with an accent tried to call to sell me a house, I'd probably hang up on them too! I am successful because I really care about my clients. Some agents would sell any house, but I tell people if it's not a good choice, maybe too close to the freeway.

"After Derrick died, I went into a real decline. I was very fragile, I was a big mess. This little boy's death was harder on me than when my own father died. And I feel responsible there too because I wasn't with him. I broke my father's heart by moving so far away. None of my co-workers really understood what I was going through. I even felt responsible for the fact that Derrick's parents' marriage was falling apart, even knowing that things were rough before they moved. By November, I was still in bad shape, not working well, not making much money. Finally, I said to myself, 'You have a *choice* here. You can pull yourself together or you can stay home all day and cry.' I thought of the Japanese character *Gaman,* which means patience or endurance. I remember when my first baby was born, the doctors said I could scream. But I didn't. I endured. And little by little, started to heal.

"Yesterday was the anniversary of Derrick's death. I went to the service in his honor and I spoke. I said, 'We have so much to be thankful for because of this little boy. I've made new friends. Derrick's mom is like my own sister. We're all so close now as a result of this tragedy.' And I got the idea of starting a Japanese lending library in my office in Derrick's honor.

"The other day, I took Susan to a Buddhist temple to do a ceremony in honor of her son. We buried incense, we said a prayer. I did it to help her get through her grief. But I also did it for me."

Sometimes, it doesn't take a death to bring about a loss. Laura's mother was mentally ill and unable to provide her children with adequate mothering. In essence, Laura lost her childhood to the heartless and unrelenting exigencies of her mother's condition. Complicating a difficult picture was the traditional reluctance of Asian families to talk about feelings, the inability of the father to acknowledge what his daughter was enduring.

"I'm in a one-year residency program now, trying to decide where I'd like to settle. Here in Missouri, everyone seems to be into 'nesting,' choosing sometimes to forgo attractive career opportunities in order to stay close to home and family. I have no such compulsion. I see my father and his wife maybe once a year, communicate with my two younger brothers three or four times a year. We are not really close as a family and I have no real hopes that we will ever be. I'm also divorced, have no children, and feel no urgency to create a family of my own.

"Perhaps this is unusual for Asians, but in my case I think it is understandable. My parents met at a church outing and my aunt has told me that my father was attracted to my mother because 'he believed she would make a good parent for his children.' Not that he loved her. Unfortunately, even this did not prove to be true. My mother was a paranoid schizophrenic who used to wake me up from a nap in order to spit in my face, and who would attack my furniture with kitchen silverware. Even before her symptoms became flagrant, there were signs of problems. She would 'forget' to pick us up. Or we would get home, find the house locked, no sign of my mother. As a child, the only way I could understand this was to believe that I did not matter to her. I didn't count at all.

"The same aunt who pointed out my father's motivations in marrying also explained to me that she thought my mother felt threatened by having me—another woman—in the house. So she reserved the full brunt of her wrath and cruelty for me. My brothers were largely spared. I also had to contend with the fact that all her sisters blamed my father for the whole mess. They did not believe she was sick.

"I remember having to take care of my mother. Making sure she took her meds. At the same time, she never was a real mother to me. I have photos of her holding me, giving us birthday parties, normal stuff like that, but I have no memories of those events. She never expressed any hopes for me, if she had any. Mostly she criticized, told me I could stand to lose a few pounds (which is not true). She was also very focused on sex and her fear that I would be sexual. Whether that was a part of her illness or not, I'm not sure. But she used to ask me, 'Do you know about such-and-such . . . ?" and I was clueless.

"The only way for me to survive was to be as independent and self-reliant as possible. After I left for college, I basically did not return. My father eventually decided that he had to get a divorce. I can understand that, but I still have a hard time with the way he did it. He planned the whole thing very carefully, met a woman, bought a house with her. Then, after filing, when my mother was in the hospital, he and his second wife-to-be came in one day, cleared out half the possessions. I was so mad I refused to attend their wedding.

"I didn't get a lot of support from my father either. He never wanted to acknowledge the things I had endured as a child. He would only say, 'Your mother was sick,' and leave it at that. When I applied to Dartmouth, he told me I was too stupid to get in. Well, we weren't, after all, a family that communicated effectively with words. But we did buy incredibly expensive Christmas presents for each other.

"Now that I'm a doctor, however, my dad is gushing all over the place. I think it's only recently that he has stopped addressing every possible communication to me as "Dr. . . ." This doesn't feel great either. And even now, when I talk to him, I still get so upset. So much between us is unsaid, so much swept under the carpet.

"In 1979, my mother got breast cancer. Her voices told her not to do chemo, radiation. But I was able to convince her otherwise. When my mother was not psychotic, she was a very sweet, gentle person. And in her fight with cancer, she was very vulnerable, scared. I really felt for her. This woman, who so many times in my life I had wished dead, now commanded my sympathy. Still, our interactions were guarded, superficial. She'd ask me what I was doing. I told her I was in medical school. I don't think it registered with her. 'Oh, yes?' she'd say.

"Four or five years ago, my brother, who was living at home, noticed blood on the kitchen floor. My mother had an ulcerated breast mass. I had been planning to take a few months off med school to be with her, but I never had the chance. I didn't find out until four days after her death. No opportunity for closure.

"Now, I live mostly in a white world. Sometimes I wish I was closer to my culture, but on a day-to-day basis, I think about being Chinese only when I look in the mirror. Still, I'm aware that the Chinese part of me is very deep-rooted, especially when I'm in need of comfort. That's when I search out Chinese food! And as difficult as my relationship is to my father, I still feel obliged to help him out when he gets older. I just finished sending him some mail. Advising him to get a financial planner and look into long-term care."

Grief has a way of putting things in perspective for all of us. That which was suspected before is now made evident. That which was secure is now irreparably altered. And sometimes grief bears its own bittersweet gift: a new way of looking at the world, a new appreciation for the evanescence of life and the power of love.

17 IMMIGRATION STORIES

Women who are immigrants to the United States have a unique perspective on the intersection of Asian and American culture. For recent immigrants, the emphasis is on survival, and the task of adjustment involves mourning what has been left behind and deciding how much of the new culture to embrace. This can take several years or more, but once a degree of stability has been attained, including the acquisition of adequate language skills, women in this position can comment on the traditions in their country of origin—that which is essentially Asian—and contrast these to the prevailing beliefs and attitudes in America. Here are some stories, told from the heart and from the soul.

I will start at the beginning: the story of my mother's immigration. Although I was clearly not present at this event, my mother's story is a part of mine. What she left behind, what she brought with her, how she was changed in the process—all are ingredients that season the making of my life. In listening to her, I have gained a better sense of who I am, and in the telling, she has had an opportunity to share an important part of who she is. Not inconsequentially, we are brought closer by the giving and the receiving of the story.

"After I finished college, I had an opportunity to go to Strat-ford-upon-Avon to study Shakespeare. This seemed like a tre-mendous opportunity for me, almost too good to be true. I still think about it sometimes today, but I also know that my father was right: We could not possibly have accepted the money my professor was offering us to finance the trip. So instead of En-gland, I was sent to the United States to finish my education.

"Before I left China at the age of twenty-one, I had many different thoughts. For one thing, I was excited that I would go to a country where the government leaders were cleaner. I hated the corruption in the Chinese government. I was also excited because I had heard many good things about America, about how nice it was. On the other hand, I was afraid that I wouldn't fit in because I couldn't speak English very well. I had learned English in school, but it was an academic, textbook English, not useful in everyday conversation. I also had some apprehension about what I heard were the sexual appetites of American men. Someone warned me that they were all 'sexpots' and I would have to be careful when I got to the United States. One thing I didn't worry too much about was missing my family, with the exception of my mother. I never got much love from my family, so leaving them wasn't too hard. But I did worry about my mother. She was an old-fashioned woman who didn't seem to fit into my father's sophisticated world. I worried about her dur-ing the entire trip over.

"I was seasick for the whole two weeks of my ocean voyage. I hardly ate a thing and I lost a lot of weight. To this day, I'm not too thrilled about traveling on big boats. The day I arrived in San Francisco, touched land in America for the first time, I was still sick, but also hungry. I went into a coffee shop looking for some-thing to eat. I saw a sign on the wall that said, 'Ham and Cheese Sandwich, $1.50.' So I ordered one and paid the man $150. You see, I was thinking about Chinese money, which at that time was worth very little. Servants would have to push a whole wheelbarrow full of yuen just to buy a pair of stockings. The man behind the counter looked at me like I was crazy and told me, 'That's *one dollar* and fifty cents! Here's your change.' I was so happy! This man was so honest! He could have kept the money. In China, that's exactly what would have happened. I'm sure of it. But to me, the important thing was that, naive as I was, Americans still wouldn't take advantage of me! At that moment, my ideas about the quality of the people in this country were set.

"Leaving San Francisco, I traveled to Baltimore, where I was to attend the University of Maryland and study geography, of all things. I had a room reserved in a boardinghouse. My landlady was friendly, and started a conversation with me. I told her my story so far, and that I was to register for classes the next day. She asked me my name. I told her, Mao Y Tung. She asked, 'What kind of a name is that? No one at the university will recognize it. I'll tell you what. *I'll* give you a name. You sound like a very brave young woman to have gone through what you've already experienced. How about Diana? She was a goddess who represented strength.' So I became Diana, and remain Diana to this day.

"Now I have lived here many more years of my life than in China. Looking back, I feel quite sure that coming here was the right thing to do. If I had stayed in China, I think my life would have been like my two sisters'—years of suffering in silence through the Cultural Revolution and after, and trying my best to get my children to the United States. I have had a much happier life here. I think in this country, the standard of living in every respect is the envy of the world, unparalleled to anything I know of. This surely gives people the happiness they like. Also, I believe people here are much more compassionate. If they see someone lying down in the street, they will try to help. In China, you just walk away.

"I guess the only thing I don't like about America is its liberalism. Young people, not old enough or mature enough, are given such freedom that they can't handle it. And in this country, the old are not respected, they are 'looked down upon,' cast away because they no longer produce. Things are much, much different in China, where the old get the best of everything. In that respect, I guess you could say I lost out. I cared for my mother as best I could until the day she died, sending her almost all the money I earned as a clerk in a library and lugging heavy Smithfield hams to the post office so she could enjoy the salty taste in her soups. I was old-fashioned Chinese in that way. My children, on the other hand, are modern Americans and don't feel the same obligation to look after me. So I do the best I can for myself. I just accept that."

Phillie emigrated to the United States from Vietnam. Her story of trying to make a life for herself in the new country while feeling the influence of values and attitudes from the old is a common theme in the lives of immigrant women. Often, children learn English more quickly, establish friendships with American peers, and thus assimilate more readily. This sets the stage for generational conflicts.

"We escaped from Vietnam by boat and lived with my older brother and his wife in New Jersey for exactly two weeks until the night he locked us out of his house. Things had been tense, but all I knew was that his Taiwanese-born wife and my mother had a very hard time getting along. We were forced to move out on our own and find an apartment. I was thirteen or fourteen at the time and I remember that period of my life as one of sheer misery. The kids I went to school with had never seen a Vietnamese refugee before and they were very cruel to us, teased us to the point where I thought, 'I'd like to go back to Vietnam. Life under the Communists would be better than this.' To this day, I have a hard time relating to teenagers.

"I had already experienced prejudice. Back in Vietnam, kids would be mean to us because we were Chinese. But at least there, I was able to talk back to them. And I did. In New Jersey, things were so bad I forgot about what happened at home. Kids here looked at me like I was some kind of alien, not fully human. One day, a boy at school went beyond name-calling and hit me on the head. I told the teacher, but I was so enraged that I also challenged him to a fistfight after school. You know that perception that all Asians do kung fu? Well, I was planning to have my brother confront him. But he never showed up, and luckily I never heard from him again.

"My mother was a single parent, struggling to survive and provide for all her children in an unfamiliar country. So, it was without question that we would do whatever we could to help her. She started a small grocery store in Chinatown, and even though it meant a four-hour bus ride each way, I came home from college every weekend to help out. I never had a moment of what you would call free time. This I accepted, it was OK. What I found increasingly difficult to handle, however, was my mother's attempt to control my life. I probably wouldn't have felt this way about her back in Vietnam, but here, things are different.

"One day, I told my mother I needed to go to the library to get some books for a class I was taking. She said, 'OK, but just for one hour.' It took me several hours to find everything I needed and when I got back, she was *furious*. I decided at that moment that I wasn't going to let her run my life anymore. So after college, I joined the Peace Corps as a way to get out on my own. When I returned, she didn't say much to me except to let me know she felt my two years abroad were a waste of time. But I would catch her peering at me when she thought I wasn't paying attention, as if to say, 'Who *is* this girl I don't know anymore?'

"The truth is, I was changing in ways she had a hard time accepting. Becoming more American. For example, I'm very independent. Right now, I'm thirty-three years old, single, and living alone. My mother can't understand this and neither can anyone else in my family. She thinks I should move in with her, but there's no way I would do that. Hey, I'm a water buffalo. Stubborn and independent. My mother says a woman without a husband is like a home without a foundation.

"For many years, it was difficult even to consider the idea of marriage, no matter how much pressure I felt from my family. My own parents' divorce was very hard on me. My mother stuck it out as long as she possibly could—that's the Chinese way. All I remember is the fights, never any happy times between them. But I still didn't want them to divorce. I'd pray to the fat Buddha.

'Please keep Mommy and Daddy together and I'll buy you a banana.' When my father finally did leave, it made life very painful for me because I had always been his favorite. My mother would try to talk me into marriage and I'd explain to her that it's hard for me to trust men. She didn't want to hear that, just brushed it off. Then she tells me again how important it is for me to be married, and my brother joins in, saying, 'It's bad for a girl to be alone.'

"But now I feel differently. Something seems to have resolved itself after the death of my father. I'm finding it easier to consider the possibility of long-term commitment. I've dated both Caucasian and Vietnamese Chinese, but I'm finding it hard to be serious about the latter. They don't think a woman needs to be highly educated. When I said I was getting a master's degree, they asked, 'What for?' And now I want my Ph.D.! The Caucasian men I am attracted to generally have an interest in Asian cultures and Asian affairs. So when the last guy I dated told me he lived in San Jose, but had only eaten Chinese food once in his life, I was shocked! I almost stopped seeing him.

"I am now working as a social worker in an agency that serves the chronically mentally ill. I really enjoy my work. When I first started, I was shy, I lacked confidence. But now I am continually surprising my colleagues by speaking up and through my humor. I get along very well with my white co-workers. It's the two male Chinese M.D.s on staff that give me the biggest headache. They don't treat me like a colleague, they treat me like a sister or perhaps as a wife. Once a doctor found out a client of mine was no longer going to be in treatment. But instead of telling me, he told my supervisor. I decided I had to sit down with him and tell him how I felt. This was hard for both of us, but unfortunately, the beneficial effects of such a conversation seem to last only a short time. Then we're in conflict again.

"But in other respects, I carry certain Asian values with me on the job. I like to maintain harmony, so that if someone else took credit for something I did, I would just let it be. I'm not really comfortable pursuing a raise or a promotion. In fact, my friends have suggested I ask for a raise right now, but I told them I just got one, I don't deserve another at this time.

"And I'm Asian in the sense that family, for all the conflicts we may have, is still very important to me. I respect the family hierarchies. If, for example, I felt I needed to say something to my older sister that might appear at all confrontational, I would never approach her directly, I'd ask another sister to tell her. It's just not my place to do that. I still speak to my eldest bother in a way that recognizes his role in the family. I have a hard time with American informality, this business of addressing teachers or others in a similar position by first name. It feels to me like a loss of boundaries, a lack of respect.

"In the Peace Corps, I told people I was 'Chinese Vietnamese American.' But here, I say I am 'Chinese Vietnamese.' I do not feel I truly belong here. Not because I have the sense that I'm not wanted or because I'm not comfortable here, but because I know that part of me will always carry certain Chinese cultural values."

Chantale left China at an early age and lived in Hong Kong and Macao before coming to the United States. She now holds a high-level position with the federal government and has hopes of running for elective office herself: clear evidence of her ability to assimilate into mainstream U.S. culture. What is not so apparent, however, are the psychological wounds incurred in the escape from mainland China.

"You could describe my life in cinematic terms, complete with elaborate costumes, stage sets, characters who are larger than life, even a tearful reunion scene. But as colorful as it may appear, it's different to live it. I've been through years of therapy in order to try to come to terms with my experiences, my issues of abandonment and loss of family.

"I left Shanghai when I was five years old, at the time of Mao's 'Let 100 Flowers Bloom' campaign. To be more precise, I escaped with my eighty-year-old grandmother by hiding in the bottom of a boat. My parents had sent us out alone because they felt we had the best chance of reaching our destination safely.

We were headed for Hong Kong, where my beautiful and flamboyant aunt lived her life in the society pages. She was married to a very wealthy businessman. Several years later, she created a scandal by falling in love with a clerk in her husband's textile factory, selecting a man who was well known as a gigolo. We were eventually forced to leave the country.

"In the intervening years, I was sent to boarding school in Macao. Santa Rosa de Lima. A huge gothic building standing alone at the top of the hill. When the massive wooden door at the entrance closed behind me on that first day of school, I felt I was leaving my old life behind. Something like entering a convent. The dormitories had twenty-foot ceilings, and at night, bats would swarm over our heads. Apocryphal stories had it that if one pissed on your hair, you'd go bald. When I walked in the door, my name was Irene. But they said too many Chinese girls at school already had that name, so they renamed me Chantale. My first word in English, which I repeated to myself for three hours straight in order to get it right.

"The nuns at Santa Rose de Lima painted for me a tapestry of colors—Joseph and his coat, elaborate rituals—which very much appealed to my child's eye. The China we had left was drab and gray and full of hungry people. So I embraced the religion. I still practice Catholicism today and currently attend an all-black church.

"My aunt's new husband was not a nice man. He cherished the daughter she bore for him, but he beat the shit out of me. Bad as that was, the thing I cannot forgive is that Uncle C. T. also hit my grandmother. After we left Hong Kong, we went to Okinawa, where I was required to work in the family business for two years before my uncle relented and let me attend high school. While attending school, I got active in civic affairs, even got to know the governor of Guam. So I was not entirely without resources when my aunt died during my junior year and Uncle C. T. declared to me, 'You are no longer my responsibility.' He did, however, support me in finishing high school, but then I was on my own.

"Because of my connections, I was able to get a four-year scholarship to study civil engineering at the University of

Hawaii. In some ways, living in Hawaii was a strange experience
for me. I realized that, all my life, I had valued the feeling that I
was unique. Here, I looked just like everyone else. But the simi-
larity was only skin deep. Inside, I *knew* I was different.

"For one thing, I had had a love affair with my cousin's wife
while my aunt was sick. For many years, I had tried to deny this
part of myself, dated men to prove my feelings were otherwise.
But now, at the age of forty, I am coming into my own, I am
comfortable with who I am. My only real problem is how to come
out to my parents. I think they suspected that the black woman
I was living with was more than a friend. But we don't discuss
things openly. Perhaps it's surprising, but my concern is not how
my parents will react. I know they will understand and support
me. They are wonderful people. But I'm very concerned about
what their *friends* will say, how their friends will treat them when
they find out. I'm planning to return to San Francisco (the city
they settled in when I was finally able to bring them here from
China) in a few years and run for political office. Then, the truth
about my sexual orientation will be known and I fear for my
parents' standing in their community.

"But that gets ahead of my story. First, I must describe 'The
Scene.' After twenty-one years of being away, after not having
seen my parents once in all that time or having laid eyes on my
own brother, I was returning to China. I let my family know of
my plans, and then I get this telephone call. They presented me
a laundry list of the items they wanted me to bring: a TV, VCR,
and tennis rackets. I did the best I could, but they didn't understand how far a graduate student's budget could stretch. I took
a three-day train trip from Hong Kong. It was very hot. I arrived
at the station, with a gazillion people milling about. How *would* I
be able to recognize them in this crowd? Here's where the violins
come in. My father calls out my name. We hug. I turn around,
and this guy is standing there. 'This is your brother.' I'm not sure
what to do, so we make an awkward attempt at a hug. My
mother was still waiting in the station because only two family
members had tickets to be out on the platform. I walk over there,
she spots me and bursts into tears. But the emotion is mostly on
her part. I didn't feel much connection to her, having been away

for so long. Even as a child, I didn't see much of my mother, I was cared for by my wet nurse.

"It was miserable and hot where my parents lived. I was constantly taking baths. I told my mother I planned to stay for ten days. Her response: 'Not even one day for each of the twenty-one years you have been away?' She tried to mother me, but I wouldn't let her. I'm more comfortable being the mother, taking care of others.

"Walking around the city, I felt some sense of familiarity. There were scenes from childhood that came back to me, but they didn't have the power to pull me in emotionally. During the trip, I was aware of not wanting to be identified as Chinese. I looked down on these people—they were poor, had no indoor plumbing, etc.

"When I returned to the U.S. in 1984, I got involved with the Gary Hart campaign. My first taste of politics. I also met a woman whom I consider a soul mate. She introduced me to the Chinese American Democratic Club and the notion of what it means to be an Asian American, what it means to be a person of color. I loved it! I had found myself a Cause. Eventually, however, I got burned out on San Francisco politics and headed for Harvard, where I got a degree in public policy. I met Alice Rivlin there and worked my way to Washington, D.C., first as a special assistant to the head of the EPA (Environmental Protection Agency) and then as a senior advisor to Alice. I'd characterize myself as pretty aggressive for an Asian woman.

"I'm also not like other Chinese immigrants who are masters at scrimping and saving. I love to spend money! Friends of my parents would chide, 'You should be saving money so you can bring your parents over here.' This always made me feel guilty, but I didn't change my ways. However, I did manage to put together enough cash to get them out of China about four years ago."

18 GROWING OLDER:

Looking Ahead, Looking Back

I've always known that old age would arrive,
and suddenly now I witness its encroach.
This year, luckily, I've not weakened much
but gradually it comes to seek me out. . . .

Of those whom the ancients called "immortal saints"
no one is left today.
I only wish for fine wine
and friends who will help me pour.
Now that spring is drawing to a close
and peach and plum produce abundant shade and the sun lights
  up the azure sky
and far, far the homeward goose cries,
I step outside greeting those I love,
and climb to the western woods with the aid of my staff.
Singing out loud is enough to cheer me up;
the ancient hymns have over tones.

LIU TSUNG-YUAN (773–819)

One of the best-known and most striking differences between the Asian and American cultures is the attitude
toward elders and the aging process. In the China of my mother's
time, small children were the last to be considered, the last to be
served at the table. The best, the tastiest food was always reserved for the eldest family member. Children were expected to
sacrifice in order to make their elders more comfortable. Respect

was not something an older family member had to earn, it was a *given*, an incontrovertible fact of life. Here, we tend to view our aging relatives as a problem, even an inconvenience. I still remember a college buddy's statement about his grandparents. "You know what other people's grandparents do? They die sooner or later. *Mine* just came back from a two-week cruise to Alaska!" (He was hoping for his share of the inheritance sooner rather than later.)

In this country, we do not turn to our elders for wisdom and guidance. The fact of having lived in another era is seen as a detriment, not a benefit. How, we ask, could anyone with a Depression-era mentality have anything relevant to say about the current state of affairs? Youth is revered, and whole industries thrive by supporting the illusion that we can stay "forever young." Since my friends and I are moving inexorably toward middle age, I have been invited to my share of "Over the Hill" birthday parties, complete with hearses, tombstones, and the obligatory gag gift of Geritol. In China, really good birthday celebrations don't *start* until you reach sixty or seventy.

What is it like, then, for Asian American women to grow old in America? Some may attempt to hold on to the privileges they would have been accorded in their country of origin. And who can blame them? Reaching a venerable age is one of the few compensations for the injuries and privations suffered by women at earlier points in their lives. But achieving the position of matriarch is difficult to do here. One cannot rule without subjects, and American-raised sons and daughters are unlikely to feel obligated to perform expected duties. Ask me, I know. I feel guilty, but guilt is the price I pay for freedom to concentrate primarily on the needs of my own family.

Most older women understand that they cannot recreate the situation from back home. They don't expect their children to care for them the way they cared for their own parents. "Oh, my kids are too westernized for that," they would say. Instead, these women adjust their expectations downward, angling for expression of concern—phone calls, letters—if not checks and gestures of obeisance. And yet, among my mother's acquaintances, one of the favorite topics of conversation is how they ended up with the short end of the stick: relating to their parents in the old way (my mother sent money faithfully to her parents on a $1.50-an-hour salary even though they never really paid much attention to her) but expecting little from their children in return.

The process of aging also brings with it the opportunity to reflect on the course of one's life. My aunt observed that, as she grows older, she feels more and more Chinese. She has lived in this country many more years than in China, but senses a certain longing to reconnect with her origins. She shares this proverb: "The falling leaf rests near the root of the tree." The fact that most of her friends today are Chinese (this was not true when her children were younger), that she eats primarily Chinese food and speaks most often in her native Mandarin, are all evidence to my aunt of the wisdom of this saying. For other women, this is a time of life to express regret over roads not taken, gratitude for the good times, and hope—perhaps tempered by uncertainty—for the days and months ahead.

Relinquishing the old expectations sometimes yields its own rewards: the forging of a new identity based on a Western model in which self-esteem is garnered from individual accomplishments and acts of self-reliance.

Mary is a good example: a marathon runner who understands that she must look to herself, not to her children, for the help she may need as she ages.

"My primary concern now is, how am I going to live out the remainder of my days? It's a question of survival. I looked at my estimated Social Security payments recently and I know I can't live off that. So I'm making plans. I'm taking gerontology classes at night school and I'd like to consider a job as an activities director in a retirement home. Or, figure out some way to start a business that will market to seniors. I'm also learning about finance from my kids. Mutual funds, no-load, etc. It was intimidating at first, but now I really know what I'm talking about! In other words, I don't just plan to sit around and twiddle my thumbs. You know, even though I am sixty, I don't really feel old, I don't feel that my brain is deteriorating. It's only when I look in the mirror that I think, 'Say, who are *you*?'

"I started running in my forties and now I run marathons. For my birthday, my kids decided I had to go to Europe—I've never been. So they sent me and I got a chance to run the Berlin Marathon. All those people clapping, telling me 'Bravo' and 'wunderbar!' I look at my daughter and ask, 'Is all this because I'm Chinese? Because I'm old?' Who cares! It was a great feeling for whatever reason.

"I grew up in a small town in Mississippi, 1,100 people. My parents came from a poor Chinese village. When my dad landed in San Francisco, the only job he could get was as a porter. Some friends told him that he should go to the South and start a business serving blacks. They will buy from you. So he opened a general store and he did get lots of black customers. Because these customers themselves only got paid once a month, Dad let them buy stuff on credit, unlike the cash-and-carry stores owned by whites. The prejudice against blacks was very strong. Blacks treated us well, but when my oldest sister was ready to go to school and my mother tried to register her, the white officials said, 'Oh, she can't come here, she has to go to the nigger school.' My mother refused and she found this Christian lady to teach my sister. That woman suggested that my mother take us to church and then we would be accepted by whites and allowed to go to their schools. This is what happened, but I always believed they let us in because they felt they had to, not because they really wanted to.

"Life was very hard. We'd go to the store directly after school, put our books down on the cases of food, and try to catch up with our studies when there were no customers. There were no child labor laws then; there should have been. Many days we'd work until midnight or later. My own kids don't know about sacrifice. I remember my daughter asking if I had a doll when I grew up. *Doll?* We played with cardboard boxes, rocks, bits of broken glass. However, my brother—being the only son—got a new toy every time he went to the doctor. But that's another story. I used to be mad at my parents for making us work so hard. But later in life, when we got their oral history and I learned how hard their life had been, I understood better.

"I never had a chance to go to college. Neither did my ex-husband. But I was determined that my children would have the opportunity, and this is one of the things that came between us. We had operated a successful real estate business until the eighties when the market went sour. We guaranteed the business with our house and lost everything. At the time, I tried to get my husband to church, to get some comfort there, but he wouldn't listen. He just wanted to blame God, blame everyone. The kids were in college and I was adamant that they be allowed to finish, even if it required student loans. He refused to see that it was necessary. On the one hand, he wanted them to get their degrees, but he was also jealous of their knowledge. He treated me that way too. I was taking some business courses at night and I'd come home with a new idea or a suggestion. He would never listen to me because I was a woman. Then, several years later, some male friend would tell him the same exact thing, and of course, he'd listen with great interest.

"I went to a therapist. She gave me this assignment. Write down all the things you want to happen in your marriage on the left side of your paper. Then, on the right, write whether you think it's likely to happen or not. This made it really clear to me. When I told my husband I wanted a divorce, he was against it. His reasoning was, 'You don't have another man in your life, I don't have a woman, so it must be money that's the problem.' I said no, we just think differently.

"Anyhow, we got a divorce, and so here I am in my late forties, broke, no job, no Social Security. But I went forward with my life. I have faith, I ask God to stand beside me. My kids are very supportive, they think it's great I get up every morning at 5:00 to run for an hour before work. Now my ex used to say, 'Hey, you're not a teenager anymore, you know.' One day I got so angry I said, 'Why can't you just say something like, good luck!' My kids and I get along great. I respect them, they respect me. I don't try to influence who they marry—it's their heart.

"My daughter married a white man who is a paraplegic. I don't care about the color of his skin, but I was concerned about his being in a wheelchair. I said to her, 'You know, most couples fight about sex or money.' She told me, 'Sex is not a problem and if we can't have children, we can adopt.' I also don't try to tell them what career to choose. I have Chinese friends who foot the bill for double degrees and then their children are indebted to them for the rest of their lives. I also have friends who are married just for the financial security. None of that for me.

"As you can see, I'm not your typical Chinese woman. Actually, I'm kind of a rebel. As a kid, I was the one who got the most spankings. But even then, I didn't mind because I'm sure I was enjoying whatever it was I was doing wrong! But I do continue to celebrate Chinese holidays and I taught my kids Chinese values such as the importance of education and respect for your parents. Recently, my youngest told me he was sitting around with some friends who were all talking about how much they hated their parents. He was kind of shocked, and he told me so.

"Back to the issue of growing older. My mother is ninety-four years old, and lives by herself in Oakland's Chinatown. Theoretically, my brother's supposed to be taking care of her. After all, he's the one who always got the best of everything, but it is actually us sisters who do all the work. I'm hurt, not because he inherited the bulk of the money, but because he tells my mother that the girls wouldn't even come over at all unless he *instructed* them to do so. She believes she is comfortable only because of her son. She tells us that. She is from another generation, that is how she sees things and believes they should be. But for myself, I'll never get into this kind of situation, because I know I have the capability to do things on my own. I've even designed my house so that, if I need to, I can take in a tenant to help pay the expenses. I'll survive."

May, a professional woman in her mid-seventies, has very definite ideas about how to face the end of her life. She was born in China, but her personal philosophy is of her own making.

"This is what I've told all my friends, my family, even my husband. If you walk into my house and find me lying on the ground of a heart attack or stroke, leave immediately and close the door behind you. If you come in, you'll feel you have to do something, and I'd rather you let me drop dead on my own. I've lived a very full life, I consider myself extremely fortunate. I have had a wonderful professional career as a college professor, I've eaten in the finest restaurants in the world. When it's my time, I don't want to hang on unnecessarily. I even have a picture of myself standing next to Dr. Kevorkian. I'm clear about how I want to live my life and I have the courage to face ending it if my health declines to the point where I can no longer do the things I want to do or be the person I am.

"I know from personal experience what it's like to have a parent be an emotional burden on a daughter. Especially after my brother died in his early twenties, my mother concentrated all her attention on me. I had moved to the U.S. by then, to work on my Ph.D. When I was away from her, I'd vow to be a better daughter, be nicer to her. But within a few days of each trip back to Taiwan, I'd be climbing the walls, ready to leave again. Mostly what my mother wanted was to rehash the past and to gain my sympathetic ear. She would tell me over and over again her interpretation of her life, how she might have gone to college or had a promising career as a pianist, but instead devoted her life to staying home and raising my brother and me. By day three of my visit, the only way I could survive was to fortify myself with an armload of books, sit in the living room reading while she sat in the bedroom feeling sad. I do not believe it is right for the mother to demand sympathy from her children. And so my policy with my own kids is to leave them alone. Plus, I believe God will take care of all of us, so there is no need for me to intervene in my grown children's lives.

"Today, at times I regret that I wasn't more affectionate with my children, more 'lovey-dovey.' I'm the first to admit that in some ways I've been a terrible mother and grandmother. My mother was so proud of all my accomplishments—my precocious grasp of concepts, my straight A's—that she was constantly bragging about me to her friends, which made me very embarrassed. Sometimes she'd compare me to other classmates whose parents she knew and I'd be left to deal with the feelings of bitterness and envy those children experienced.

"So I have been very careful to keep my personal accomplishments to myself, not go around broadcasting them, and I do the same with my kids. I'd never think of saying 'Oh, my daughter is such-and-such.' Having received so much of that as a child and not liking it, I went the opposite direction with my children.

They may complain bitterly, but they know how I am. And bottom line, I don't really think I could change that part of myself even if I wanted to. The Chinese have a saying, 'It's easier to move a mountain or change the course of a river than to change a person.' I'm the mountain that can't be moved."

In terms of developmental psychology, the later years of life are viewed as a time of reckoning and a time of reminiscence. One way to make peace with a lifetime of triumphs, disappointments, joy, and grief is to believe that one has something to pass on to future generations.

Trudy looks back at her life and ahead to the future of her children.

"I think I lost my identity as an Asian after high school. I went to art school in Oakland, one of only five Asian students. I blended in with all the whites and didn't really think of myself as Chinese anymore. Yet, I know that loyalty to my extended family is probably the greatest influence in my life and certainly one of my richest joys. My husband Bill died five years ago, but I feel surrounded by family and I know I can always count on them. Frankly, I'd rather die than have to depend on my sons to support me, but I still know that if I needed them, they would be there.

"We still gather as a clan many times a year to celebrate important events. I had a big party on my sixtieth birthday—more than 150 people showed up—and we had a wonderful time! Usually, you wait until seventy, eighty, or ninety, but I had already been invited to so many other parties I felt it was time to reciprocate. This is always a lavish affair at a Chinese restaurant. In my family, we take time for speeches about the birthday person. Ordinarily it is number one son who talks but we usually invite the sisters to speak also. One year I remember telling a story about my brother when he was three. I saw him running back and forth through the house with little teacups full of water. Curious, I followed him and found out that he and a cousin had started a fire in the bathroom. They were trying to put it out one little cup at a time! Our clan also celebrates each new baby's first-month birthday with the red egg party. I must have attended more than a hundred already!

"I do expect my two sons, Neal and Brook, to attend all these events. Brook is always willing, but sometime Neal hesitates. Once he told me he'd go to 'make me happy.' That's not what I want to hear. He wants to break all the strands except those that connect him to me and to his brother. But I tell him he *needs* to remain an integral part of his extended family. As long as I'm alive, they'll go. But once I die, they're on their own. If they choose not to carry on these traditions, it will be their decision.

"My parents felt it was very important for me to know about my cultural heritage. So my mother drove us six days a week to Chinese school, half an hour round-trip. I tell my students this, and they are amazed. You know, I came back from school every day at 3:00, had a snack, then went to Chinese school from five to eight. Returned home, had dinner, and then did my homework. I'm glad for myself that I had that exposure, but for my sons, *no way!* Bill and I even decided not to teach our children Chinese. He thought it would 'impair their English.'

"Whether or not they speak Chinese doesn't matter to me, but I do care about them attending family functions. And I *made* Brook go to his commencement. It was fashionable at the time to skip it, but I said, 'Go for me. We've worked hard to put you through college and we want to attend the ceremony.' Otherwise, I try not to interfere. Brook is thirty-six now, living with a lovely Chinese woman who has children of her own. I treat her just like a daughter-in-law, buy her jewelry, close to her kids, etc. But he doesn't want to make the commitment of marriage and I don't press him. I only asked once, after my husband's funeral. Brook said no, he wasn't planning marriage, and no, he didn't want to discuss the reasons. I don't say anything else although I am sad not to be a grandmother. And my other son, Neal, is pretty rebellious. He has long hair—once all the way down his back—and he looks like a punk rocker. After high school, can you imagine, he ran off to join the carnival. Managed the corn dog concession with lots of scroungy, dirty carnival types. Bill and I were worried sick. But we kept in touch with him as they traveled around the country and never threatened him in any way. After a year, he abruptly quit, came home, and said he was now ready to go to college. Which he did. Big relief!

"I am very close to my boys. They call me every week. I don't ask them to, I don't intrude, but I really appreciate their concern. I also try to help them however I can. We Chinese believe in assisting our children financially, paying for college, helping with down payments, etc. I have a white friend who told me, when her son turns eighteen, she's 'kicking him out of the house.' It's hard for me to hear things like that. It's certainly not how I feel.

"I am also glad to be who I am, living at this time. I look back at my grandmother's life and I feel very sad for her. She was this gentle, intellectual woman, but I found out later that her husband beat her regularly. And she was so submissive that she didn't protest when he decided one day to give their youngest daughter to a close scholar friend who couldn't have his own children. I can just imagine how she felt."

Mary, a seventy-four-year-old Issei, has the time to reflect on her life and the choices she made. Or did not make.

"Today, I look back on my life and how I've raised my four children and sometimes I think I should have pushed them a little harder. Not just always let them feel free to make their own choices. I also regret that I didn't do more to keep the Japanese traditions going. I recently bought a book about Japan and it's interesting reading, but in a way, I think it's too late. At seventy-four, it's hard to honor customs that haven't really been part of your life.

"My father came to the U.S. with the hope of making enough money to go back to Japan and live comfortably. But, as a farmer, he was never able to do that, so we ended up here permanently. My mother came as a 'picture bride.' We lived in a small town on the outskirts of Denver, and while we did go to Japanese school every summer, I didn't ordinarily have a lot of exposure to Japanese ways. Mom and Dad spoke a little English, we spoke some Japanese, so our language at home was half and half. They never gave us the idea that speaking Japanese exclusively would have been better. As a child, I just didn't give much thought to being Japanese. White children at the school treated us well, I guess we just saw ourselves as 'one of them.'

"I've never experienced any real discrimination or feelings of being different. The closest it came to that was during World War II. Luckily, Colorado treated its Japanese citizens very well and we were never sent to the camps. But I do remember as a teenager, eating in a restaurant and all of a sudden noticing a man holding a newspaper with huge headlines about Pearl Harbor. We hadn't even heard about it before. My friends and I got nervous and walked out of the restaurant. However, it turned out that a few people might eye us suspiciously, but on the whole, no one gave us any flak.

"When it came to marriage, my parents arranged for my oldest sister to marry the son of a Japanese family they knew. But for me, I wouldn't go along with such a thing. I always knew I'd marry someone Japanese, but I wanted to be the one to make the choice. I guess I was kind of—what would you say?—spoiled, had too much freedom. My oldest daughter Jan is like me. When she and her brothers and sisters decided not to go to the Buddhist church anymore, I didn't argue. Maybe I should have impressed it on them more, I don't know.

"My parents always stressed the value of education. It was seen as a way to get ahead. Even more important than food on the table, I also tried to show my kids the same value, but when Jan decided after one year of college to quit and work instead, I didn't try to stop it. I didn't like it, but I couldn't really force her to do something she didn't want to do. Now I'm not so sure that was the right choice. Maybe I should have been stricter. We raised our kids to be independent but I also think they need guidance at times.

"One way my parents were definitely Japanese was that they expected their oldest son to take care of them when they get old. They didn't talk a lot about this, but it was known, and so my brother did take our parents in to live with him. For myself, I don't have the same expectations. I want to be independent, not a burden to my kids. Even if they wanted me to live with them, I think I'd always feel guilty, always wonder if they were doing this because they really wanted to, or because they felt they have to.

"Recently, my sister-in-law and I were talking, feeling some regret that we didn't learn more about our Japanese traditions while our parents were still alive. Somehow, it never dawned on us to ask while we had the chance. But even if I am over that, I also know that in many ways I appreciate being American. I enjoy my white friends and our activities. With them, I feel more free. I can open up, I don't have to be so reserved. And we have more fun. Come join our line dancing some time!"

Lily is at the age and stage of life where she could be considered a role model for younger generations of Asian American women. She shares her views about success and achievement.

"Maybe I'm naive, but I've never felt different from other people because I was Japanese. And I really never experienced much discrimination or had the sense that I was being treated differently because of my ethnicity. Today at the age of seventy-six, I can look back at a lifetime of achievements, honors, and wonderful opportunities, at the rich life my husband and I have created together, and feel very blessed. Not that I'm ready to slow down, however!

"My parents were Issei, but in some ways I see myself as more Sansei than Nissei. They met in Santa Barbara, fell in love and married, which is already very different from other families created out of an arranged marriage. Their thinking was very modern and their lifestyle up-to-date. You know how Asians are generally reluctant to show physical affection? Well, not in my family. My dad was in the insurance business and I remember running to the door every evening when he came home from work; he would smother me with hugs and kisses. I used to send him letters when he traveled and would always sign them XOXOXO. One day he said, 'I know the Xs are kisses, but what are the Os?' 'Those are hugs, Daddy!' I told him and he included these on every postcard he sent after that day.

"My father was interested in ballroom dancing and got me involved as well, which led to the opportunity at age sixteen to do bit parts in movies. Once, I was supposed to double for Anna May Wong, but she refused when she found out I was Japanese. That's one of the few instances of discrimination I have really faced in my life. In 1936, I rode on the city of Long Beach's float as the first Asian American woman ever to take part in the Tournament of Roses Parade. It was a beautiful piece of work, dragons with orchids trailing out of their mouths.

"Within the year, however, the war started. My new husband and I were interned at Santa Anita Racetrack. Pat was bitter about the whole thing, but I primarily remember being in a state of shock. It all happened so fast. I just kept believing that God would watch over us, not let us down. And he did. We were rescued by Father Flanagan, who took us to Omaha, Nebraska, to try to start a new life. At first we ran into a wall of resistance trying to buy a house, get established in the community. I remember my husband saying, 'I don't care what people say. I'm going ahead with what I want to do.' Now I really appreciate his aggressiveness, his ability to stand up for what he believes in. But early in our marriage, my views were a little more traditional and I suggested not to try so hard to fight this. Over time, things would work out fine.

"I have been very fortunate to always have good jobs come to me. I'm aware as I say this of my mother's reminder not to boast about my achievements. Secretly I knew my parents were very proud of me, but they still believed it was important to keep me simmered down. One time I remember a woman I was interviewing for a job. I asked her, 'What are your shortcomings?' She answered very confidently, 'I have none.' That really got to me. I've had a number of high positions, including executive director of the Okura Mental Health Leadership Foundation, which my husband and I created. Things have come easy for me, but I *never* felt it was because I was Asian or a woman. I know the effort I have made, and I don't hesitate to bring that up when people suggest that I've gotten ahead because of my race or sex.

"My parents were very much ahead of their time compared to other Issei. But certain things they did care about. They spoke only Japanese at home and wanted us to know the traditions of our culture. I'm glad I had this exposure and right now, in fact, I'm teaching a class on the art of Kimekomi, the first royal dolls, made from wood by Imperial Guards and dressed in materials from their own clothing. Modern Japanese from Japan haven't even heard of these dolls, but I'm working to keep the tradition alive. My mother also had strong feelings about an appropriate marriage partner for me. She didn't say anything directly, but at one point when Caucasian friends might ride their bicycles over to visit me, my mother would remark at dinner. 'Well, if Lily married a Caucasian man, she would get very embarrassed with *me* because I wouldn't even be able to speak with my new son-in-law!'

"Someone once called me a role model for younger Asian American woman. I like that. If I had advice to give it would be along these lines: Don't limit your possibilities by thinking that because you are Asian you can't get as far as you'd like to. If you want to act Asian, that's how people are going to treat you. I think the secret to my success is that I've never seen myself as any different from anyone else. I think that if a woman, especially an Asian American woman, wants to succeed in the professional world, she has to look the part. Maybe I'm just old-fashioned, but it makes me mad to see these young Japanese girls walking around the streets with holes in their jeans. What impression are they giving? People already look at you and say, 'Here's this Asian face.' Don't make it harder on yourself by dressing like you don't care. I also have to say I feel this attitude that you can't succeed because of racial discrimination against Asians is not always in a person's best interest. I knew this Chinese fellow who had just been fired and was suing the company for discrimination. He couldn't understand why he couldn't get a new job and refused to think his personality or work habits might have anything to do with it.

"I'll say this. Believe in yourself. Don't see yourself as Asian in a way that limits you, don't expect others to see you that way either."

AFTERWORD

A recent dinner conversation at my house went something like this:

"Elisa and I are always joking in pre-algebra about how Asians are so smart. So, when she's all, 'Did you get problem number ten,' I said I had to ask my dad for help. Elisa told me her parents yelled at her when she did that, and I said, 'My dad yells at me too.' Hey, I *should* have said, 'It's because I'm only *half* Asian, and so it's *your* fault I'm having trouble with math!' Elisa and I started cracking up."

My husband's response:

"You know, Rebecca, that is a racist thing to say. Not all Asians are smart. Not all whites are stupid."

Instead of blurting out the first thing that came to mind, I decided for some reason to sit quietly and think about what had just transpired. What I thought about was the fact that my husband had a valid point that would have to be addressed. Someday. But for now, I was happy just to hear that Rebecca feels so comfortable with the Asian half of her heritage. If she wanted to make a case for the superior intelligence of Asians, who was I to stop her?

Moments like this, I am aware that I have been the beneficiary of much healing in my life. The world has changed a lot in thirty years, and so have I. Today, I love listening to my mother tell my children stories of what life was like when she was a young girl in China. A measure of healing takes place here as well: by understanding more about my mother's life and the cultural context in which she was raised, I have a clearer picture of this courageous and resilient woman who struggled to raise her children in what was essentially alien territory. I encourage my daughter to explore her Asian roots and take pleasure in her sense of connection with Asian friends. I may still dream about what my life would be like if I were smarter or more outgoing, but at least I never dream anymore about not being Chinese.

Writing this book has been an important part of the healing process. When I started committing my thoughts and feelings to paper, I made the same vow to myself that I ask of clients who enter therapy with me: I would try to be as honest as possible, painful though it might be, and trust that the outcome would be good. It has been. And as in therapy, part of the healing is related to the fact that this process is a *dialogue,* not a monologue. I have listened to other women tell their stories, sometimes stoically and dispassionately, sometimes with laughter, and sometimes with tears, and together we have gained insight into our separate journeys as Asian American women, and into our connectedness.

Perhaps the most important lesson I learned in writing this book is that the inability to integrate ethnicity with identity has prevented me from achieving a sense of wholeness. It promotes fragmentation, and like any other form of denial, requires psychic and spiritual energy for sustenance. Energy that could be used in much more productive ways. That is one reason I am so happy to see my children growing up, so far at least, without the burden of trying to deny an important part of who they are, the Asian half of their ancestry.

I have also come to believe, as a result of my work, that having an ethnic identity is not exactly the same thing as understanding how one's ethnicity influences identity. There is a subtle but important distinction between the two concepts. Ethnic identity could be defined simply as a person's acknowledgment of her cultural ancestry, as in, "I am a first-generation Chinese American woman who feels proud of my rich heritage." Some women I interviewed grew up with this attitude; many others came to such a place later in their lives, often in young adulthood. A few stragglers, like myself, took years to get here.

But I believe there is more we can learn than simply to be proud of our culture of origin. We can become more intimately acquainted with our true selves when we understand the ways in which ethnicity has shaped our identity. True, I am Chinese American, but *what* part of me is Chinese? In other words, when faced with a choice, what cultural messages from my mother lurk at the edge of consciousness? When am I more likely to follow the way of the dominant culture? And at its most developed, Asian American ethnic identity allows a woman not only to be aware of the relative importance of both cultures in her life, but also to understand how each is inexorably transformed by contact with the other—how Asian values introduced to American soil yield strange and wondrous new fruit.

Leaving Deep Water is essentially an inquiry into the interactions between ethnicity and identity. After their interview with me, more than a few women told me they had never really looked at their lives this way before. They were able to see themselves with the clarity of a new lens. ("Perhaps my family wasn't crazy after all, just Chinese!") For the opportunity to be part of their journey, I am deeply grateful.

The ancient Chinese philosopher Lao-tzu said in a poem, "Fish cannot leave deep water." Although I have no real understanding of Taoist philosophy, I was drawn to this line as a title for my book because it speaks to me about the natural order. Perhaps there is a specific safe place, a comfort zone for all living things. Leaving deep water means losing that natural security. But, in a sense, all of us Asian American women have left deep water. Whether by choice or necessity, we are in this country, and it behooves us to make the adaptations that permit us to survive, and then hopefully to thrive. Even if the waters are murky and unclear. Even if they are shallow.